The Rise and Fall of Repression in Chile

The
RISE and FALL
of Repression
in Chile

PABLO POLICZER

University of Notre Dame Press   Notre Dame, Indiana

Library of Congress Cataloging-in-Publication Data

Policzer, Pablo.
The rise and fall of repression in Chile / Pablo Policzer.
    p.   cm. — (From the Helen Kellogg Institute for International Studies)
Includes bibliographical references and index.
ISBN-13: 978-0-268-03835-9 (pbk. : alk. paper)
ISBN-10: 0-268-03835-X (pbk. : alk. paper)
1. Political persecution—Chile—History—20th century. 2. Dictatorship—
Chile—History—20th century. 3. Chile. Dirección de Inteligencia Nacional.
4. Chile. Central Nacional de Informaciones. 5. Chile—Politics and
government—1973–1988. I. Title.

F3100.P646   2008
983.06'5—dc22

                                                                    2008039253

♻ *This book is printed on recycled paper.*

TO ANDRÉ, NICO, AND HANNA

Contents

PART I

PART II

PART III

Tables and Figures

TABLES

FIGURES

Acronyms

ACHA	Acción Chilena Anticomunista Chilean Anti-Communist Action Group
ANC	African National Congress (South Africa)
APDH	Asamblea Permanente de Derechos Humanos Permanent Assembly of Human Rights (Argentina)
BIM	Brigada de Inteligencia Metropolitana Metropolitan Intelligence Brigade (Chile)
CC	Comando Conjunto Joint Command (Chile)
CChDH	Comisión Chilena de Derechos Humanos Chilean Human Rights Commission
CNI	Central Nacional de Informaciones National Information Center (Chile)
CNRR	Corporación Nacional de Reparación y Reconciliación National Reparation and Reconciliation Corporation (Chile)
COAJ	Comité Asesor de la Junta de Gobierno Junta Assistant Committee (Chile)
CONADEP	Comisión Nacional sobre la Desaparición de Personas National Commission on the Disappearance of Persons (Argentina)

COPACHI   Comité por la Paz en Chile (Comité Pro Paz)
                Committee for Peace in Chile

D.L.   Decreto Ley
                Decree Law (Chile)

D.O.   *Diario Oficial*
                Official Gazette (Chile)

DICOMCAR   Dirección de Comunicaciones de Carabineros
                Carabineros Communications Directorate (Chile)

DINA   Dirección de Inteligencia Nacional
                National Intelligence Directorate (Chile)

EM   External monitoring

FPMR   Frente Patriótico Manuel Rodríguez
                Manuel Rodríguez Patriotic Front (Chile)

GAP   Grupo de Amigos del Presidente
                President's Group of Friends (Chile)

GDR   German Democratic Republic (East Germany)

IC   Izquierda Cristiana
                Christian Left (Chile)

IM   Internal monitoring

MAPU   Movimiento de Acción Popular Unida
                United Popular Action Movement (Chile)

MfS   Ministerium für Staatssicherheit
                Ministry of Security

MIR   Movimiento de Izquierda Revolucionaria
                Revolutionary Left Movement (Chile)

NP   National Party (South Africa)

| PC | Partido Comunista |
| | Communist Party (Chile) |

| PDC | Partido Demócrata Cristiano |
| | Christian Democratic Party (Chile) |

| PR | Partido Radical |
| | Radical Party (Chile and Argentina) |

| PS | Partido Socialista |
| | Socialist Party (Chile) |

| SADF | South African Defense Force |

| SAP | South African Police |

| SED | Sozialistische Einheistpartei auf Deutschland |
| | Socialist Unity Party of Germany (East Germany) |

| SENDET | Servicio Nacional de Detenidos |
| | National Detainees Service |

| SERPAJ | Servicio Paz y Justicia |
| | Peace and Justice Service |

| SICAR | Servicio de Inteligencia de Carabineros |
| | Carabineros Intelligence Service (Chile) |

| SIDE | Servicio de Inteligencia del Estado |
| | State Intelligence Service (Chile) |

| SIFA | Servicio de Inteligencia de la Fuerza Aérea |
| | Air Force Intelligence Service (Chile) |

| SIM | Servicio de Inteligencia Militar |
| | Military Intelligence Service (Chile) |

| ZK | Zentralkomittee |
| | Central Committee (East Germany) |

Note on Translations

Unless otherwise indicated, all translations from Spanish to English are mine. Also, *Report of the Chilean National Commission on Truth and Reconciliation* (1993) is the English translation of *Informe de la Comisión Nacional de Verdad y Reconciliación* (1991), popularly known as the *Informe Rettig*. I have drawn from both versions. Where I have used the English translation I cite the English title, and where I have translated from the Spanish version I cite the Spanish title.

Preface and Acknowledgments

I did not know it at the time, but this book began with the military coup in Chile on September 11, 1973. I was eight years old, and the coup marked me, as it did every Chilean. My parents had supported the Allende government, my father spent eighteen months as a political prisoner after the coup, and in 1975 he and my mother fled to Canada as refugees with my two sisters and me.

This book goes to press almost a year after Augusto Pinochet's death, when many of his henchmen are in jail for crimes committed during the dictatorship. Although he avoided prison himself, Pinochet was dogged by the courts in his final years, especially after being arrested in London in 1998, thanks to the efforts of a dedicated Spanish prosecutor making full use of an increasingly restrictive international human rights legal regime. During his final years Pinochet also lost a great deal of support as a result of financial scandals, which demonstrated that contrary to widespread popular belief his regime was not free from corruption and he and his family took advantage of their power to enrich themselves personally. Many of the dictatorship's crimes remain unpunished, and many Chileans still support, if not Pinochet, then many of the dictatorship's overall goals. Yet compared to a generation ago, Pinochet and the dictatorship are much more thoroughly discredited than in the past, the regime's misdeeds are well known, and the legal noose around its principals continues to tighten.

The intellectual origins of this book can be traced in part to the work of Max Weber, which I read as an undergraduate at the University of British Columbia and came to especially appreciate in graduate school at MIT. Weber (like Hobbes before him) understood that coercion is at the center of politics—one of the fundamental insights of the social sciences. If coercion is central to politics, it is especially central to authoritarian

xvi Preface and Acknowledgments

regimes, which use coercion more freely than democracies. In graduate school in the 1990s the world appeared to be on an inexorable path toward democracy, but from the perspective of the early twenty-first century this path seems less certain and the resilience of authoritarian regimes more striking. Unfortunately, by comparison to democracy we still know very little about authoritarianism. One reason is that the operations of authoritarian regimes, especially regarding the use of force and coercion, are more secretive. Does this mean that a fundamental part of politics is destined to remain in the shadows?

In this sense, studying the Chilean dictatorship presented a number of challenges and opportunities. On the one hand, it was a coercion-intensive and secretive regime well known for its abuses, especially during its first few years. On the other hand, the regime at one point restrained its repressive apparatus as part of an institutional reform that had not, I felt, been adequately studied or understood. Of course, the regime did not stop abusing its citizens then, and scores would continue to be tortured; but it killed fewer people, and this new restraint opened some political spaces that had previously been closed. This book is written in the hope that a better understanding of the rise and fall of repression in Chile will shine a light on a critical yet little understood part of the politics of still too many regimes in the world.

Various parts of the research for this book were carried out with support from the Canada Research Chairs Program and the Social Sciences and Humanities Research Council of Canada, the Canadian Foundation for Innovation, the Aspen Institute, the American Historical Association, the Inter-American Foundation, the I. W. Killam Trusts, the Massachusetts Institute of Technology, the University of British Columbia, and the University of Calgary.

In addition, this book owes its existence to the advice, critique, help, and support of many people, none of whom are responsible for the resulting analysis but all of whose input has been invaluable. I am especially grateful to my advisors at MIT, Josh Cohen, Jonny Fox, and the late Myron Weiner, who exemplify the highest standards of analytical rigor and moral purpose in scholarship. Phineas Baxandall, Max Cameron, Ram Manikkalingam, Chap Lawson, and Tony Pereira gave the project crucial boosts at critical moments, and without them this book would not have come into being. I am also grateful to Sandra Aidar, Ariel Armony, Estela Barnes, Robert Barros, Mabel Belucchi, Brian Burgoon, Marcelo Cavarozzi, Diane Davis, Jorge Domínguez, Ricardo Domínguez, Agustín Fallas, Robert Fishman, Archon Fung, Clelia Guiñazú, Frances Hagopian, Darren Hawkins, Waleed Hazbun, Lisa Hilbink, Dick Johnston, Loren King, Mirna Kolbowski, Dan Kryder, Liz Leeds, Gerry McDermott, Andrés Mejía Acosta, Mercedes Mignone, José Molinas, Patricio Navia, Melissa Nobles, Phil Oxhorn, Susana Pérez Gallart, Enrique Peruzzotti, Dra. Alicia Pierini, Eduardo Rabossi, Phil Resnick, Anny Rivera, James Rosberg, Ricardo Salvatore, Catalina Smulovitz, Mario Sznajder, Arturo Valenzuela, and José Miguel Vivanco.

In Chile, during a research trip in 1995–97 and other shorter trips since then, I benefited from the help of Rose-Marie Bornard, Fernando Bustamante, the late Jaime Castillo Velasco, Juan de Castro, Enrique Correa, Andrés Domínguez, Roberto Durán, Gonzalo Falabella, Hugo Frühling, Claudio Fuentes, Juanita Gana, Manuel Antonio Garretón, Roberto Garretón, Alejandro González, Mónica González, José Miguel Insulza, Luis Maira, Carlos Maldonado, Violeta Morales, Juan Pablo Moreno, Tomás Moulian, Elías Padilla, Alejandro Rojas, Héctor Salazar, Augusto Varas, Alex Wilde, José Zalaquett, and especially Carlos Huneeus, whose work on the dictatorship informs my own (even where we come to somewhat different conclusions).

Thanks also go to Carmen Garretón, who guided me through the archives of the Vicaría; Neville Blanc and Juan Guillermo Prado, who helped me through the Biblioteca del Congreso; the staff of the Jaime Guzmán Foundation; and Rosa Palau in Asunción's "Archivo del Terror." Even though much of the information I found there ended up on the cutting-room floor as the book took shape, it greatly enriched my understanding of the Chilean and other authoritarian regimes.

Raúl Bertelsen, Sergio Fernández, Mónica Madariaga, Miguel Schweitzer, and Generals (ret.) Jorge Ballerino, Carlos Donoso, Alejandro Medina, Odlanier Mena, and René Peri generously shared their reflections and perspectives as participants in the military regime. They may not agree with the arguments in this book, but they helped me better understand how the dictatorship worked from the inside.

I am especially grateful to Max Cameron and Brian Job at the University of British Columbia for their friendship and unwavering support and for stimulating many new ideas. I am also grateful to the University of Calgary, and especially my colleagues in the Political Science Department. Jan Boesten, Alejandro García Magos, Alex McDougall, and Juliana Ramírez provided valuable research help, and Shawn England and Peter Larose excellent editorial assistance.

My parents, Adam and Irene Policzer, set a wonderful example of a life dedicated to helping others and nurtured my love of books and learning. I owe my biggest debt to my wife, Lara Olson, who has seen this project emerge and develop, if not quite from the early beginnings, then for far longer than she bargained for. This book would not exist without her love and patient support, or her sharp intellect and wise counsel. I dedicate the book to our three children, André, Nicolas, and Hanna. May their lights shine brightly.

PART I

ONE

The Dark Spaces of Politics

Ad mala patrata haec sunt atra theatra parata. [Dark theaters are suitable for dark deeds.]

A motto of the Papal Inquisition, ca. 1233

Coercion—the threat to employ brute physical force and the actual employment of such force—is central to politics. In a foundation that stretches from Hobbes to Weber, it defines our basic political institutions. But despite its importance, analyzing how various types of coercive institutions operate—and why they differ across time and space—remains difficult. Coercion often takes place in the dark spaces of politics, concealed from public scrutiny. Even in relatively open societies, coercive institutions such as the police and military forces tend to be secretive and mistrustful of any efforts by outsiders to oversee their operations. In more closed societies, such as those ruled by authoritarian regimes, secrecy is the norm, making coercion in these cases that much more difficult to observe and understand.

This book is motivated by the conviction that understanding the coercive tyrannies that are common in the dark spaces of politics is both urgent and possible. The urgency is straightforward. Authoritarian regimes have been by far the most successful and common sorts of regimes in history, and recent events in places such as China, Russia, Syria, Belarus, Zimbabwe, Iran, and Pakistan, among many others, show that authoritarianism shows no sign of going into history's dustbin any time soon. Democracy has made great advances in recent decades, yet by 2007 only 90 of the world's 192 countries were classified as "free countries" that enjoy the civil liberties and political rights associated with democratic regimes (Freedom House 2008). Authoritarianism is also not

3

restricted to states. Many if not most armed nonstate groups, including guerrillas, rebel groups, criminal gangs, terrorists, and national liberation movements, are more authoritarian than democratic (Policzer 2006). Such groups routinely exercise de facto, if not de jure, control over large numbers of people and territory. Anyone who cares about the welfare of people forced to live under the tyrannies common in the dark spaces of politics must at some point attempt to understand coercive force, whether employed under authoritarian regimes or by authoritarian nonstate groups.

The task of understanding authoritarian coercion is less than straightforward. When secrecy is the norm and dissent regularly punishable by death, information on coercive institutions is not often freely available. But despite such constraints, a surprising amount of information is available on the operations of coercive organizations like the military and police forces under authoritarian regimes. In some cases, independent monitors, such as human rights organizations, have built impressive archives of crimes committed under different dictatorships. In other cases, dictatorships themselves produce and keep records that become available at some future point.

It is also possible to learn about authoritarian coercion without discovering a previously untapped archive. Indeed, preexisting information can be analyzed in new ways to shed new light on old problems. For example, all authoritarian rulers face a crucial dilemma regarding coercive institutions like the military and the police. On the one hand, they have to create an organization powerful enough to help them achieve their goals, such as gaining and maintaining power, pursuing their enemies, and controlling the population. On the other hand, the military and police cannot be made so powerful that they threaten—or even depose—the ruler. Authoritarian rulers need to calibrate their need for a powerful coercive apparatus against their interest in self-preservation and maintaining control. A great deal has been written about the (often massive) violence and human rights abuses in various authoritarian regimes, but the dilemma that authoritarian rulers confront in *organizing* coercion is a fundamental issue of governance that has received little scholarly attention.

Asking new questions of familiar data can result in surprising findings.[1] For example, authoritarian strongmen often justify their rule with the promise to "get rid of politics" by replacing corrupt or ineffective civilian politicians with a more disciplined cadre.[2] But a close look at the organizational dilemma faced by authoritarian rulers belies this justification. At one level coercion in authoritarian regimes might be thought of as the least political of activities precisely because it takes place in the dark spaces of politics, well beyond the scrutiny of overseers such as parliamentary representatives, judicial authorities, and members of civil society. In most authoritarian regimes these institutions are immeasurably weaker than those in democracies, if they exist at all. Yet politics does not take place only in formal institutions like parliaments. Even in closed dictatorships rulers must decide how to resolve the dilemmas inherent in organizing coercion, which involves trade-offs among different organizational options. Such trade-offs are unavoidably political. They require foreclosing some options and opting for others, often at great political cost. In other words, contrary to authoritarian rulers' own claims and justifications, organizing even the most emblematic of authoritarian functions—coercive force—requires making inherently political choices.

At one level, rulers in any political system face similar choices. Democratically elected rulers as well must calibrate the organization of military and police forces so that they can exercise coercion effectively but without running amok as they do so. Yet there is a difference. Because authoritarian regimes are fundamentally repressive—because coercive force in many ways defines the nature of their governance—the stakes involved in calibrating the organization of coercion are much higher for them. Dictators can often summarily execute their enemies, an option not available to democratic rulers. At the same time, dictators can themselves be summarily executed by their enemies if they lose their grip on power. Coercive institutions are critical to maintaining that grip, yet designing and organizing these institutions is fraught with pitfalls, often involving choices between life and death.

Dictatorships normally shroud their coercive practices in secrecy, but peering behind the shroud—by obtaining whatever information is available and by asking the right questions—reveals wide variation in how rulers in these regimes organize coercion. In some cases, they construct highly bureaucratized hierarchical institutions (such as a secret police force) with the power to gather information on all aspects of the state, including the lives of its citizens. In others they rely on a varied and decentralized set of agents, such as independent task forces or death squads, which operate with a great deal of autonomy and over whose activities rulers have little direct knowledge. In some cases executives monopolize power by repressing all alternative sources of power. In others at least some alternative power sources are tolerated: for instance, in the other branches of the state, in the media, or in the form of some limited political opposition. Here the coercive institutions operate under accordingly greater constraints, watched over by a wider range of actors. Moreover, sometimes coercive institutions remain relatively stable throughout a single regime's tenure in power, and other times they fluctuate widely as one autocratic ruler replaces another.

This book develops a framework to make clearer sense of the different ways coercive force can be organized in different regimes and at different points in time. The point of departure for this framework is the observation that no ruler can rule alone. Even in highly centralized regimes, rulers rely on others to carry out orders and implement edicts. Ruling thus involves the sharing and delegation of power, which in turn requires rulers to work out the terms of these relationships. Some rulers may not want to share power, with the possible result that disputes arise with those who are excluded. Other rulers are happy to share power, but they must coordinate this with great care. Nevertheless, whoever the rulers happen to be, and however they happen to rule, they face a common fundamental problem: that of monitoring the operations and behavior of their own agents, the very people they entrust with carrying out certain unsavory tasks. This is certainly not the only problem of ruling or of building and running an organization: among other things, rulers have to decide how and where to recruit agents, how to train them and finance their operations, and how open or closed to make their organization. Yet monitoring agents' performance is a fundamental problem of ruling, one that all rulers face.

Rulers need to gather information to assess the behavior of their agents, and then they must evaluate whether it conforms to their own goals. Rulers have essentially two options for this. They can choose to gather information from within their own organization through such mechanisms as reports or databases, or from outside information sources such as the press, the courts, or even watchdog groups. I call the first strategy *internal monitoring* and the second *external monitoring*.

Plotting degrees of internal and external monitoring along vertical and horizontal axes (using criteria such as the quality and frequency of reporting) yields a readily measurable typology of the different organizational options, and we can use this to analyze the organization of coercion across different cases.[3] Rulers can rely on internal monitoring to the exclusion of external monitoring or on some combination of the two.

There are costs and benefits to different monitoring choices. For example, reliance on only one overarching internal monitoring source makes rulers vulnerable to the problem of bias. By contrast, external monitoring requires rulers to accept limitations on their power by relaxing constraints upon the activities of other groups and institutions outside the executive that may or may not support the ruler. The costs and benefits of different monitoring options can prompt rulers to rely more heavily upon one information source or the other, which in turn affects both the quality and severity of coercion in an authoritarian regime.

Authoritarian coercion can take unexpected twists and turns. For example, if external monitoring is truly "external," even authoritarian rulers are not entirely capable of directly controlling or regulating it. Because it involves independent actors such as watchdogs or citizens' organizations, external monitoring is often highly contested. Authoritarian rulers can decide whether to tolerate or ban these groups altogether, but by definition they cannot control the operations of external monitors once they exist. One of the key differences between authoritarian and totalitarian regimes is the existence of at least limited pluralism in the former (Linz 1975). This means that there is likely to be a politics of external monitoring in authoritarian regimes, turning on the conflicting interests between rulers who want to retain control and independent watchdogs who want to oversee the government's coercive practices. Like politics in other areas, the outcomes of these conflicts can be quite surprising and at the same time highly consequential for future interactions among the opponents.

Even more central to this book, the information gathered by external monitors in some cases reverberates inside authoritarian regimes.[4] Others have documented how information gathered by watchdog or "advocacy" groups can pressure authoritarian regimes into restraint by publicizing their abuses (Sikkink 1993; Keck and Sikkink 1998). This book complements such research by focusing on how information of this nature helped shape one particular regime's repressive institutions, but it also departs from that research in significant ways. First, it shows how information gathered by external monitors can have unintended consequences inside an authoritarian regime. Rulers can use such information to monitor and even regulate the activities of their own coercive agents. For example, for a government that wants to maintain its operations secret, a watchdog's report on human rights abuses committed by the government's own agents is a signal that secrecy has not been achieved. This does not mean that watchdogs deliberately collude with authoritarian rulers; rather, the watchdog's information in some cases can have unintended consequences inside the regime, depending on the goals and intentions of the government.

Why should this matter? Human rights advocacy groups commonly assume that calling attention to abuses is part of a linear process whereby "naming and shaming" automatically results in fewer abuses. More information, in other words, should result in less violence. Otherwise, why publish information about a government's abuses? Yet we still know very little about how such information actually interacts with the internal debates or decisions of an authoritarian or indeed any other type of regime. In some cases, as suggested above, rulers may have an interest in restraining their repressive apparatus: for example, if they seek support from a community that might withhold it as a result of a watchdog's report. In other cases, however, more information may result in more rather than less violence: for example, if a "shamed" ruler decides to crack down on his enemies even more harshly in order to avoid future embarrassment. The connections between information provided by monitors and the behavior of coercive organizations, this book suggests, can reveal a great deal about this darkest side of authoritarian regimes.

The second way this book departs from the work on transnational advocacy networks follows from the first: the principal focus is not the advocacy networks but on how particular authoritarian regimes organize coercion at different times. In some cases external information shapes a regime's coercive operations, and in other cases it does not. But in most cases, external information is refracted through domestic institutions and intraregime politics, sometimes with uncertain consequences.

Until now I have outlined the problem of authoritarian coercion in general and largely abstract theoretical terms, but this book examines how one particular authoritarian regime grappled with the dilemmas inherent in the organization of coercion. The early part of the military dictatorship in Chile (which lasted from 1973 to 1990) offers a rich case study for analyzing the organization of coercion. During a period of great institutional flux between 1973 and 1978, coercive institutions were organized in three different ways. When they overthrew the Allende government in a violent coup in September 1973, all four branches of the armed forces carried out widespread campaigns of unrestrained terror and repression, from mass arrests to summary executions. By 1974, the application and organization of coercion came under tighter central control under a single secret police agency, one given broad powers not only to carry out its own operations but also to oversee those of the other branches of the military and police. And less than five years after the coup, between 1977 and 1978, a second shift took place. The junta replaced its notorious secret police with a different organization that operated under greater restraint. This resulted in even fewer people killed or arrested. Although violent suppression of opposition groups continued until the end of the regime in 1990, after 1978 the regime carried out coercion under greater constraints, and new independent actors made use of increasing opportunities to contest the regime's coercive practices. Through the lens of internal and external monitoring, this book examines the causes of the different ways in which the Chilean dictatorship organized coercion.

This book adopts an unapologetically narrow focus on a single case, especially targeting a period of great institutional flux during the early part of the regime. The fundamental advantage of this single in-depth case study is its ability to trace how one factor or mechanism evolves and shapes outcomes over time (Russett 1974; Abbott 1992; Bennett 1997; Ragin 1997). This book shows how the key actors during each of the periods I discuss faced a distinct set of problems with respect to organizing coercion and how they addressed these by drawing on a limited set of organizational alternatives. The trade-offs involved in the various alternatives meant that in most cases the principal actors managed to address one set of problems while at the same time creating a series of new ones. In other words, a single case study such as this can show how the problem of organizing coercion operates as a mechanism, with distinct causes and consequences over discrete periods of time.[5]

Another important benefit of a single case study is that it can serve as a test for the large body of already accumulated knowledge about the particular case (Eckstein 1975; Ragin 1997; George and Bennett 2005). A great deal has been written about the military regime in Chile and about its main historical turning points, including the creation of some of its major coercive institutions. My aim in this book is not to contribute another history of the regime but to focus primarily on one five-year period of significant institutional flux. Through tests of alternative hypotheses and counterfactual analysis,[6] this book explains why and how the regime organized its coercive institutions at different points in time, specifically tracing the rise and fall of the main repressive agency, the Dirección de Inteligencia Nacional (DINA).

The authoritarian regime in Chile is a case that most analysts assume can be satisfactorily explained by existing arguments, which include examinations of international pressures, factionalism within the regime, and personal power accumulation by Pinochet, but none of these arguments have been subjected to a systematic test. In some cases, these hypotheses do a reasonable job of illuminating certain aspects of the organization of coercion, such as explaining why some sectors may have been interested in a particular form of coercion, or in shifting from one to another, but they fall short in important ways. Perhaps most significantly, they do not disaggregate the conflicts and strategic inter-

actions among different actors over how to organize and reorganize coercion. Some sectors may have been interested in particular forms of
coercive organization, but even powerful actors in a strong authoritarian
regime like Chile's did not always get what they wanted. Indeed, an examination of the clashes over organizing coercion reveals winners and
losers, as well as paths taken and others foreclosed.

One hazard of a single case study is the danger of focusing on a
mechanism that may be highly significant in one case but not in others
(Lieberson 1992; King, Keohane, and Verba 1994).[7] To avert this hazard,
the book is grounded in a theoretical framework, sketched above and
presented in greater detail in chapter 2, that can be used beyond the
Chilean case. Principally, it is built around categories that are mutually
exclusive and jointly exhaustive of the possible ways to organize internal
and external monitoring in coercive organizations. There is a limited set
of organizational options that are clearly distinct from one another, and
all conceivable cases can be plotted as having more of one or less of another. Thus we can compare and contrast how different cases, across different times, organized their coercive institutions. Indeed, in chapter 8 I
demonstrate this by analyzing the organization of coercion in three different authoritarian regimes: Argentina between 1976 and 1982, South
Africa under apartheid, and East Germany.

The bulk of the book (chapters 3 through 7) explains how the Chilean regime used data from both internal and external monitors to adapt
the organization of coercion in Chile after the 1973 coup. Chapter 3 describes the volatile initial period, characterized by breakdowns in hierarchy, ideological conflicts inside the military prior to the coup, and
confusion as to exactly which powers the junta had taken as a result of
the coup. Not surprisingly, given the extent to which the armed forces
used executive power to control the state and the country, they were able
to drastically limit the level of external monitoring of state coercion.
More surprising is the absence of a high level of internal monitoring,
given the long-standing traditions of military discipline and hierarchy.

The new military regime ran into trouble when the different
branches of the armed forces failed to coordinate their activities in crucial areas. Often one branch did not know what the others were doing or
which prisoners were being held where. Even inside the army, the largest

and most powerful branch, officers disagreed on key issues, including whether a state of war existed to justify their actions. In some places local commanders took a hard line against opponents and prisoners, while in others they adhered to strict codes of conduct. This led to divisive internal fights over how to apply coercion, a crisis made all the more threatening amid growing international pressure against the new regime over its many human rights violations.

By early 1974, as chapters 4 and 5 show, the organization and application of coercion shifted dramatically. Coercion came under tighter central control under a single new agency, the DINA, which operated until 1977. The DINA was given broad powers not only to carry out its own operations but also to oversee those of the other branches of the military and the police. Under the DINA, coercion was applied more consistently according to the regime's goals. Fewer people were targeted, and assassinations were carried out in a much more strategically secretive manner. The DINA carried out hundreds of "disappearances," which gave the regime a thin curtain behind which to deny responsibility for the human rights violations that were increasingly being reported.

An analysis of internal monitoring under the DINA, however, reveals only a slight increase in the regime's ability to scrutinize the actions of its coercive agents. The DINA centralized functions and was given broad powers but still did not achieve very high levels of internal monitoring. As it grew in power and as its operations broadened in scope (even extending to acts of international terrorism in South and North America, as well as in Europe), the DINA ran amok. Policing the police became an increasingly urgent problem for the regime.

External monitoring increased somewhat during this time, making the DINA's excesses all the more apparent. Groups of human rights lawyers working under the protection of the Catholic Church presented hundreds of *recursos de amparo*[8] for those who had been detained by the regime. Even though the courts ignored the overwhelming majority of these petitions, all the information collected by human rights groups on each of the cases—gathered from witness accounts and from former prisoners—formed the basis for what increasingly became the most systematic record of the regime's coercive activities (Frühling 1983, 1984).

Observers inside Chile and abroad relied on this information to report on human rights violations and to pressure the regime.

Chapter 6 analyzes a second shift in the organization of coercion, which took place from 1977 to 1978. In 1977 the DINA was replaced by a different institution, the Central Nacional de Informaciones (CNI), which was initially staffed by former DINA officials. However, in 1978 this group was dismissed by Pinochet and his cadre of advisors at the same time as other reforms to the coercive apparatus were implemented. Most critically, restrictions on civil liberties were relaxed, and the CNI came under tighter central control as it worked under stricter civilian supervision inside the regime. These reforms resulted in a marked drop in the number of people killed by the state's coercive agencies.

This shift is commonly explained as a response to international pressures (especially from the United States, then pursuing a more aggressive human rights policy under President Carter), or as a result of the push by soft-liners to institutionalize the regime, or both. However, an analysis of the organization of coercion suggests a more complex set of factors. The broad political-level factors, such as the changing balance of power among international or domestic actors or the push to institutionalize the regime, at best explain *why* the regime may have been interested in reorganizing coercion. But they fail to provide an adequate account for *how* this reorganization was carried out or for explaining which direction it took.

Chapter 7 shows that internal monitoring increased after 1978 as the regime imposed greater constraints on the CNI and supervised its activities more closely. For example, instead of reporting directly to the president, as the DINA had done, the CNI reported to a civilian minister of the interior. This civilian ministry was staffed by a new cadre of advisors to the junta, who had expressed their discontent with the high levels of repression under the DINA. While they favored strong authoritarian rule, they made clear their desire to rein in the worst abuses of the regime and to end Chile's status as an international pariah.

More surprisingly, the regime eased restrictions on civil society organizations after this time. This had the effect of de facto permitting a higher level of external monitoring, with new and unexpected consequences. New human rights organizations joined the church-based

groups in monitoring coercion and in some cases established unprecedented information-sharing networks with the CNI itself. The fact that
an authoritarian regime would offer to share information with its supposed enemies is an astonishing outcome that merits further explanation.

As indicated above, in chapter 8 I briefly compare the organization
of coercion in Chile with similar processes in three other authoritarian
regimes: Argentina during the Proceso de Reorganización Nacional
(1976–82); East Germany between the creation of the Stasi (in the late
1950s and early 1960s) and the collapse of the regime in 1989; and South
Africa under apartheid, especially between the Soweto uprising (in 1976)
and the beginning of the transition to democracy in the mid- to late
1980s.

The Argentine and East German dictatorships were subject to similarly low levels of external monitoring but sharply different levels of internal monitoring: very low in Argentina and very high in East Germany.
The absence of external monitoring in both cases permitted coercive
agents to operate freely and without restraint. The different levels of internal monitoring meant that coercion in East Germany was tightly controlled and centrally directed, while in Argentina it operated as a blunt
weapon with few internal restraints.

By contrast, in South Africa, particularly after the Soweto uprisings
of the 1970s, the regime adopted and utilized a high level of external
monitoring, a transition similar to that which occurred in Chile, and
with some of the same consequences. The judiciary and the media challenged the apartheid regime's coercive practices, and the regime at first
secretly and later more openly shared information on coercion. Indeed,
the South African regime went further than Chile, insofar as it increasingly coordinated activities with the opposition, eventually joining it in
a transitional government.

Because I focus only on authoritarian regimes, none of the cases discussed in the book displays an especially high level of external monitoring. While many human rights groups and individuals attempted to
monitor and expose the practices of these brutal regimes, countless others lost their lives in the process and were unable to report on the actions
of state officials. Only recently has much of this information become

readily available. And because I have focused on only four authoritarian regimes (and on only one case in depth) I have not covered all the possible combinations that varying levels of internal and external monitoring might yield. However, as I argue in my conclusions in chapter 8, the framework can be applied to a range of other cases, from authoritarian to democratic regimes. Indeed, this book provides the foundation for a more systematic analysis of the huge variation in coercive institutions, along with the causes and consequences of their utilization.

Finally, it bears stressing that the goal of this book is to understand how authoritarian regimes organize and in some cases reorganize their coercive institutions. The premise of this exercise is not to excuse repression under dictatorship but precisely the opposite. If we are to have any hope of improving the lot of people forced to live under the tyranny of authoritarian rule, we have no choice but to try to shine a light on these, the darkest spaces of politics.

TWO

The Coercion Problem

A clarification about what this book is not. It is not a book about why the military or the police take power. Political interventions by the armed forces in many parts of the world during the 1960s and 1970s spurred scholarly interest on this problem (Stepan 1971; O'Donnell 1973; D. Collier 1979; Lowenthal and Fitch 1986). In some cases I refer to these works, but overall this literature is concerned with a broader problem than what I tackle here: whereas it asks why military forces take power, I am concerned with how they deal with one specific problem— organizing coercive institutions—once they have power.

This is also not a book about the role of coercion in state building, a problem most centrally associated with the work of Charles Tilly (Tilly and Ardant 1975; Tilly 1986, 1992). Tilly's work has (deservedly) been very influential (e.g., Davis 1994; Reno 1995, 1998; Herbst 2000; Centeno 2002; Davis and Pereira 2003). However, it focuses on a different level of analysis, namely the effects of coercive force on the process of state formation in the long run and vice versa (i.e., "States make war and war makes states").[1] By contrast, I am concerned with a problem at once both narrower and broader. On the one hand, I have conceived of a way to better understand how some authoritarian regimes organize coercive institutions, which is a phenomenon of far shorter duration than the processes Tilly describes. On the other hand, I also want to systematize the general organizational alternatives available for coercion, as well as their trade-offs, and the consequences of adopting one or the other.

With this in mind, it is well understood that dictatorships are political regimes that tend to use coercion much more freely than democratic governments in order to pursue their goals. Indeed, coercive force in many ways defines dictatorship—it is a basic tool of unconstrained power. Yet organizing coercion presents all rulers, even dictators, with a series of dilemmas. Very generally, rulers need to address such questions as: How much force should be used against enemies to maintain domestic order? Which institutions should use force, and how much power should they have? How can the ruler ensure that the levels and kinds of coercion employed do not critically undermine support for the regime or for its political goals?

Compounding these problems are the standard dilemmas of governance stemming from the fact that all rulers must necessarily share power and rely on others to carry out their commands. No ruler, in other words, rules alone. Rulers must delegate, and those to whom they delegate must also delegate. But delegating to agents or institutions complicates the business of ruling because rulers cannot always directly observe their agents' actions. How do rulers ensure that agents perform in a manner consistent with the rulers' goals? Or that the agents carry out the rulers' goals and not their own? How can the ruler ensure that they even do their jobs at all? When agents operate outside the principals' direct oversight, the latter must rely on some sort of information-gathering mechanism to know whether the agents are doing their jobs. Agents also often have incentives to withhold information from their superiors. For instance, the agent may wish to withhold information about his qualifications or lack thereof. He may also want to mislead his superior about the quality of his work or the degree of enthusiasm with which he approaches it (Jervis 1976; Wilson 1989, 155; Allison and Zelikow 1999).

Principal-agent theory addresses these problems by analyzing how different incentives and cost-benefit calculations influence actors' choices and shape economic and political outcomes (Alchian and Demsetz 1973; Ross 1973; McCubbins and Weingast 1984; Calvert, McCubbins, and Weingast 1989; Williamson 1990; Kiewiet and McCubbins 1991; Krehbiel 1991; Macey 1992).[2] Among other things, principals need to determine optimal wages or other incentives to attract and keep agents and to ensure that they perform their work according to the principals' aims.

At first pass, we might expect principal-agent problems to be more likely to occur in democratic regimes than in dictatorships, since there is more likely to be a divergence between the interests of the principal and those of the agent in a regime with embedded multiple interests, such as a democracy. By contrast, dictatorships, especially highly centralized ones, might have less trouble carrying out their goals than democracies. Instead of having to account for myriad embedded interests, dictators can simply issue orders in the expectation that they will be followed. Indeed, that is often one of the key reasons that dictators themselves give to justify taking or holding on to power: that they are better able than democrats to "get things done," or, according to the myth surrounding Mussolini, to "make the trains run on time."

When scrutinized carefully, however, these conjectures turn out to be less than straightforward. First, it is true that in authoritarian regimes superiors tend to have more power over agents' careers and sometimes over their lives. The stiff penalties that they impose for disobeying result in greater incentives to obey orders. But these same penalties also greatly increase the stakes, resulting in greater incentives to hide the mistakes and transgressions that do occur, for fear of far more severe consequences.

Second, the closed nature of authoritarianism means that there are likely to be fewer independent sources—such as free courts, political parties, press, or social groups—that can accurately report on agents' performance and act as feedback mechanisms for the ruler. If these institutions existed, and if they were truly free, the regime in question would not be authoritarian. The absence of accountability mechanisms in authoritarian regimes is likely to multiply principal-agent problems. In other words, dictators may be powerful, but they are often also information-poor.

In short, ensuring that agents perform according to the ruler or principal's goals is a critical function of governance, but there are good reasons to believe that gathering information on agents' performance in authoritarian regimes is likely to be more difficult than in more open regimes. In a system with higher punishments for transgressions there are likely to be more disincentives to accurate reporting; in authoritarian regimes, accurate monitoring is less likely than in pluralistic regimes that tolerate or encourage independent monitoring.

These difficulties become apparent when we examine the specific mechanisms available to rulers for monitoring agents' performance. Mc-Cubbins and Weingast (1984) describe two possible monitoring strategies: "police patrols" and "fire alarms." The first refers to reliance on a specialized set of agents or agencies created by the ruler for the purpose of monitoring the performance of other administrative agents or agencies. The second refers to reliance on information provided by the population at large: for instance, in the form of complaints about a given institution or set of agents. In police patrol monitoring, special agents actively seek out information on agents' performance. In fire alarm monitoring, special agents or institutions may collect and systematize information, but the "eyes and ears" are the population at large who call attention to specific agents' performance.[3]

I adopt the distinction between these two kinds of monitoring but assign them different labels. I call police patrols *internal monitoring* and fire alarms *external monitoring*. In my view, these labels better capture an important aspect of the difference between the two kinds of monitoring, namely the different relationship of each to the ruler. Internal monitoring is that of specialized agencies created within the boundaries of the bureaucracy and still under the control of the ruler, while external monitoring relies on information from outside the bureaucracy and outside the ruler's direct executive control.[4] This can involve a range of institutions, from other branches of the state to groups in society at large that gather and publish information on the operations of the various agents.

The distinction between internal and external monitoring has a strong resonance in long-standing debates over the merits of internal versus external review in ensuring police accountability: "Internal review involves police oversight of police; commanding officers and administrators investigate the public's complaints of police corruption, abuse, and violence and mete out appropriate discipline. External review typically involves either government-appointed administrators, civilian review boards, or the creation of politically powerful blue-ribbon committees of inquiry (such as in South Africa after the 1976 Soweto riots, Russia after the 1991 coup, and Los Angeles after the Rodney King beating)" (Tanner 2000, 116). The proponents of internal review typically argue that those who are most familiar with the operational details of police work (such as other police officers) are best equipped to carry out investigations. Moreover, supervisors are especially well equipped to mete out punishments to agents in the form of reassignment to undesirable posts or denial of career advancement. By contrast, proponents of external review point out that outsiders are likely to enjoy greater legitimacy and that the information they gather is likely to be more trustworthy. Officers can find themselves torn in terms of loyalty when investigating fellow officers, a position that can compromise their investigations (Hudson 1972; Chevigny 1995, 85–116; Tanner 2000, 116–17).

In the following sections, I describe internal and external monitoring in greater depth, providing criteria to measure their degree. These are proxies at best, and here I aim at distinguishing broadly between low, medium, and high monitoring levels.[5] Such a distinction is useful to analyze observed differences in institutional organization and whether these differences correspond to given trade-offs as well as organizational strategies and choices.

Internal Monitoring

Principals normally lack constant direct oversight over agents.[6] It is not possible for them to know 100 percent of their agents' operations 100 percent of the time. As a result, they need to rely on other ways to gather information on them. Internal monitoring (IM) is one available option. It relies on information gathered from within the principal's same organization. Principals can carry out internal monitoring themselves by personally observing agents' behavior, requesting reports, and ensuring that agents fulfill their goals. If the number of agents is relatively small, it may be possible for principals to monitor agents' operations directly. But as the number of agents grows, it becomes increasingly difficult for the principal to do this, and it is likely that principals will rely on a special kind of agent—a monitor—to gather information on the operations of other agents. The monitor may be assigned strictly monitoring duties, or the monitor's tasks may combine monitoring with operational duties that resemble those of other agents. Regardless, the main criterion that makes this monitor "internal" is that it remains under the principal's direct control.

Principals are interested in the breadth and depth of information gathered. How well the monitor itself performs, based on how well it is gathering the information it is supposed to gather, is a central problem for the principal. For instance, is the monitor reporting all the relevant cases? Is it reporting them in sufficient depth to allow the principal to make decisions for the purpose of pursuing his goals and implementing his policies? Are the reports regular and accurate?

It is possible to turn these questions into indicators that measure the extent to which a regime adopts internal monitoring of coercion. I have distinguished between two broad kinds of criteria: process and outcome. The first refers to procedural measures of how well the given organization performs, and the second to agents' behavior; both serve as indicators of the quality of monitoring.

For instance, process criteria includes how frequently and how well agents report to their superiors on their activities (IM1), as well as how regularly monitors report on agents' behavior (IM2). An information clearinghouse (IM3), which receives and disseminates regular updates on operations to the relevant parties, also indicates that a ruler is relying on internal monitoring to keep track of agents' operations.

Internal monitoring is also likely to be higher where the ratio between monitors and agents is higher (IM4). It is reasonable to expect better information overall when more monitors are keeping track of fewer agents than when the situation is reversed. For simplicity, I have designated a ratio of less than 1 (when the number of coercive agents exceeds the number of monitors) as an indicator of a low level of internal monitoring, and the reverse (greater than 1) as an indicator of a high-level of internal monitoring.

Outcome criteria include indicators such as how much trust principals have over their agents (IM5), and how well intra- and interbranch coordination takes place (IM6). If principals do not trust their agents, this is likely to reflect an internal monitoring problem. The same is true when coordination is poor—where it is difficult for the relevant parties to obtain the information necessary to perform their duties. Also, corruption and coercion carried out for personal ends (such as revenge or extortion) are likely to reflect a low level of internal monitoring, as agents place personal ends over organizational ones (IM7).

For the sake of simplicity, I have distinguished roughly between "low," "medium," and "high" internal monitoring. Table 2.1 lists the criteria that serve as indicators of each.

It is important to note that these criteria are different from simple measures of greater or lesser central control by principals over agents. Indeed, internal monitoring can be centralized or decentralized, insofar as it is possible for a principal to receive information from a variety of decentralized internal monitors or from a single centralized one. All things being equal, it is likely to be easier and more convenient for a principal to receive information from one centralized source than from many decentralized ones; however, there can be significant disadvantages to centralization. For example, reliance on a single source of information can make the principal perilously dependent on a monitor that may be unreliable or one that puts its own interests above those of the principal.

The level of centralization in any particular case can be captured by some of the indicators presented in table 2.1. For example, centralization would almost necessarily imply an information clearinghouse that gathers and disseminates information to the relevant parties. Also, centralization is more likely when the total number of monitors (or overseers) remains low. If there is a single overseer, this is likely to reflect a high level of central control, but this does not necessarily translate directly into a higher level of internal monitoring. An indicator of the level of monitoring is not the centralization of monitoring per se but rather the ratio between the number of monitors and the number of agents. A single monitor may have to look after dozens, hundreds, or even thousands of different agents. It is reasonable to expect that having to keep track of a large number of agents is more difficult than having to keep track of a few. In this case, the level of centralization is a handicap to high levels of internal monitoring.

Also, in principle monitoring involves only information gathering, but in practice—particularly in coercive institutions—internal monitors can often take on operational functions as well. Secret police forces frequently do more than simply monitor others' operations: often they

Table 2.1 Internal Monitoring Indicators

	Low	*Medium*	*High*
PROCESS			
Internal reporting by agents to superiors on their activities (IM1)	Reports either nonexistent or ad hoc and unreliable	Reports may be reliable but ad hoc, or regular but unreliable	Agents deliver regular, detailed, and accurate reports on their activities
Monitors' briefings on agents' operations to principals (IM2)	No briefings	Ad hoc briefings	Regular briefings
Information clearinghouse (IM3)	None	Ad hoc	Present
Number of monitors divided by number of agents (IM4)	< 1	$= 1$	> 1
OUTCOME			
Principal's self-reported trust in agents (IM5)	Low	Medium	High
Intra- and interbranch coordination (IM6)	Poor; frequent delays, relevant parties often lack adequate and timely info	Moderate delays	No delays; parties usually have adequate and timely info to carry out ops
Corruption and coercion for personal ends (IM7)	Frequent	Occasional	Rare

carry out coercive operations of their own. No doubt combining functions can make some problems (such as dependence by the principal on a single monitor) all the more serious. However, while many actual internal monitors combine both functions, it is important to separate them analytically.[7]

External Monitoring

The second information-gathering mechanism is external monitoring (EM). This involves information that comes from sources outside the direct control of the principal or ruler. One possibility is for the principal himself to gather such information. For example, principals in some cases allow appeals and information from the population at large, through special audiences or other mechanisms.[8] Another possibility is for the other branches of the state outside the executive, such as human rights commissions, ombudsmen, congressional committees, courts, or special panels (so long as they remain truly independent) to carry out external monitoring. Independent groups in society, including the media, watchdogs, and other citizens' coalitions, could also do this. International human rights groups, such as Human Rights Watch and Amnesty International, have also increasingly played a significant role as external monitors of coercive agents in different states.

In democratic regimes that purport to uphold the rule of law, this information is an important—and often routine—check on the operations of coercive agents. Still, external monitoring can also occur in the context of authoritarian regimes. It may be less routine, and the relationship between rulers and external monitors may be more conflictive, but it exists nevertheless.

The activities of external monitors may increase during periods of intense coercion,[9] which has the dual effect of not only exposing and pressuring the regime but also making information on the activities of its agents publicly available. Authoritarian rulers may challenge this information or claim that human rights organizations are biased against them, but they are aware of this kind of monitoring. Whether or not a dictator uses the information as a control on the operations of his agents is a matter of choice. Some dictators reject such information out of hand as a matter of principle, but not all of them do.

As with internal monitoring, principals of whatever stripe (whether democratic or authoritarian) are concerned about the breadth and depth of information obtained through external monitoring. External monitoring is likely to be higher, all things being equal, where there are more available sources of information on agents' operations, where these sources operate under fewer constraints, and where there are regular and reliable information-sharing mechanisms between the executive and outsiders (Rosberg 1995, 41–51).

It is therefore also possible to roughly measure the quality of external monitoring in the same way as internal monitoring. External monitoring is likely to be higher in cases where there is an ombudsman or interlocutor that outsiders can refer to and rely on than in cases where no such nexus exists (EM1). However, this interaction need not be formalized. Informal networks between insiders and outsiders indicate the presence of what in effect is information sharing between unofficial interlocutors and outside groups.

External monitoring is also likely to be higher in cases where outsiders have the legal right to obtain regular access to prisoners held by the coercive agency (EM2). In addition, a principal's level of trust in outsiders' reports can be an indicator of their quality (EM3), though this should be measured carefully. Principals may deeply mistrust outside observers' reports about coercive agents even though the reports may in fact be accurate and useful. Or principals may claim in public to mistrust reports or agents themselves, while in private (especially if the reports are useful) treating them as an invaluable information source.

The presence of human rights agencies and how freely they are able to operate is an important gauge of external monitoring. The more agencies there are with an established presence, and the more freedom they have to operate, the higher the quality of external monitoring is likely to be (EM4). The same is true with respect to independent media (EM5). The media cannot serve as an external monitor unless they are free from official restrictions and executive control.

Also, the other branches of the state can serve as external monitors provided that they are not directly manipulated by the executive. With respect to the legislative branch, a signal of high external monitoring would be the presence of dedicated standing committees to check the executive's use of coercion (EM6). Ad hoc (or nonexistent) committees would normally indicate lower levels of external monitoring. By the same token, external monitoring is likely to be higher where the judiciary has full jurisdiction over relevant cases pertaining to coercive force (EM7). In situations where a country's supreme court abdicates jurisdiction over coercive institutions, for instance to the military courts, external monitoring is low.

Last, the quality of external monitoring is likely to be reflected in the quality of a regime's freedom-of-information laws. The more that outsiders have legally protected access to a wide variety of documentation and information on government policies and practices, the more likely it is that they will be able to monitor effectively (EM8). Table 2.2 summarizes these criteria.

Just as internal monitoring can be complicated when a monitor adopts both information-gathering and operational functions, something similar can be observed in external monitoring. Monitors can become political actors, carrying out operations in their own right. These are not necessarily coercive operations (except in some very rare circumstances: for instance, when other branches of the state besides the executive carry out coercion) but may be other forms of political activity related to coercion. Groups can carry out protests or mobilize in support of—or more frequently against—the government. This can result in situations where the same group that monitors the executive's use of coercion is also mobilizing against it. In extreme cases such a group may itself use coercion against the government. In other cases the executive's coercive organizations may be called upon to patrol a march or to break up a demonstration by a group that may also be acting as a monitor. Although this may complicate external monitoring in specific situations, it is important for analytical purposes to keep external monitoring distinct.

Table 2.2 External Monitoring Indicators

	Low	*Medium*	*High*
Interlocutor or ombudsman for outside groups (EM1)	None	Only on ad hoc basis	Present and accessible full time
Outsiders' access to prisoners (EM2)	None	Legal but not necessarily granted	Legal and granted
Principal's trust in monitor's reports (EM3)	Low	Medium	High
Human rights agencies (EM4)	Not present or forced underground	Limited presence, may operate in public but often repressed	High presence, and their rights respected
Independent media (EM5)	Not present	May be present, but not very effective	Present and effective
Legislative oversight (EM6)	None	Ad hoc	Standing committees
Judicial jurisdiction (EM7)	None	Partial (some cases)	Full (all cases)
Freedom-of-information laws (EM8)	None	Ad hoc or ineffective	Broad and effective

Variation According to Internal and External Monitoring

Internal and external monitoring are not mutually exclusive options. Many regimes rely on combinations of both. Each can be considered an axis in a matrix depicting a political and policy space pertaining to how principals use information in the organization of coercion. In some cases coercion is organized with very low internal and external monitoring and in other cases with higher degrees of one or both.

Regimes that score very high on internal monitoring and low on external monitoring are those where the top executive leadership is likely to have a great deal of information on coercion but where this information is not available outside the executive. There are unlikely to be any strong groups or institutions that oversee the coercive power of the executive and that are independent of it. Executives have de facto and likely de jure monopoly control over the organization of coercion in a given territory in these cases and can exercise this control unchallenged by other power centers.[10] I have labeled this space *bureaucratic coercion* to denote the monopolization of information at the top of the leadership hierarchy and the fact that this type of coercion is likely to generate myriad reports and a great deal of paperwork. The high degree of internal monitoring and the absence of external monitoring often results in more systematic and widespread coercion that is more nakedly brutal and thus more "effective" at pacifying the principals' opposition. In this area lie some of the best known examples of strong dictatorships in recent history, such as Nazi Germany, Stalinist Russia, Iran under Reza Pahlavi (and the Savak), and East Germany, especially after the creation and consolidation of the Stasi (a case that I will discuss in chapter 8).

By contrast, regimes that score low on both internal and external monitoring are those where neither the leadership nor any other groups or institutions are likely to be very informed about the activities of the coercive agents. Where this information is available, it is at best patchy and ad hoc. Agents in such regimes operate with neither internal supervision nor the expectation of accountability to outside groups. For this reason I have labeled this space *blind coercion*. The lack of information and coordination in these cases often results in more haphazard and unsystematic coercion (though it is often no less brutal). Such examples include coercion in countries like Liberia during the Taylor regime or within the Democratic Republic of the Congo.

Diametrically opposite this space, scoring high on both IM and EM, are cases where the executive leadership as well as other institutions and groups in society are likely to have broad and deep information about the operations of coercive agents. I have called this *transparent coercion* to denote the fact that coercion here takes place in a fishbowl, in which a large number of actors and institutions have a great deal of access to information on all aspects of the executive's use of coercion, from the principal's policies to the agents' actions. This is especially common where civil society groups—such as human rights watchdogs—have mobilized and operate without a critical degree of repression by the executive. Such conditions are more likely in democratic regimes, in countries such as Canada or the United Kingdom. The result of agents' knowing they are under strict scrutiny is that they apply coercive force in a more disciplined manner, targeting only those they are allowed and only to the extent permitted by law. Consequently, there are fewer associated deaths and human rights violations in such states.

Where the organization of coercion scores high on EM and low on IM, information on the operations of the coercive agents is likely to be widely available to different groups and institutions but not particularly deep. No one is likely to know very much about the details of the operations themselves, given that there is little or no direct oversight. Indeed, the principals in such cases may deliberately not want to exercise very much oversight: for example, if the agents are carrying out controversial missions or ones likely to carry a high political cost. The principals' primary mechanism to learn about their agents and check whether such operations have achieved the desired results is outsiders' reports: for example, in the media. Information on the outcomes of coercion—such as the number and type of people killed—is likely to be readily available. Indeed, coercive agents in such a regime are likely to try to hide their actions, as monitors will try continually to uncover their actions. I have therefore labeled this space *hide-and-seek coercion*. Table 2.3 illustrates the possibilities.

Table 2.3   Types of Coercion

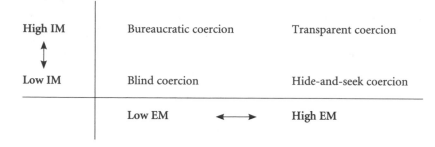

High IM	Bureaucratic coercion	Transparent coercion
Low IM	Blind coercion	Hide-and-seek coercion
	Low EM ⟷ **High EM**	

To summarize: We can use the criteria in tables 2.1 and 2.2 to measure degrees of internal and external monitoring. Both types of monitoring can be combined, and different cases can be placed along the matrix indicated in table 2.3. I have described what are in essence the cardinal points of the internal and external combinations. With the adoption of essentially an ordinal scale that measures levels of monitoring, cases can lie anywhere in the matrix or can shift from one place to another. These shifts can happen as a result of external monitoring pressures (e.g., from independent monitors) or as a result of a decision to reorganize internal monitoring.

The reader will notice that the matrix is not only applicable to authoritarian regimes. Any sort of regime—from authoritarian to democratic—can be measured according to internal and external monitoring and placed on this matrix. As the levels of external monitoring grow, no doubt the likelihood of authoritarianism diminishes. An authoritarian regime with high levels of external monitoring, especially external monitoring by other independent branches of government, would be almost a contradiction in terms. Because this book focuses on the organization of coercion only in authoritarian regimes, the cases I select do not reflect high levels of external monitoring.[11]

Table 2.4 provides a rough summary of where the various cases discussed in this book (Chile and the three cases discussed in chapter 8) lie on the matrix and suggests other possible cases in brackets. I will explain

Table 2.4   Regimes Placed on the Coercion Matrix

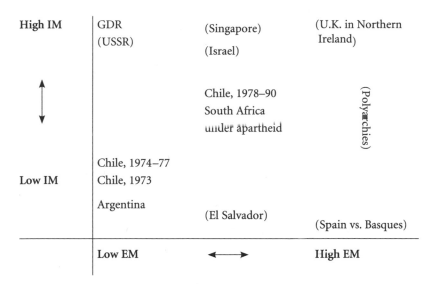

the categorization of each of the different cases in later chapters. In the Chilean case, the bulk of the analysis will be devoted to measuring monitoring levels in the main periods discussed and to using these measurements to analyze the reasons for the shift from one way of organizing coercion to another, as well as the overall effects upon the targeting and intensity of coercion. I build a key part of the tool kit for this analysis in the next section's discussion of the various trade-offs among different types of monitoring.

Trade-offs

The preceding discussion raises the questions: Why would a ruler, if given the choice and the possibility of implementing his choice, choose one type of monitoring over another? What advantages and disadvantages does each type possess?

Bureaucratic coercion presents the ruler with many obvious advantages. With high internal monitoring scores on all criteria, orders are likely to be followed and transgressions are likely to be reported (and punished). Leaders utilizing such a system can trust their agents. Under bureaucratic coercion, organizations act with a unity of purpose. There is a low level of corruption and a high capacity to coordinate activities, either within the organization's branches or together with other institutions. Moreover, because of the low level of external monitoring, a ruler in this kind of organization need not be concerned with independent power centers either inside or outside the state.

But there are also costs to bureaucratic coercion. With internal monitoring, as we have seen, principals monitor their agents' performance using only channels from within their own organization. They have two options to do this. Either they gather information themselves, or they delegate the monitoring task to a special agent (the monitor). When organizations are small and there are relatively few agents, it may be possible for principals to carry out internal monitoring themselves. As organizations grow, however, it is increasingly likely that principals will rely on specialized monitors. Bureaucratic coercion regimes are likely to rely on relatively large and complex organizations that tend to become increasingly totalitarian because of their need to both repress and scrutinize.

This raises a dilemma. With high internal monitoring (a condition that defines bureaucratic coercion), the agents are ultimately under the ruler's command and remain dependent on him for promotions, funding, and perks. While this gives the ruler a high degree of control, it also creates a potentially counterproductive set of incentives. Agents who do something they are not supposed to do have few incentives—and many disincentives—to accurately report their transgressions to their superiors and ultimately to the ruler or principal. Yet information on precisely these sorts of transgressions is critical. Without it, the principal may not be able to accurately gauge what agents are doing. In these cases, rulers may be rich in control but poor in information.

One option to address this problem is for the principal to create a separate agency, a specialist in internal monitoring. If the principal wants to keep track of Agency A, he may designate Agency B to do so. While this may resolve the immediate problem vis-à-vis A, so long as the incentives governing B are similar to those governing A, the problem has not ultimately been resolved. If B is still dependent on the principal for funding and promotions, B's agents will have similar disincentives to report accurately on their performance if they are involved in transgressions. Keeping track of B's operations now becomes a problem in its own right. No doubt, a ruler who becomes suspicious of Agency B may decide to create Agency C to keep track of B. But again, this does not really resolve the problem, insofar as Agency C also remains dependent on the ruler and retains the same incentives and disincentives. Rulers can keep layering monitors overtop of monitors, but the effect of this strategy is simply to ratchet the problem up to different levels.[12] This dilemma can be understood as a problem of "monitoring the monitor."[13]

The second cost of bureaucratic coercion can be understood, then, as an attempt by the ruler to avoid the "monitoring the monitor" problem. A ruler who wants to avoid this problem and still retain the advantages of high internal monitoring and low external monitoring could decide not to rely on a specialized monitor. In this scheme, all the monitors (or the combinations of monitors and agents) monitor each other. By definition, this requires a relatively decentralized monitoring mechanism, where the principal receives direct information and reports from many different sources.

But careful scrutiny reveals that this situation does not necessarily resolve the principal's basic problem of ensuring readily available, accurate, and reliable information. It merely replaces the ratcheting problem (of adding layers of monitors in hierarchical fashion) with the problem of having to decide which among the myriad monitors he will now listen to and figuring out how to make sense of the multiple sources. The various monitors may have different standards, agendas, and ideologies, in which case using them effectively may require considerably more work and perhaps a great deal of luck.

In other words, while it is more convenient to rely on only one trusted source, as that source attains a monopoly on information its trustworthiness becomes suspect and the principal's vulnerability increases. Multiplying the number of internal monitors is likely to increase the overall quantity of information available to the principal, but it makes that information perhaps only slightly more reliable, and getting it now becomes a highly difficult task. In short, the principal trades convenience for effort and quantity.

Increasing the level of external monitoring and adopting transparent coercion offers a way out of this dilemma. Instead of having to trust a single monitor, the principal now empowers multiple monitors (and indeed the population at large) to scrutinize the state's coercive agencies via such institutions as the courts, the press, or watchdog groups. He is still likely to be faced with countless new reports from many different sources, but a high level of external monitoring offers him a way out of the dilemma highlighted above. With high external monitoring, the "monitoring the monitor" problem is avoided, insofar as the external monitors are by definition not under the principal's direct control. The need to repress and potentially alienate larger segments of the bureaucracy in a more totalitarian manner in order to gain more control and unity is also avoided. Therefore, the principal can afford the convenience of a specialized monitor without the vulnerability that this option imposes in bureaucratic coercion. The internal monitor's information can always be checked against that of the external monitor(s).

To be sure, not all the information gathered by external monitors is likely to be accurate. In many cases, for a variety of reasons (from deliberate disinformation to simple mistakes) reports are likely to be inaccurate. Or, in some cases, external monitoring sources are likely to reflect the concerns of only one portion of the population, with a resulting information bias. But there are two ways to address this problem. One is simply by the sheer quantity of information; the more information there is, the greater the likelihood of checking errors against other independent accounts without the biases of intentional misreporting of enemies or competitors inherent in bureaucratic coercion. Moreover, the greater the protections in place to allow delivery of accurate reports (e.g., protections for freedom of speech and for witnesses in court), the more incentives there are for more people to report and to provide accurate information (Rosberg 1995).

However, a high level of external monitoring in transparent coercion presents rulers with a new and different set of problems. The most obvious is that as external monitoring increases, often beyond the control of the principal, limitations are placed upon his autonomy. When external monitors are given more leeway, more violations are exposed, and elements both within and outside the state become increasingly vocal in their opposition to the regime. Rulers that are already in this area (e.g., in an established polyarchy) may simply assume these costs as a given and not question them; but a ruler who wants to maximize his own power and minimize the power of other institutions either inside or outside the state is likely to try to avoid moving in this direction. With low external monitoring, rulers do not have to negotiate the limits of their coercive agencies with other independent institutions or suffer the risks of sanctions or other punitive measures from the international community.

Blind coercion, with minimal internal and external monitoring, yields diametrically opposite sorts of trade-offs. Here rulers do not need to accept limitations on their power from external sources, but they are unlikely to receive very much information on their agents' operations from *any* source, internal or external. Why would any ruler choose this?

One reason is cost. It is cheaper to set up blind coercion than to create the complex bureaucratic apparatus required for high levels of internal monitoring. In some cases rulers may also deliberately not want to know what their agents are doing, especially if they are carrying out operations that are politically costly. Indeed, most coercive operations (from detentions to killings) arguably fall into this category. Not knowing may be a good option for rulers who do not want to bear the costs of the "dirty work" their agents may be doing. Blind coercion, in other words, provides rulers with more plausible deniability.

At the same time, blind coercion is likely to involve more difficulties in coordinating inter- and even intrabranch activities, and this may be a severe disadvantage to those rulers or principals for whom such coordination may be important. Also, the likelihood that agents will deviate from their organization's task and engage in corruption and coercion for their own purposes is extremely high in blind coercion. With neither internal nor external monitoring as a check, it is hard to imagine how principals can effectively prevent this. Because agents in blind coercion do not have to worry about being watched, they are less likely to try to op-erate in secret and more likely to conduct themselves as if they enjoyed a high degree of impunity.

Hide-and-seek coercion, with low internal and high external moni-toring, is as unlikely to occur in authoritarian regimes as transparent co-ercion. In this type of organizational pattern, a ruler may deliberately want to have no direct internal knowledge of the details of his agents' operations. He may be interested only in whether the task is done (e.g., were the intended targets arrested or killed?), and this information can be provided reasonably effectively by external monitors' reports—for example, in the media. However, the problems of exposure and opposi-tion inherent in situations of high external monitoring remain. And even though hide-and-seek coercion provides a ruler with more checks (through available external monitoring reports), coordination of agents and agencies in this case may remain difficult.

The costs and benefits of these different patterns of monitoring may prompt rulers to shift from one to another, but the shifts themselves may also impose additional costs. For example, a ruler who wants to change his strategy of bureaucratic coercion because of the pitfalls associated with it may decide to allow or even facilitate higher external monitoring. Doing so increases the available information, but it has costs of its own. Increasing external monitoring necessarily requires accepting some new limitations on a ruler's power. It is also likely to mean engaging openly with political foes that in a previously closed regime the ruler could simply have disposed of. While these new constraints pose obvious dif-ficulties for an authoritarian regime, they may also present new oppor-tunities for alliance building and competition.

The shift from high to lower external monitoring is also likely to be extremely costly. It necessarily requires closing down or seriously hob-bling independent groups or institutions, which may strongly resist the executive's actions. Enhancing internal monitoring is also likely to im-pose other costs. For example, creating a strong specialized internal monitoring agency may be difficult in cases where executive power is shared among two or more players. In these cases, the creation of an in-ternal monitor may be extremely costly, insofar as it requires the agree-ment of the main players, who may need to put aside mutual distrust and fear that the others will use the new institution to their own advantage. By the same token, getting rid of a strong specialized internal monitor is also likely to be politically costly, particularly when other actors have an interest in keeping it.

For all of these reasons, the middle area in the matrix is likely to be an extremely contested space. Because coercion is so central to politics, and to different types of regimes, this middle area is also likely to be an important contested space in cases of regime transition from authoritarian to democratic rule. To be sure, the shifts to greater or lesser degrees of internal and/or external monitoring are not the only factors likely to matter during regime transition. Other factors, such as the struggle for power among different political actors and institutions, are also important during this time. But the politics of different forms of monitoring in the organization of coercion is a crucial factor that has received relatively little systematic attention. In the following chapters I use this framework to analyze the politics of organizing and shifting from one type of coercion to another during the Chilean dictatorship.

PART II

THREE

The Overthrow and Turmoil

The Chilean Armed Forces overthrew the Allende government on the morning of September 11, 1973, with swift and overwhelming force.[1] They launched a massive assault on La Moneda, the presidential palace, through a combination of air and ground attacks. They disbanded Congress and banned all other independent political organizations, including the country's main parties.[2] Allende himself held out against the assault for several hours in the presidential palace with a small group of allies, but by early afternoon he was dead and much of the palace was reduced to rubble. By this time also hundreds of people, including most of his key cabinet ministers, were in prison, and scores of others had been summarily executed. All independent media sources, including newspapers as well as radio and television stations that did not support the government, were either closed or taken over.[3] Allende was able to deliver his final address on Radio Magallanes, a pro government station, at 10:00 a.m., shortly before the station was taken over by military forces.

A state of siege was quickly imposed, meetings of more than a handful of people were banned, and strict curfews were enforced.[4] Planning for the coup had been taking place for months, and the armed forces were helped in their preparations by having previously successfully infiltrated the top leadership of the main left-wing parties.[5] Within days, most of whatever armed resistance remained had been dealt with, and the military's control of the country was nearly total.[6]

This chapter describes the background to the coup, focusing on three factors that shaped the organization of coercion afterward: breakdowns in military hierarchy, ideological contradictions, and confusion over which powers the junta had assumed after the coup.

Breakdowns in Hierarchy

The 1973 coup took place in the aftermath of a long and divisive struggle within the armed forces over two central issues: whether to get involved in politics at all and what stance to assume toward the growing influence of Marxism in the country. These struggles had been taking place within the armed forces for decades, but they reached a crisis point with the election of Salvador Allende.

The standard view of the debate regarding the political involvement of the Chilean military casts the "constitutionalists" as those sectors that provided unconditional support for the constitutionally elected government and the *golpistas* as those who favored overthrowing the Allende government (Arriagada Herrera 1986; Sohr 1989). This is how many key players are usually characterized in Chile, and I will similarly use the terms as they are most commonly applied. However, the conventional use of these terms is not altogether accurate. Chilean political history and the 1925 Constitution did not provide an unambiguously apolitical role for the armed forces.[7] The armed forces were supposedly a "nondeliberative" institution obedient to the executive, but the constitution stipulated that they enjoyed a special role as guardians of the institutional order (Loveman 1993).

By the late 1960s many officers openly discussed politics, challenging both the principle of nondeliberation and the military lines of command. In April 1968 approximately eighty officers and students of the Academia de Guerra (the army's war academy) resigned in protest over poor wages, a move that resulted in the downfall of Defense Minister Juan de Dios Carmona. These tensions continued, and in October 1969 a retired general named Roberto Viaux, in direct challenge to the orders of the top army command, took control of the largest munitions regiment, the "Tacna," in protest over the defense minister's wages and retirement policies. This was the most serious crisis and the most serious breach of discipline inside the military since the 1930s. The crisis resulted in the downfall of the minister of defense, the commander in chief of the armed forces, and the head of the Joint Chiefs of Staff *(jefe del estado mayor de defensa nacional)*. General René Schneider took over as commander in chief of the armed forces and General Carlos Prats as head of the Joint Chiefs of Staff. Both had a reputation inside military and civilian circles as strict constitutionalists who would put a brake on the growing politicization of the armed forces.

Then Senator Salvador Allende of the Socialist Party won a narrow plurality among the three contending candidates in the September 1970 presidential elections. In a system without runoff elections, when no single candidate obtained a clear majority, Congress had to approve the appointment of the president. Because no Marxist candidate had ever obtained a plurality before (though since the 1952 elections Allende had been the perennial "also ran" candidate), Allende's appointment provoked a serious crisis inside the Christian Democrat–dominated Congress. Rumors of a military coup were widespread. Nixon's then–national security advisor, Henry Kissinger, privately declared that the United States could not simply stand by and let a country turn Marxist due to "the irresponsibility of its own people" (Hersh 1982, 35). The Central Intelligence Agency (CIA) during October 1970 made numerous contacts with various military and paramilitary groups to work out the possibilities of a coup (Sigmund 1977; Hitchens 2001a, 2001b). The biggest stumbling block to these plans was General Schneider. According to a 1975 U.S. Senate report on covert activities during this time, since it was not possible to remove Schneider by retirement or resignation, the coup plotters decided to kidnap him (U.S. Senate, Church Committee 1975; U.S. Senate, Select Committee 1975).[8] On October 22 several cars surrounded Schneider's car; armed young; men approached and broke the car windows. When Schneider reached for his gun, the young men opened fire. Schneider died in the military hospital three days later (Prats González 1974, 184–89).[9] On October 24 the Congress confirmed Salvador Allende as president-elect after reaching an agreement with the Christian Democrats that Allende's Popular Unity (Unidad Popular) government would promise, among other guarantees, not to clean house in the army. On October 27 the outgoing president, Eduardo Frei, named General Carlos Prats, next in seniority, as commander in chief of the armed forces.

Apart from the obvious significance of the murder of a commander in chief, the Schneider assassination signaled an unprecedented breakdown in hierarchy and discipline. The investigations into the crime revealed that several officers, including General Viaux, were behind the attempted kidnapping that resulted in the assassination of Schneider. Their purpose was to create instability in order to block Allende's appointment as president (Prats González 1974).

Prats was a constitutional "loyalist" (in the sense that he did not favor coup plotting), but he did more than any other commander in chief to bring the armed forces into overtly political deliberations. Under his command, in order to defuse growing civil-military tensions, Allende invited officers, including Prats himself, to take part in the cabinet. Also, he repeatedly requested official proclamations from his generals backing a "negotiated" resolution to the deepening political crisis inside the government and the country. In his memoirs he wrote that "we were in the paradoxical situation that I myself was living through: we were deliberating (which was forbidden to us constitutionally), but moved only by the patriotic and sincere desire to avoid [a situation in which] not finding a democratic formula [for the resolution of the political crisis] would drag the institution into a coup" (Prats González 1974, 403).

There was an abortive rogue coup attempt on June 29, 1973, popularly known as the *tanquetazo,* in reference to the light armored vehicles *(tanquetas)* in the street.[10] One army unit, led by Colonel Souper, attacked La Moneda Palace and the Ministry of Defense Building, but the attempt quickly broke down when no other units from within the army or the other branches of the armed forces joined the effort. General Prats went in person, automatic rifle in hand, to put a stop to the attempt (Prats González 1974).

After this incident, Admiral Patricio Carvajal, head of the Joint Chiefs of Staff and later a defense minister under the military government, proposed the creation of a group of generals and admirals to coordinate the application of the Arms Control Law during the searches and investigations that followed the coup attempt. General Prats approved the creation of this group, with the stipulation that it restrict its activities to this one task and keep strictly within the limits of the law. Prats wrote in his memoirs that such specialized meetings were "unprecedented" in the armed forces because the coordination of policy normally already took place at several levels. Clearly, he thought, the real purpose of these meetings was "deliberation," but he allowed them to take place nonetheless. Disallowing them would have shown a lack of confidence in the generals concerned and would simply have driven such activities underground. He also notes that "because the head of the *Estado Mayor* of the army, General Pinochet, in whom I had full confidence, took part in all these meetings, he would be in charge of informing me of any deviation from discipline" (Prats González 1974, 403).

The abortive attempt of June 29 and its aftermath revealed not only that there was obvious discontent with the Allende government but also that in many ways the lines of command had broken down. Repairing them would prove insurmountable for Prats, and this problem would continue to plague Pinochet later on. General Prats offered his resignation to Allende immediately after putting down the attempt. Allende accepted this only by the end of August, after it became clear that Prats had lost the support of an important section of the army. The trigger was an aftereffect of the long ongoing truckers' strike. General Cesar Ruiz Danyau, commander in chief of the air force as well as minister of the interior, offered his resignation as minister to Allende in mid-August after repeated failures to resolve the strike. Allende accepted his ministerial resignation but insisted also that he resign his post as commander in chief of the air force. Ruiz refused initially and bunkered himself and some troops in two air force bases. Eventually Ruiz accepted the resignation, but this provoked a strong reaction against Prats from within sectors of the army who believed that "Prats had conspired with Allende to get rid of Ruiz, and had threatened Ruiz with the full might of the army if he did not resolve the rebellion" (Prats González 1974, 480–81). Prats asked Pinochet, then second in command of the army, to come up with a document in which the top generals would show their full support for Prats. Pinochet failed to secure the required support and instead informed Prats that Generals Sepúlveda and Pickering, two key Prats supporters, had offered their resignations. Prats writes that at this point, with two pillars of support gone, he saw he had no option left but to resign, which he did on Friday, August 24 (Prats González 1974, 480–89).[11]

Allende replaced Prats with the army's second in command, General Pinochet. This change in command provoked serious worries among the coup plotters, given that they did not know whether Pinochet would support them. On his first meeting with the generals in the "Group of Fifteen" after the resignation, Pinochet said that "what they've done to my general Prats will be washed with the blood of generals" and asked for their resignations. Generals Arellano, Palacios, and Viveros did not hand in their written resignations, however; instead they began to plot a possible coup for Wednesday, August 29, bypassing the commander in chief. On Monday, August 27, Pinochet put a stop to the plots by announcing that he would not insist on the resignations and by hinting at the possibility of a "military intervention" (Verdugo 1989, 16) of his own devising.

Getting Pinochet on board would have facilitated the smooth execution of their plans, but the plotters could have gone on without him. General Arellano, described as "the singing voice of disenchantment" within the army,[12] visited Pinochet on September 8 to tell him that the coup was in its final stages of planning and to offer him a last opportunity to jump on board. He did so only the following day, after further pressures from air force commander in chief General Gustavo Leigh and Admiral José Toribio Merino, commander of the navy (Verdugo 1989, 16).[13]

Pinochet's treason has been the subject of some debate, and his own memoirs contribute to the confusion by rewriting his own history and participation in the preparations of the coup (Pinochet Ugarte 1979). One view suggests that Pinochet should be understood less as a "traitor" than as someone who was "one-hundred percent military."[14] To rise within the army, Pinochet learned to follow the currents, to learn "which way the wind was blowing." In an interview conducted prior to the downfall of Allende's government, for instance, he portrayed himself in a manner far removed from the anti-Marxist crusader he would become less than a year later.[15]

Pinochet jumped aboard the coup plots only at the last minute, calculating, we can speculate, that the days of the Allende government were numbered.[16] Early in the morning of the coup, September 11, 1973, before the identity of the new junta members was known, Hortensia Bussi, Allende's wife (and soon to be widow), was reportedly overcome with worry, asking, "Where is Augusto?" Ironically, she was fearing the worst for a trusted friend.

Pinochet was not only taking part in the coup that morning but leading the tactical operations and showing a remarkable degree of callousness and disregard for the welfare of the many people who had been taken prisoner, including a number of former colleagues and members of the Allende executive. Recordings of the communications between Pinochet and Vice-Admiral Patricio Carvajal, the navy's chief operations officer and the second-in-command during the coup attack,[17] reveal that when Carvajal suggested that the prisoners, including several former cabinet ministers, simply be held in custody for the time being, Pinochet replied: "All right, but if we keep them we give them time. I think we have to consult with [air force commander General Gustavo] Leigh. My opinion is that we take these gentlemen and we send them by airplane anywhere, and even, during the flight, we can start throwing them outside."[18]

I take this detour on the issue of Pinochet's personality to illustrate several points. The first is what might be labeled the "definitional vacuum" at the center of the coup and of the new military government. The man who would become arguably the most powerful figure in Chilean history was very likely a latecomer to the crucible event of his political career—the "Decisive Day," according to the title of the book that gives his own account (Pinochet Ugarte 1979). An analysis of Pinochet's role at this time therefore confounds theories that explain outcomes according to a particular actor's interests: in this case the principal actor was arguably an opportunist still searching for his political interests during the time of the coup. The coup was not a power grab by one man but a highly complex operation by a set of institutions—the Chilean armed forces—ostensibly to carry out what they saw as their constitutional mission to safeguard the country's institutional order. There was no blueprint for this type of action, nor was there consensus within the armed forces about the purpose of the mission or even whether it should be carried out in the first place.

As the preceding discussion illustrates, the coup could also not have taken place without a deep breakdown in military hierarchy. There were tensions and breakdowns (and assassinations) prior to the coup, and the command chain of the new military hierarchy was not altogether clear. Merino took over command of the navy from Admiral Montero on the day of the coup, but Montero had been one of the key coup instigators and appeared to have the confidence of their top officers. Leigh had been commander of the air force prior to the coup and also appeared to have the confidence of his top staff, who trusted him to protect them in case of a purge by Allende. Pinochet, as we have seen, although he had been the commander of the army and of the armed forces as a whole, was a latecomer to the plot. He assumed a leading role during the attack essentially because the army was both the largest and the most central institution within Chile's armed forces. The army is also the only institution besides the Carabineros that has a truly national presence and reach.[19] The navy and air force have bases in only certain areas, seaports and airports, and lack the manpower and infrastructure to cover the entire national territory. While this fact alone does not necessarily guarantee that the army should assume a leading role in any joint operation, it strongly weighs in its favor. In addition, General Mendoza's position within the Carabineros was not altogether secure, given that he took over the institution by jumping over more than a dozen generals who preceded him in seniority (Cavallo Castro, Salazar Salvo, and Sepúlveda Pacheco 1989, 21).

The group of generals that took power proclaimed that their actions were required by a constitutional mandate for the armed forces to protect the country's institutions. With the coup they essentially defeated those within the military who argued that respecting the constitution meant staying out of politics and backing the elected government. But it would be inaccurate to suggest that the entire military body was of one mind about the coup. Instead, the kinds of tensions that were a precondition to the coup continued to haunt the new military government as it tried to establish control.

Anticommunism and Counterinsurgency

There were tensions within the armed forces not simply over whether to become involved in politics but over what kind of "war" it should fight in Chile. Should the military simply depose the Allende government in order to call for elections? Or should the coup be a first step toward a more a more widespread and intensive campaign against Marxists? On the day of the coup, air force commander General Gustavo Leigh declared that the armed forces would "struggle against Marxism and extirpate it to the last consequences" from the Chilean body politic (Constable and Valenzuela 1991, 36). What, in practice, did this mean? What kind of campaign did the armed forces intend to carry out against Marxism, and was there agreement on how it would be done?

Once again, notwithstanding the overwhelming use of force employed by the armed forces, there were serious divisions behind the scenes over how to carry out the campaign against Marxism in Chile. The disagreements went beyond differences over tactics against a given enemy. There was disagreement over exactly who the enemy was. In other words, the military was deeply divided over some basic issues, such as defining exactly whom it purported to defend the country against. To understand these divisions, I focus on three elements of the military's ideology: anticommunism, counterinsurgency, and national security.

First, anticommunism has been at the center of the modern Chilean military's ideology since the end of the nineteenth century. The army traces its institutional roots to reforms carried out in 1885 by Emil Körner, a Prussian army captain and professor at the German *Kriegsakademie*. Harsh discipline and strict respect for hierarchy modernized the Chilean army, but at the same time the Prussian reforms had two consequences: they eroded the army's traditional respect for civilian authority, and they infused it with a strong sense of anticommunism. Newly professional officers, many of whom had trained in Prussia with the imperial guards, came to resent any civilian involvement in military promotions, a process often tainted with patronage (Constable and Valenzuela 1991, 41). European-trained officers also became much more directly aware of the central debates of the day in Europe, such as the conflicts between the Second International and European national interests prior to the First World War. The Prussian army's strong anticommunism during this time was reflected in the Chilean and Argentine armies.[20] There were growing socialist and anarchist movements in Chile and throughout the Southern Cone, and the army railed against these as enemies of the fatherland and the national state. The Russian Revolution further heightened these tensions (Arriagada Herrera 1986, 183–84).

Anticommunism was openly central to the Chilean military's ideology until 1931. That year marked the end of a period of military polemics and involvement in politics, which included two separate military governments (1924 and 1927–31). In 1931 the military officially "returned to the barracks," and its anticommunism since that time is more difficult to detect openly. Officers during the four decades between 1931 and 1973 did not typically make political declarations, preferring to adopt a much more neutral stance toward the constitution and accepting civilian control as an essential piece of the political order. This stance was reflected in officers like René Schneider and Carlos Prats, the two commanders in chief of the armed forces prior to Pinochet, both of whom opposed the idea of a coup (Arriagada Herrera 1986, 14; Constable and Valenzuela 1991, 40–44). Nevertheless, anticommunism remained important inside the barracks. For instance, in 1949 former commander in chief of the armed forces General Indalecio Téllez asked whether military intervention in political affairs might not be justified in some circumstances: "The first duty of the army is the defense of the fatherland. Against whom? Against any enemy that endangers national honor, peace, or integrity. Could the army, invoking its duty not to intervene in the country's internal affairs, allow the government to fall in the hands of communism? Does the country have any greater enemy than this? From here we can deduce that when it comes to enemies of the fatherland, the army cannot make distinctions" (Téllez 1949, 229–30).

Anticommunism might have remained no more than an ideological preference within the military, but it was honed into a much more systematic strategy as a result of the theories of counterinsurgency developed in France and the United States after the Second World War. The French fought against insurgencies in Indochina (1945–54) and in Algeria (1954–62), and this experience led a generation of officers to radically question traditional methods of war making (Ambier 1966). The French theory of counterinsurgency can be summed up as follows:

> The nuclear balance of power beginning in the 1950s made nuclear war highly improbable. Instead, the most likely kind of war that the West would fight would be a war of insurgency against revolutionary or liberationist movements.

A war of insurgency is different than a traditional war. The objective is not the defeat of an opposing army, but rather a moral victory over a given population.

International communism is carrying out a global war of insurgency.

To defend itself against this, the West must adapt some of the techniques of the enemy, especially propaganda, political indoctrination, and clandestine organization. (Ambier 1966, 309–10)[21]

Instead of a conventional war of armies against armies in open battle, counterinsurgency is a war against a more secretive enemy who turns his weaknesses (e.g., the lack of heavy equipment such as artillery, tanks, or aircraft) into relative strengths by operating in areas where traditional armies have trouble operating. Insurgents can blend into the local population, for instance, making it extremely difficult to even identify enemy fighters. Information about the organizational makeup of the insurgency, therefore, becomes especially critical in this kind of conflict.

The French theories of counterinsurgency were influential throughout the armed forces of the Southern Cone. The works of Colonel Roger Trinquier, in particular, were published and widely distributed. Trinquier argued that every kind of soldier has his "venom": the antiaircraft gun stops the pilot, and the machine gun stops the infantryman. The main weapon to stop terrorists, he argued, is torture, because that is the best way to obtain information about the captive terrorist's organization.[22]

There are several problems with torture as a military tactic, however. The first is that, contrary to Trinquier's assertions, torture is a highly inefficient method of obtaining information. Prisoners may lie to stop the punishment, and there may be a flood of information from a tortured prisoner that ultimately proves to be useless. Or, knowing that torture and extraction of information is a possibility, insurgents can organize to anticipate it. They can prepare themselves not to "crack," and they can compartmentalize information in such a way that no one agent can reveal all the key secrets.

Apart from its dubious usefulness as a truly effective weapon, there is ultimately a much more serious problem concerning the use of torture within a military institution. Unlike other kinds of warfare tactics, torture is an activity normally carried out by one person directly, in secret quarters, against another person who is completely defenseless. Most human beings are usually incapable of causing this kind of sadistic suffering. By contrast, a pilot drops bombs on an "abstract" population, and an infantryman fights against enemies who are armed as he is. Militaries impel their agents to torture by exaggerating the dangers the victims pose. The soldier is conditioned to believe that he faces, not a helpless victim, but a dangerous insurgent. No doubt many torturers actually believe this and punish with full conviction, but such people are exceptions. In most armies torture is one of the "dirty" tasks that is difficult to get everyone in the institution to carry out as a matter of organizational policy.[23]

Explaining the psychology of torture is beyond the boundaries of this book. I bring this up simply to illustrate the following point: a central outcome of the military ideology of counterinsurgency and its concrete application into action required a kind of activity—torture—that is notoriously difficult to implement as a matter of policy. Torture is a messy business. The widespread adoption of one of the main weapons in the arsenal of counterinsurgency, in other words, makes it much *more* difficult for elements within a military establishment to act in unison. Who carries out the dirty work? How are these operations coordinated with the rest of the institution? Is this the kind of work that needs to be kept secret even from members of your own institution? Torture raises a number of issues that any military establishment engaged in counterinsurgency has to resolve, and a resolution becomes far more urgent in cases where the military assumes full political power.

A further complication is that torture is one area where the work of the military begins to overlap with police work (Stepan 1986).[24] Police forces throughout Latin America have carried out torture against criminals, and trying to extract information about criminal organizations is a normal part of police work; however, by widening their scope to include activities previously carried out by the police, the Chilean military created new problems. Does the military simply adopt the techniques of the police? Who is best suited to carry out these techniques, the police or the military? Or should military and police forces cooperate in joint operations? If they do, how should they coordinate their activities, given that they have only rarely operated in unison?

There are important differences between police work and military work. Police forces employ coercion, sometimes including torture, as a matter of normal daily activities. The actions of the police are a normal part of the functioning of the state to ensure respect for the law and to capture criminals. The aims of the police forces are not, usually, the outright extermination of criminals. Their aim is not to "win" conflicts but to capture criminals and deter the population from criminality. By contrast, militaries employ coercion against other armies in occasional conflicts that are the exception rather than the rule. Their aim is not to defuse conflict but rather to achieve complete victory. In this sense, a technique like torture is not likely to be used in the same manner by the military as by the police. Militaries are much more likely to blur the distinctions between the extraction of information and outright extermination (Bayley 1975, 1985; Marenin 1990; Bailey and Dammert 2006).

In a similar vein, there was a great deal of confusion over exactly what kind of war the Chilean military thought it was fighting.[25] The ideological shifts inside the military prior to the coup resulted in a redefinition of their standard roles, blurring an internal long-standing division of labor between the military and the police. Added to all these confusions was the fact that a central coercive practice—torture—was notoriously difficult to monitor. These tensions might have remained theoretical debates inside the barracks, but they became very relevant once the armed forces took power and were faced with a series of concrete problems concerning the organization of coercion.

Confusion over Powers

The Chilean military did not stage the coup of September 1973 with a clear plan of what they intended to do in power once they got it.[26] Other than restoring order and ridding the country of Marxism, there was no blueprint for government. A further source of confusion, aside from the breakdowns in hierarchy, a lack of agreement over the proper treatment of members of the previous regime, and bewilderment over basic goals, concerned determining exactly which powers the military had taken over on the day of the coup.

There was no precedent for a military government in Chile. Many believed that the military was properly the "guarantor of the institutionality" of the country (Loveman 1993, 1999; Policzer 2003).[27] But there was no living memory of political involvement by the military forces. Beyond restoring order, it was unclear what "guaranteeing the institutionality" of the country would actually mean. Moreover, it is unlikely that any broad-based agreement over the terms of government took place within the armed forces prior to the coup, particularly when the participation of such a central figure like Pinochet was guaranteed only two days beforehand.

On September 12, the military *auditores,* the chief legal counsels, were given the task of preparing a constitutional act. Navy admiral (and lawyer) Rodolfo Vio, president of the committee of *auditores,* gave the task of coming up with the new document to one of his assistants, navy captain Sergio Rillón. According to Rillón, his instructions had been to draft a document that would give the new junta "total power" (Cavallo Castro, Salazar Salvo, and Sepúlveda Pacheco 1989, 9; Barros 2002). Rillón quickly typed a document, the "Acta de Constitución de la Junta de Gobierno," which declared that the junta had taken over the "supreme command of the nation" *(mando supremo de la nación)* in order to "restore the destroyed *chilenidad,* justice and institutionality." The document was adopted with only one correction[28] and with the addition of two separate articles: one to appoint Pinochet as head of the junta and one to guarantee the independence of the judicial branch.[29]

A commission of constitutional and legal experts appointed by the junta in the first weeks after the coup pointed out the difficulties in defining the exact meaning of the junta's declaration on the day of the coup that it had taken "supreme command of the nation." Some commissioners suggested, on the basis of Article 60 of the 1925 Constitution, according to which the president was the "head of state and supreme commander of the nation," that the junta had only taken control of the presidency but not the legislature. Even if they granted legislative power to the junta, the commissioners continued to disagree over whether it had therefore also assumed the constitutive power *(poder constituyente)* to draft a new constitution. The junta had not demonstrated the intent to rewrite the 1925 Constitution at the time of the coup.[30] In response to these doubts, the junta issued a clarification in the form of a *decreto ley* on November 16, 1973, which stated that "the supreme command of the nation includes the legislative and executive powers, and as a consequence the *Poder Constituyente* that corresponds to these."[31] In an interview, Rillón later admitted that the original term had been a mistake made out of haste (Barros 1996, 27 n. 15).

A second source of confusion stemmed from the relationship between the military and the former political authorities that supported the coup. Opposition politicians supported the military overthrow of Allende with the understanding that a prompt transfer of power would take place. During the final months of the Allende government, Patricio Aylwin, in particular, played a leading role. As president of the Senate and as the ranking Christian Democrat in the legislature, he was the key opposition figure responsible for leading the negotiation attempts with the Unidad Popular to try to avert the possibility of a coup. All such negotiation attempts failed. To opposition leaders like Aylwin it appeared, prima facie, that the military should have embraced them as natural allies.

Such an alliance did not materialize. Christian Democrats, led by Senator Patricio Aylwin (who would later be elected president in December 1989), held a meeting with the junta on October 10, 1973, to discuss what the civilians hoped would be a prompt transfer of power.[32] The minutes for this meeting *(Actas de la Junta)* indicate that the delegation led by "Sr. Alwing" *(sic)* stressed the Christian Democrats' marked anticommunism and its agreement that the "military pronouncement"[33] was a "legitimate defense, in view of the attitude of the forces of [the previous] government illegally armed." The delegation, according to the minutes of the meeting, also noted that many Christian Democrats would be willing to cooperate with the junta "individually." According to Aylwin, Pinochet indicated during this meeting that the military would be in power for a total of eight months.[34] Not surprisingly, no specific mention of this is found in the minutes. Instead, they record the following as the junta's reaction to the delegation: "The president and each of the members of the Junta de Gobierno make comments in reference to the materials discussed, note the responsibility that this party [the Christian Democratic Party] also has for the chaotic situation in the country, and clearly establish the true principles *[postulados]* that guide [the junta]."[35] What went unrecorded was perhaps a clearer indication of the military's intentions: Aylwin later recounted that navy commander José Toribio Merino had placed a large revolver on the table during the discussions.[36] No cooperation between the military and the Christian Democrats was established, and no power transfer was discussed again.

A third source of confusion surrounded the appointment of Pinochet as primus inter pares within the junta. Pinochet had played a relatively minor role in the planning of the coup, but as the top military leader in the country he was the natural choice to be appointed head of the junta. The intent of this appointment, according to the junta's original declarations, was to share the leadership equally among all four junta members on a rotation basis (Comisión Nacional de Verdad y Reconciliación 1991, 47). In practice, no rotation ever took place. Pinochet assumed the title of "supreme commander of the nation" (Decreto Ley [D.L.] 527) by the end of 1973, and by December 16, 1974, he consolidated his position by having himself appointed president (D.L. 806). As the top military and political figure in the country, Pinochet achieved a concentration of powers that was unprecedented in Chilean history (Arriagada Herrera 1988; Huneeus 1988).

With such uncertainty and lack of coordination among the coup's main plotters, it is clear that they had no definite plan concerning the organization of subsequent coercion. Indeed, many organizational alternatives were being considered. In the next sections I assess the levels of internal and external monitoring during this period and analyze in greater detail the kinds of concrete problems the new government faced as it attempted to organize coercion.

The Turmoil

During the first several months after the coup, all four branches of the armed forces practiced all aspects of coercion, from taking prisoners to carrying out summary executions, although the bulk of these tasks were carried out by the army and the Carabineros.[37] This early period was by far the most violent in terms of the sheer numbers of victims of the military's repression. Roughly half of all the deaths that occurred during the military regime took place in 1973. This period also witnessed about a third of all detentions and anywhere from a quarter to three-fifths of all tortures. The victims included people from a wide range of political backgrounds, from the left, to the center, to those without political affiliation, and even including some whom had been opponents of the Allende government. This was by far the broadest range targeted during the course of the regime (Comisión Nacional de Verdad y Reconciliación 1991, ch. 2; Padilla Ballesteros 1995, 45–66). And although many prisoners were held (and killed) in secret, most were kept in highly public places like the country's main sports stadiums and hastily improvised concentration camps.

Also, during this time the new junta quickly achieved almost complete control of the entire country. Throughout this process, the previous civilian authorities in the various provinces and regions either were forcibly deposed or, in many cases, peacefully handed power to military officers. The ranking officer in each area took political and administrative command.

Internal Monitoring

Notwithstanding the level of violence and the speed with which the military took control, the levels of internal monitoring during this time were surprisingly low, especially when compared with what would later occur under the auspices of the DINA and the CNI. For example, division commanders of the armed forces enjoyed a relatively high degree of autonomy from the junta and were often beyond the scrutiny of the junta principals. While the junta was nonetheless aware of the overall levels of repression and the general variations in practices between the regions, they were largely unaware of the precise methods and reporting mechanisms that regional commanders and their field agents used. Consequently there was a great deal of variation in the nature of the repression used and the degree of control exercised by commanders over their respective agents.

Competition among junta members and their respective branches of the armed forces also made coordination and consistency of reporting problematic at best. There was some confusion over who would do the actual monitoring of agents—for example, whether it would be regulated centrally or on an ad hoc basis. The default practice was that each branch of the armed forces carried out its own internal monitoring. During this period members of the junta appeared considerably more concerned over monitoring their declared enemies than in regulating their own agents consistently. While the four branches of the military worked together to depose the Allende government, the manner in which they interacted was often haphazard and without established procedures. In general, it is a safe assumption that principals trusted each of their own branch's agents and reports more than those from the other branches.

The only central information clearinghouse that existed maintained information only on detainees and did not provide systematic data on the actions of agents. Not surprisingly, no information was collected on those who were "disappeared" or executed, let alone on the officers responsible for these actions. Thus it is safe to conclude that the overall level of information on the extent of agents' actions was relatively low. On the other hand, considering the relative lack of monitoring and oversight, the early years of the regime cannot be considered particularly corrupt—at least not in terms of the rampant abuse of power for personal ends.[38]

In conclusion, the period was generally characterized by a high number of agents undertaking a broad array of coercive practices in a relatively decentralized manner and with little consistency or accountability. A more detailed explanation and breakdown of the seven categories, and the justification for each measurement, can be found in Appendix A.

External Monitoring

Most of the basic external monitoring mechanisms were essentially shut down immediately after the junta assumed power in September 1973. The opposition press was closed down, Congress was disbanded, and there were no freedom-of-information laws through which outsiders could request details about the executive's operations. While the judiciary was able to continue functioning, the vast majority of cases regarding the coup or political crimes were placed under the jurisdiction of military tribunals. Nevertheless, some sources of external monitoring remained, despite the efforts of the junta leaders.

While the military sought to maximize its discretionary powers regarding coercion, outsiders were able to achieve some measure of control and oversight with respect to certain kinds of prisoners. Family members could sometimes visit prisoners who were held in detention centers throughout the country, including those constructed or converted specifically for the political prisoners, such as the Estadio Nacional. The Red Cross was also able to monitor many of the prisoners detained in these locations and to report on the conditions of their captivity.

Perhaps the most effective method of external monitoring was undertaken by relatives and friends of opposition members in concert with human rights agencies, who utilized the country's remaining legal instruments to petition the government for information about detainees. These requests, known as *recursos de amparo,* soon constituted a large database of information that was then used by members of the opposition, human rights agencies, and international organizations to pressure the regime. However, there is little evidence that the members of the junta considered this information to be particularly accurate at this time, so they did not consider it a valuable information source to assist in the monitoring of agents. In short, despite the efforts of many organizations to monitor the actions of the junta, the early years of the dictatorship were generally marked by a lack of external monitoring (again described in greater detail in Appendix A).

Monitoring Problems

The pattern of coercion just described posed several problems for the junta. First, the visibility of the prisoners in places such as the Estadio Nacional became problematic. The regime faced a great deal of international pressure for its massive human rights violations and its treatment of political prisoners.

In November 1973 the Estadio Nacional was closed as a prison camp, and the bulk of its prisoners were transferred to Chacabuco, an abandoned mining town in the Atacama Desert. This served to remove the prisoners from the scrutiny of the international press based in Santiago and to show an improvement in the treatment of prisoners.[39] In Chacabuco prisoners were allowed greater freedom and autonomy than in the Estadio Nacional.

With respect to internal monitoring, a serious crisis took place a few weeks after the coup, once it became clear that not all military units were adopting a uniform policy versus prisoners and the enemy. According to the *Informe Rettig,* the junta at this time decided that many of the commanders in the provinces were being too "soft" on their prisoners, perhaps because they had not faced the same levels of resistance found in Santiago. They feared that such a policy might create the conditions for the reorganization of the opposition (Comisión Nacional de Verdad y Reconciliación 1991).

During October, General Sergio Arellano Stark (one of the leading instigators of the coup within the army, who had taken part in the raid on the presidential palace) led a mission to the southern and northern regions in the country. The mission visited every key military regiment, especially those where prisoners had been taken. Pinochet himself had ordered the mission. Its official purpose was to empower Arellano to "look over" prisoners' trials currently under way.[40] Its real aim, we can surmise, was to "speed up" these trials and to impose a stricter hard line throughout the military. With regard to internal monitoring, the mission would have had several purposes. It would have served as a check on local commanders' operations by a monitor personally appointed by Pinochet. It also would have represented an attempt to impose a more uniform policy of coercion, which would have made monitoring future operations easier.

The mission arrived in the Talca regiment, in the southern part of the country, on October 30, 1973. Lieutenant Colonel Efraín Jaña was commander of the regiment at that time. Upon Arellano's arrival, Jaña reported that the regiment was "without news." The subsequent dialogue is transcribed below:

Arellano: What do you mean, no news? How many casualties?
Jaña: There are no casualties or trials, general. The only problem
              we had, and which might have been avoided with timely or-
              ders, has already been resolved. The former regional gover-
              nor [*intendente*] was tried and shot.
Arellano: Don't you know we are in a war!
Jaña: I don't know what war you are talking about, general.

(quoted in Verdugo 1989, 27–28)[41]

Arellano reproached Jaña for having urged the population of Talca toward peace and reconciliation, putting aside divisions, and coming to the aid of the military government. Jaña noted, "Afterwards I understood it: I was calling for civil-military friendship at a time when this did not fit with the plans from above, precisely when it was necessary to exacerbate the military fury against the Left using the so-called Plan Zeta. But Talca did not fit with the plan. Everything was very quiet, just when many prisoners and trials were needed, to accuse them for Plan Zeta" (Verdugo 1989, 29).

Arellano's mission had already been to other regiments prior to Talca. Between October 16 and 19, it went through La Serena, Copiapó, Antofagasta, and Calama. In most of these places the local commanders had taken prisoners and were holding trials. As Arellano's mission passed through the regiments, dozens of prisoners who were awaiting trial were executed, mostly without the knowledge of the local commander. Typically, Arellano's team would remove prisoners from the detention centers to take them to "interrogations" in a different camp. The prisoners would be summarily executed in an isolated spot. The bodies were later given to the local morgue, and in most cases the military issued an official declaration that the officers in charge had applied the "Law of Escape" (Ley de Fuga), which allowed for the shooting of prisoners who tried to escape.[42]

Although Arellano's mission operated under direct orders from Pinochet, it often did so while bypassing standard military lines of command. On most occasions his men would order the removal of prisoners without the knowledge of the local commander or would directly bypass his authority, showing official documentation from Pinochet empowering Arellano to look into the trials in process.

General Lagos, commander of the Antofagasta regiment, on October 20, 1973, challenged Arellano regarding the crimes his men had committed the previous night. Arellano responded by showing him a letter from Pinochet, officially putting him in charge of looking into and speeding up the trials of the men in his regiment as well as others. Lagos states that had Arellano shown him this documentation at the outset, he would have had no choice but to comply and to give the order to all the men under his command to follow Arellano's orders in these matters.[43]

Lagos warned Arellano that he would "give account" of the incident to Pinochet, who was landing in Antofagasta that same afternoon. When Pinochet arrived Lagos explained to him the crimes that had been committed without his knowledge in Antofagasta and Calama, the regiments under his authority, and asked Pinochet to relieve him of his command. Pinochet, according to Lagos, expressed deep concern over the issue and stated that while he could not accept Lagos's resignation immediately he would do his best to accommodate by transferring him to a different unit. In February 1974, Lagos was transferred to Santiago, and in October of that year he was sent into retirement.[44]

On October 22, Arellano and his mission arrived in Arica, Chile's northernmost city.[45] Their putative purpose was to look into the trials under way in the Rancagua regiment, at that time under the command of General Odlanier Mena (who would later assume control of the CNI after the exit of Manuel Contreras). Here the same procedure took place—Arellano asked to review the trials, showing direct orders from Pinochet—but Mena stated that he had already put Arica's chief prosecutor, Humberto Retamal, in charge of these procedures and that it would be inappropriate to reveal any information regarding these trials, including the number of prisoners held or their names, since that task was already assigned to someone else. Arellano did not insist and, according to Mena, accepted the explanation that all procedures were being followed properly. As Arellano and his men left, one of them, Lieutenant Armando Fernández Larios, said to Mena, "Despite the explanation you gave to General Arellano, we will still approach the jail to see how things are going." Mena at this point told Larios to remember that while he and Arellano were in his regiment they were under surveillance and that if they did approach the prisoners without his permission the regiment's personnel had orders to have them arrested. Mena states that he made this decision "because, through the same sources that had announced to me Arellano's itinerary, I knew the results [his mission] had produced in the other regiments."[46]

Arellano's mission is an important turning point in the early history of the dictatorship. It indicates deep tensions inside the military hierarchy and the government over how to treat prisoners and, indeed, over the nature of the military regime as a whole. Other than the question of simply bypassing the normal lines of command, it underscored a more serious problem: many commanders felt that the kind of hard line Arellano sought to enforce was neither necessary nor in the best interest of the new government. Instead, many, like Lieutenant Colonel Jaña, had until that point believed that the new government would try to build support among the population by encouraging dialogue and reconciliation.

The Arellano mission is often seen as an example of the brutality of the new military regime. The *Informe Rettig* points out, "This trip to the North, with its official and extraordinary character, with the highest authority—originating in the commander in chief—that backed it up, with its aftermath of astonishing extralegal executions, and with its blatant impunity, could not fail to give the officers of the armed forces and the Carabineros [Fuerzas Armadas y de Orden] one clear signal: that there was only one command and that it would have to be carried out ruthlessly [*duramente*]" (Comisión Nacional de Verdad y Reconciliación 1991, 123).[47]

The mission no doubt exemplified a new hard line. But while dozens of prisoners were killed, what is most striking besides the impunity of the killings is the fact that well after the coup there was so much internal resistance from within the army itself to this kind of coercion. In a previous passage, the same *Informe Rettig* notes the power of local commanders regarding the application of coercion:

Especially during the first period, what took place in each region in terms of control of public order and violations of human rights had substantial differences that depended, to an important degree, on the different local conditions and on the attitude of each of the zone commanders *[Jefes de Zona]*. In this way, in some places the highest authorities of the deposed government were advised, even by telephone, to turn themselves in to the new authorities, while in others there was a rigid and far-reaching control of public order from the very first days. (Comisión Nacional de Verdad y Reconciliación 1991, 109)

Very little firsthand information is available on the debates inside the ruling circles over the differences in opinion concerning the application of coercion. We can only speculate and infer from the available sources about the causes and effects of these differences and the tensions these might have produced. There are no specific references to the Arellano mission in the Actas de la Junta and only the vaguest references to the more general problem of the uneven coercion as applied by different local commanders. On October 8 the minutes of Acta No. 17 record a discussion over the worry that very few heavy weapons *(armas largas)* had been found, given that "there is certainty that there must be buried or circulating at least five or ten thousand more."[48] The same meeting also notes a resolution to convene the War Council (Consejo de Guerra) and the Charges Tribunal (Tribunal de Cargos) to look into the trials against the main people charged with the "chaos that the country is suffering."[49]

The overall picture that emerges about the application of coercion during this time is thus not that of a tightly controlled and well-organized policy. Some key commanders, such as General Mena (in charge of arguably the most strategically important military post in Chile, next to the tense Peruvian border),[50] resisted the adoption of a hard line. But there were clearly forces pushing for this inside the military leadership.

Was the Arellano mission a success? It depends on how one evaluates it. If the goal of the mission was to assert the authority of central command, then the mission was a partial success. If nothing else, it sent a clear signal to the commanders in the field about the direction the central command was taking. Yet if the goal of the mission was to implement a harder line against the growing number of prisoners, it must be judged a qualified failure. The reason is that apart from the message that the mission might have sent, there was no systematic shift in coercion. The garrison commanders remained in place, at least in the short term.[51] Some sectors of the military took a hard line against prisoners, while others continued to be puzzled about the extent of the "war" the military was fighting. Compared to the shift in coercion that took place when the DINA began full-scale operations (which I will discuss in the next chapter), the changes in coercion as a policy were negligible after the Arellano mission.

To evaluate the importance of the mission in historical context, we need to keep in mind the connections between the mission and the DINA. Future research into now-closed military archives will better reveal the relationships between the men in the mission (such as Fernández Larios, Moren Brito, and Pedro Espinoza) and Colonel Contreras at the time of the mission. They all went on to play important roles in the DINA after it was formally organized. But we do not know whether and in what capacity they operated as part of what at that time was the Comisión DINA[52] and whether they formed part of the mission because of their DINA membership. Given the growing prominence of Contreras, and given the importance of the mission coming from the center, it is likely that these men had contact with the DINA during this time.

What possible interest might the nascent DINA have had in this mission? As I will show in the next chapters, the DINA became an agency for the systematic extermination of key sectors of the left, particularly through the practice of the disappearances. The *Informe Rettig* notes that during this first period in 1973 there were a great many disappearances but that the practice was not as systematic as it would later become. Instead, it "was a manner of hiding or covering up the crimes that had been committed, rather than the result of actions subject to a tight central control that sought to eliminate certain categories of persons" (Comisión Nacional de Verdad y Reconciliación 1991, 22–23).

Therefore, if the goal of the mission was to test the possibility of carrying out a campaign of counterinsurgency against the left, the answer must have been "not through regular military channels." In this light, the mission can be judged a relative success. By revealing the points of resistance, it showed the members of the DINA that if a campaign of counterinsurgency were to occur, it would have to take place *outside* regular military channels.

These goals—to assert central command, to implement a hard line, and to test the possibility of counterinsurgency—are not mutually contradictory, and indeed they may have been held by different sectors of the military leadership. It is perfectly consistent, for instance, for Pinochet to have devised a mission to assert his command and for Contreras, if he had anything to do with the mission, to have seen it as a testing ground for his aims. Even if Contreras had no prior connection to the mission, it would still have served his purposes afterward by revealing the resistance to counterinsurgency within the regular channels.

José Zalaquett notes that a working hypothesis in the Comisión Nacional de Verdad y Reconciliación (of which he was a member) was that Pinochet needed to stage "his own" military victory, given that he had been a latecomer to the coup.[53] He jumped on board at the last possible minute and was appointed head of the junta strictly as a formality. As head of the army, the largest unit within the armed forces, he was the most obvious choice for the post. But the real victors in the coup had been Admiral Merino and air force commander General Leigh, who had taken part in the coup plots from the beginning. Even though Pinochet was head of the junta, neither Merino nor Leigh deferred to him as a matter of course. For all purposes they considered him an equal. To assert his authority, therefore, Pinochet needed to build his own separate power base. From this perspective, Pinochet's ambitions intersected perfectly with those of Contreras, who wanted to wage a war of counterinsurgency. Contreras essentially convinced Pinochet that he could deliver a victory in "his" war and allow him to reap its political benefits.[54] The view of Pinochet as essentially an equal to Leigh and Merino is backed up by Barros's analysis of the "collegial" relationship among the members of the junta, where neither Merino nor Leigh were willing to allow Pinochet to accumulate too much power.[55]

In short, the mission can be seen as an attempt to ensure a more uniform application of coercion according to a harder line from within the preexisting military channels. No new organizations or institutions were created to try to assert the new directive. From this perspective, the mission can be judged a success insofar as it revealed to the top military command (namely Pinochet) that a harder line within the preexisting channels would face a great deal of resistance. As the next chapter will show, the lessons learned from the Arellano mission opened the way for a radically different, and far more comprehensive and severe, organizational shift.

FOUR

The Rise of the DINA (1973–74)

At the beginning of 1974, observers noticed a new coercive organization whose agents, in civilian clothing and unmarked cars, would round up people and detain them in a variety of new locations. The DINA would not receive official status until June 1974, but its detentions had become apparent several months before. As the DINA became increasingly active, it took over the bulk of operations from the other branches of the armed forces and imposed a radically new pattern of coercion. During the first several months after the coup, large numbers of people from a wide range of backgrounds had been rounded up in military and police operations and either detained or summarily executed. But by early 1974 the number of victims decreased sharply. The military and police stopped practicing large-scale and broadly targeted sweep operations. Instead, fewer victims were taken, and repression was much more selectively targeted toward communists and other members of the far left, such as the Movimiento de Izquierda Revolucionaria (MIR). Moreover, information about those who were detained during this time became increasingly rare. Indeed, human rights workers began to notice that while the number of people imprisoned and killed decreased, the new detainees were taken to new and secret locales both inside and outside Santiago. Moreover, information on those who were detained during this time became increasingly rare. Prisoners were no longer held in large detention centers, where they could be attended to by national and international humanitarian aid organizations like the Red Cross; instead, they were taken to smaller, more secret locations. They were almost always brutally tortured, and many simply disappeared.[1] While disappearances had been carried out during the first several months after the coup, under the DINA the disappearances became a much more systematic and deliberate tool of coercion. What explains the rise of the DINA and the resulting shift in how the military government organized and applied coercion? Why was there a shift at all?

To explain the rise of the DINA, analysts and observers generally refer to variations on three basic arguments, which are often interwoven in accounts of the history and evolution of the regime. The first characterizes it as a natural development in the evolution of the regime, the second as a tool for Pinochet's power consolidation, and the third as the principal mechanism for its director, Colonel Manuel Contreras, to wage an ideologically driven war of counterinsurgency. I will show that while each of these accounts explains some aspects of the DINA's creation and operation, it also leaves crucial questions unanswered. A better explanation for the DINA requires taking into account the politics associated with the costs and benefits of different patterns of organizing coercion, which I have presented in the previous chapters. The DINA was not simply a vehicle for Pinochet's or Contreras's ambitions, nor was it a necessary or natural development in the evolution of the regime. Indeed, the DINA emerged despite the serious objections to it from within key sectors of the military leadership, including members of the junta. As we shall see, they had good reason to fear it, principally because it decreased their own power. The DINA's creation, in other words, is puzzling from a pure power politics perspective, which cannot explain why powerful actors would willingly act against their own self-interest and constrain their power. Any account for the DINA has to explain why, however reluctantly, these sectors might have agreed to what essentially amounted to the creation of a powerful secret police beyond their control, run by men whom most junta members did not trust.

The Standard Explanations

The view that the creation of the DINA and the shift from random and haphazard coercive practices to more centrally planned, targeted, selective, and more effective coercive practices were part of the natural institutional evolution of the military regime has been advanced by Padilla Ballesteros (1995). It is essentially a functionalist explanation of how authoritarian regimes must follow specific patterns of coercion to survive. At first, they must impose a harsh regimen of widespread repression to eliminate all potential enemies and display their strength. After this initial stage, leaders must inevitably become more selective in the use of coercion to strategically balance the need for physical control while eliciting some degree of cooperation from members of society.[2] The principal evidence in favor of this view is that such a shift in the way the military regime practiced coercion did indeed take place.

The second common argument is that the DINA was a tool for Pinochet's consolidation of power. Arriagada describes how Pinochet consolidated power, claiming that at first "power seemed so evenly balanced among the commanders in chief that they apparently believed that the presidency of the junta would rotate at brief intervals. Pinochet told the press, 'The junta works as a single entity. I was elected [president of the junta] because I am the oldest. . . . But I will not be the only president of the junta; after a while, Admiral Merino will be, then General Leigh, and so on. I am not an ambitious man; I would not want to be a usurper of power'" (Arriagada Herrera 1986, 9).

Despite this initial division of powers, during "the months of late 1974 and early 1975 . . . the structure of the military regime changed rapidly":

> General Pinochet, the commander in chief of the army, continued to increase his power. The first and most substantial change in the power structure came with the promulgation of the Statute of the Governing Junta [Estatuto de la Junta de Gobierno]. This document reiterated that executive power rested in the military junta and that exercise of that power was assigned to the president of the junta. But this statute did not recognize the junta's prerogative to designate the president. . . . The statement signified that executive power had been placed in the hands of General Pinochet, who did not have a fixed term and could not be dismissed by the other members of the junta. (Arriagada Herrera 1986, 15–16)

Remmer (1991) subscribes to the same view as Arriagada regarding Pinochet's power consolidation, pointing out the importance of the DINA in helping him achieve this:

Even more important to the consolidation of Pinochet's control over the military was the creation in mid-1974 of a centralized military intelligence agency, the Dirección Nacional de Inteligencia (DINA). Although DINA originally drew personnel from all three services and was destined to achieve greater intelligence coordination among them, under the leadership of Manuel Contreras it reported directly to Pinochet rather than to the Junta. DINA's powers were enormous. It operated virtually without restraint, both inside and outside of Chile, repressing dissenters and eliminating leading opposition figures, including General Prats. DINA thereby played a vital role in the consolidation of Pinochet's control over the army and predominance over the other service chiefs. The myth of military unity, which discouraged outsiders from seeking allies within the military, helped to preserve the autonomy of decision makers, and bolstered Pinochet's authority, also owed much to the DINA. (129)[3]

The main pieces of evidence in favor of this view are: (1) Pinochet centralized power in a way unprecedented in Chilean history and also by contrast to other contemporary authoritarian regimes in Latin America;[4] (2) although the DINA technically depended on the junta, it answered in practice only to Pinochet; (3) Pinochet and Contreras were, at least at first, exceptionally close allies;[5] and (4) the DINA appears to have used its power to help Pinochet's allies and hurt his enemies within the ruling circles.

The third common argument to explain the DINA is that it was a vehicle for right-wing members of the armed forces, especially Manuel Contreras (director of the DINA), to pursue a war of counterinsurgency against left-wing opponents. The *Informe Rettig* describes the group that later formed the DINA as "remarkably coherent in ideology and action" (Chilean National Commission on Truth and Reconciliation 1993, 59). The group never expressed its ideology, but the commissioners write that it can be deduced "from their behavior and from the influence they received from outside the country" (Chilean National Commission on Truth and Reconciliation 1993, 60). These influences include the counterinsurgency doctrines developed continent-wide as a response to the threats presented by Che Guevara–inspired *foco* insurrections. All counterinsurgency efforts in Latin America include the following common ideological framework: (1) deep anticommunism; (2) the idea that guerrilla war is a full-scale war; (3) the conviction that the entire continent should be involved in a response to international communism; and (4) the conviction that because guerrillas do not respect the basic laws and morality of war, effective counterinsurgency should not do so either (Comisión Nacional de Verdad y Reconciliación 1991, 59–60). The main evidence in favor of this view is Contreras himself. By all accounts, he was a well-known and ideologically committed anticommunist and counterinsurgency expert prior to the coup (Constable and Valenzuela 1991; M. Salazar Salvo 1995). He used the DINA to carry out a war of counterinsurgency against leftists. Moreover, he not only did so inside Chile but took the lead in organizing a continent-wide counterinsurgency campaign (Operación Cóndor).

Also supporting the "ideological war" view is the fact that the bulk of the military leadership thought it was operating in a time of war and was therefore likely to act accordingly. During the Allende government the military believed that the Marxists posed a very serious threat to national security (Arriagada Herrera 1986; A. Varas 1987; Loveman 1999). Their fears were magnified by the isolation of the armed forces from the rest of society and by the all-too-evident mobilization and calls to arms of the revolutionary left, including the MIR (Chilean National Commission on Truth and Reconciliation 1993, 56). In other words, there were good reasons for those within the military to see its mission not merely as deposing a government but also as waging a campaign against an ideologically driven foe that posed a direct and dire threat to Chile's national security. Contreras's plans, in this sense, fit within the broad overall conceptual framework that others in the military had already embraced, even if he pushed them beyond anything originally contemplated by most fellow officers.

The previously mentioned explanations of Pinochet's attempts to consolidate power and the ideological explanation also support each other, insofar as Pinochet and Contreras were natural partners. Contreras had been Pinochet's pupil at the army's War Academy. Also, the "power consolidation" view can explain why Pinochet would want to place the DINA under his direct control: so that he could use it as an instrument to consolidate personal power inside the ruling circle. In addition, even though many within the top military leadership were critical of the DINA and feared it, the concentration of powers in Pinochet was an important motive in its creation. Pinochet was head of the army and became head of the Joint Chiefs of Staff, head of the junta, and later supreme commander of the nation (Chilean National Commission on Truth and Reconciliation 1993, 64).

Even though these views can explain various aspects of the creation of the DINA, they also suffer from serious weaknesses. None of them explains the central shift in the modus operandi imposed by the DINA: the drop in the number of victims and the increasing recourse to disappearances. It would have been perfectly possible for Pinochet to consolidate power while carrying out a war of counterinsurgency as before, with large numbers of people imprisoned and killed in relative openness, and without resorting to disappearances as a systematic tool of coercion. In fact, terror carried out in the open would have been as useful a tool of power consolidation, as it has been for dictators elsewhere.

Another shortcoming of the "natural evolution" and "ideological war" explanations is that the DINA and the disappearances it carried out were not the only options available to the regime. As shown below, other sectors within the military proposed alternative plans to change the pattern of coercion. An account of a natural evolution in the pattern of coercion during the military regime leaves little room for remaining tensions and clashes over the precise details and applications of coercion among different sectors of the military and the government.

An additional glaring problem is that the timing of the DINA's creation is not what the "power consolidation" argument would predict. The DINA was approved and began operations (in late 1973 and early 1974) *before* Pinochet consolidated his position as the center of power in Chile (in mid- to late 1974). Moreover, the scope of the DINA's operations is different from that expected by the power consolidation view. If Pinochet had amassed such sweeping powers, and if the DINA had served his interests in this way, we would expect the DINA to have played a far more prominent role than it did. In fact, the DINA never achieved a complete monopoly on coercion. Other intelligence and security services continued to operate, and there were power struggles between these and the DINA. The DINA failed to completely monopolize coercion, and it failed to neutralize Pinochet's enemies within the regime.[6]

Perhaps most problematic for the "power consolidation" argument is that during the period when the DINA began operations (at least as early as November 1973, still as the "Comisión DINA"), all decisions inside the junta were made unanimously, with each of the four junta members having only one vote.[7] In other words, even though Pinochet would later manage to centralize power, at the time when the DINA was created and permitted to operate, he was still only primus inter pares within the junta. This was only by virtue of his position as head of the largest branch of the military, rather than because of his personal charisma, skill, fame, public popularity, or leading role in the coup—none of which elements he could claim. At that time he did *not* have the power simply to impose his will on the other junta members.[8] Any explanation for the DINA must take account of this and explain why the rest of the junta would agree to its creation.

This raises three questions. First, why would the other junta members have agreed to the creation of an institution whose sole purpose was ostensibly to help Pinochet consolidate power? There were deep tensions between Pinochet and the other leaders (especially air force commander Gustavo Leigh), and they were suspicious of his ambitions.

Second, while the DINA was a military institution, it lay outside the formal hierarchy of the armed forces. Why would the leaders of the other branches of the armed forces agree to the creation of an institution outside the military chain of command? Moreover, each branch of the armed forces already had an intelligence department.[9] The creation of a new overarching intelligence organization threatened to usurp the functions of the preexisting institutions and embroil all of them in potentially divisive rivalries. The DINA was also subordinate, not to the other branches of the armed forces, but technically only to the junta (though in practice it answered only to Pinochet). This independence meant that Contreras, a colonel, became more powerful than most generals. Perhaps the leadership of the armed forces believed that it was better to place the DINA under a lower-ranking officer, but this would be yet a further signal of the potential threat that the officers understood an organization of such magnitude might pose. In retrospect, Contreras's lower rank did not prevent him from accumulating power, given that the DINA as an institution lay outside the main military structure.

Third, why would the leaders of the other branches of the armed forces agree to the creation of the DINA when there were other options? Contrary to the assumption behind each version of the standard explanations, the DINA was not the only alternative available to the junta leadership. It would have been possible to set up a coordinating committee across the separate intelligence services, for example, or to impose a more uniform coercion policy directed from within the junta itself. What did the DINA offer, in short, that the others did not?

None of these questions can be satisfactorily answered according to standard accounts of the DINA's creation. In this chapter I present an alternative explanation for the creation of the DINA that answers them better. Indeed, it depends on an understanding of the relatively equal balance of power among the four junta members during the early months after the coup and on a consideration of the relative merits of different options available, based on the needs of the junta leaders to monitor and coordinate the actions of their agents.

The DINA as a Response to the Coercion Problem

The DINA was neither a natural nor an obvious development in the evolution of the regime; nor was it simply a tool for Pinochet to accumulate power or simply a blunt weapon for right-wing members of the armed forces, like Contreras, to wage a counterinsurgency campaign against the left. It is unlikely that it would have come about had it not also plausibly promised to address the organizational problems analyzed in the previous chapter. During the first several months after the coup coercion was applied relatively unevenly and publicly, with the result of a large number of casualties. The junta faced a great deal of political pressure, especially at the international level, for these grave violations of human rights. Attempts to address the problem from within the preexisting channels (such as the Arellano mission) did not succeed. The creation of the DINA must be understood in this context of institutional uncertainty and flux .

Another alternative besides the Arellano mission that was floated at this time was to put the Allende leadership on trial. Indeed, part of the international pressure against the regime had to do with the arbitrariness of the detentions and the war tribunals. General Leigh, in particular, supported the judicial path rather than the coercive one. It was never adopted, however, because the junta could not find an adequate legal mechanism to carry it through. Instead, the junta adopted a series of legal ruses so that it would appear to be acting in a more orderly manner, while at the same time it expanded its emergency powers (Barros 1996, 105–10).

Setting up the DINA was a new and costly operation for the military regime. It was also an unprecedented and uncertain experiment for the Chilean military. As shown below, it meant giving a virtual carte blanche to an organization situated outside the normal chains of command and endowing it with a huge amount of material and personnel resources.

Contreras and Pinochet probably persuaded the other junta members that they could better resolve the organizational problems with an organization like the DINA. The main problem concerned balancing the perceived need to consistently and firmly repress the opposition with the need to limit exposure to criticism from domestic and international monitors. We know that the junta recognized these problems as such because of the efforts from inside the junta to fix them, such as the Arellano mission and Leigh's plan to jail the entire Allende administration. What the DINA proposed was to take over the bulk of repression and to oversee the rest. In other words, it would centralize coercion under a single internal monitor. This level of control would allow it to carry out repression much more efficiently than had been possible during the first period, when the various branches of the armed forces had carried out almost all aspects of coercion, often with different and contradictory goals and methods.

This greater efficiency would also allow coherent and consistent application of a new modus operandi to address the problem of external political pressure: the disappearances. While bodies had been made to disappear from the first days after the coup, the practice was carried out haphazardly, as an attempt to cover up tracks after the fact. By contrast, the DINA applied the policy of disappearances much more evenly and effectively as part of its overall grand design to wage a war of counterinsurgency. Why disappearances? The most likely reason was to allow plausible deniability.

In making this argument I do not altogether dispense with the standard views. Indeed, the explanations of Pinochet's power ambitions and the desire of members of the armed forces, especially Contreras, to wage a war of counterinsurgency against all members of the organized left are perfectly consistent with my explanation. But by themselves they are insufficient, for the reasons I indicated above. It is impossible to explain the DINA without understanding the organizational challenges the junta faced in organizing coercion, the changes the DINA proposed, and why the members of the junta agreed to allow the DINA to implement its plans.

The Beginnings of the DINA

Prior to the coup, each branch of the armed forces had carried out intelligence activities in a decentralized manner through their own specialized intelligence departments. Throughout the 1960s, and particularly during the Allende government, intelligence gathering focused on perceived internal threats to national security, particularly political leaders and party organizations of the left and far left. Gathering this kind of information became even more urgent for the military once it took power.

Shortly after the coup, General Nicanor Díaz Estrada of the air force was given the task of coordinating the different intelligence agencies belonging to the different branches of the armed forces and the Carabineros. Díaz Estrada gathered the heads of the four intelligence services: the army's Servicio de Inteligencia Militar (SIM), the navy's Servicio de Inteligencia Naval (SIN), the air force's Servicio de Inteligencia de la Fuerza Aérea (SIFA), and the Servicio de Inteligencia de Carabineros (SICAR) (Archivo Chile n.d.).

At the same time, if not earlier, a secretive group of (mostly army) majors and colonels began intelligence operations from the army's War

Academy as the "Colonels' Committee." Ideologically, the members of this group shared an unusually consistent (for the Chilean military) mix of anticommunism and counterinsurgency doctrine (Comisión Nacional de Verdad y Reconciliación 1991, 59–61). The most prominent among this group was army Lieutenant Colonel Manuel Contreras, who, with the rest of the group, argued against Díaz Estrada's plan to coordinate the preexisting intelligence services, claiming that the preexisting decentralized intelligence institutions were inadequate for effectively neutralizing the regime's many enemies (Comisión Nacional de Verdad y Reconciliación 1991, 471–72). Contreras pushed for the creation of a new institution that would centralize the tasks of the existing agencies and to which they would be subordinate (Archivo Chile n.d.).

By November 1973, even before obtaining full authorization from the intelligence services, the newly created National Detainees Service (SENDET) incorporated this group into its organization as the Comisión DINA. In the SENDET, the DINA continued to carry out intelligence functions, including interrogation procedures and classification of prisoners. Indeed, Ensalaco points out that "some of the men who later became DINA personnel had been interrogating and classifying the thousands of prisoners held in the National Stadium and other sites from the very beginning" (1999, 55).

Colonel Contreras, who led the DINA, was a security specialist who had received training on counterinsurgency at Fort Benning, Georgia.[10] The DINA would not gain formal status until June 1974, when the *Diario Oficial* announced its creation. But by December 1973, when Contreras moved the DINA to separate headquarters, he had already begun recruiting staff and setting up new operational centers from which to carry out detentions, interrogations, tortures, and executions.[11]

The minutes of junta meetings first mention Contreras on November 12, 1973. There are few details of the meeting, but the record reveals (1) that Contreras was seriously lobbying the junta and the senior military leadership to centralize intelligence operations under a new organization and (2) that the junta gave at least a provisional go-ahead to Contreras's proposal at this time, conditional on determining personnel allocation. The minutes read: "Army Lieutenant Colonel Manuel Contreras is received, and he makes a detailed presentation regarding the organization of the National Intelligence Directorate before the junta, the minister of national defense, and the chief of the Military Academy, and the personnel directors of the four [military] institutions, the director of Investigaciones, and director of Army Intelligence. It is accorded that before creating his organization, the personnel directors of the institutions must meet to determine how to obtain the numerous personnel required."[12]

This was probably not the first time that Contreras spoke to the junta. It is unlikely that the junta would have allowed Contreras to address them unless they had already informally agreed to go ahead with his proposal in some form or other. Nevertheless, the final sentence suggests resistance to the DINA from within military ranks. Indeed, Contreras's efforts were opposed by leading officers such as Interior Minister (General) Bonilla, as well as by Colonel (later General) Odlanier Mena, the head of army intelligence (the SIM). Both feared that the new organization was a "Gestapo in the making" that would usurp many of the preexisting institutions' powers.[13] Given this opposition, resolving to have all the intelligence services meet to determine how to allocate the personnel required by the DINA before approving its creation was likely a bureaucratic delay tactic or foot dragging.

The record of the creation of the DINA is sketchy, but it is a reasonable assumption that placing the DINA under the SENDET was another compromise between the interests of Contreras and those of the officers who feared giving him too much power. Nevertheless, suggests Ensalaco, even this compromise solution "brought Contreras' dream closer to realization" (1999, 56). While the early history of the DINA probably reflects a series of compromises between competing interests, we still need to answer the crucial question of how Contreras and Pinochet managed to convince skeptical senior officers to allow the DINA to establish operations in the first place. Pinochet would eventually amass a great deal of power, but during this period in 1973 he lacked the means to force his will on the other junta members. Pinochet and Contreras did not coerce the junta into accepting the DINA. Notwithstanding their reservations, the junta members eventually agreed to it.

Until more archives and records of the period surface,[14] we cannot know for certain the precise details of the conversations that took place at different levels over the creation of the DINA. But we can better use the available evidence to infer the most likely reasons why the junta and the top military leadership allowed the DINA, even when it represented such a serious risk.

The *Informe Rettig* speculates on a number of reasons why the DINA prevailed. These include the following:

1. The DINA operated in secret, and many officers were unaware of the true magnitude of its operations.
2. Many skeptics were probably persuaded at least to withhold judgment for a time and see the DINA as a necessary evil in a time of war.
3. Many feared that confronting the existence of the DINA would only draw attention to the problem of human rights violations, which they knew was a major source of international critique.
4. Many officers were found by the commission to have had insufficient knowledge of the laws and morality of war, which may explain why they paid insufficient attention to the activities of the DINA at the time.
5. The DINA maneuvered inside the military to cut short the careers of those officers deemed to be soft; this led to fear of dissent inside the ranks.
6. Political authority was concentrated to a great extent in the hands of the president. The head of the armed forces became the supreme commander of the nation (D.L. No. 527), an unprecedented concentration of power. (Comisión Nacional de Verdad y Reconciliación 1991)

These speculations are not altogether incorrect. For instance, it is true that the DINA operated secretly, and it is also very likely true that many officers remained unaware of the full magnitude of its activities and its ultimate plans. But even though many officers were probably caught unaware by the DINA's activities, this description does not apply to some key figures such as Bonilla or Mena.

Moreover, the timing is inaccurate. As we have seen, Pinochet consolidated his position by June 1974, well *after* the DINA had begun operations at the end of 1973. At this time the DINA moved into new headquarters and began to build the physical infrastructure to operate and hire staff. This could not have been done had the junta not specifically allocated the DINA the funds it required.

Contreras most likely appealed to the junta regarding three areas: uniformity, secrecy, and targeting. First, we know that the different branches of the armed forces were applying coercion in a highly uneven manner. Local commanders had a great deal of discretion over whom to target, how to treat prisoners, and how to implement the war tribunals. Indeed, the military leadership remained deeply divided over such fundamental issues as whether the new regime was in fact engaged in a war. Moreover, the Arellano mission and the Leigh plans are evidence that the senior military establishment, inside the army as well as the junta, worried about the uneven implementation of coercion and made efforts to establish a more uniform procedure to target enemies and to deal with prisoners. They probably worried about whether future disagreements over inconsistent policy and implementation would lead to internecine battles. And we also know that these efforts to address the problem largely did not work.

This is the context in which we can deduce that Contreras, with Pinochet's support, argued that pursuing trials, in however orderly a manner, was at best a partial response to dealing with the regime's enemies. Trials were not inherently inadequate, but they would have been at best the conclusion of a process that required first identifying and then finding and capturing the regime's enemies. Trials were not an adequate centerpiece of an overall coercive policy. Moreover, many of the regime's enemies were already in exile, and there were few prospects of extradition back to Chile, even in the unlikely event that an internationally accepted legal mechanism could be found.

More preferable, and more effective than complicated legal mechanisms, would have been the option of simply neutralizing the regime's many enemies still at large, either at home or abroad. And a more uniform coercive strategy to better target the regime's most dangerous opponents could be better implemented by a single agency than by the existing multiplicity of competing agencies. This argument, in the context of the failures of the attempted internal reforms as well as the increasingly evident costs of not having a uniform policy, must have been a powerful response to those who, quite rationally, feared the creation of a "Chilean Gestapo."

Second, uniformly applying coercion would permit a more consistent application of policies to serve the interests of the regime. In this case, it would be reasonable to expect that a regime facing a great deal of international pressure and rapidly becoming a pariah would want to find a way to ease these pressures. Even while denouncing critiques in the United Nations and other major international forums as part of a Moscow-directed conspiracy, neither the Chilean military nor its civilian supporters were ideologically or otherwise prepared to completely isolate themselves internationally.[15] An organization like the DINA could offer the political and military leadership an effective way to neutralize much of the international pressure that had resulted from the gross human rights violations.

From the very beginning, the operations of the DINA were shrouded in secrecy. Little was known about its staff or its centers of operations, and disappearances became a normal practice of the agency. Disappearances had been carried out during the initial wave of coercion but far more haphazardly, as various groups and agents sought ways to get rid of bodies. In many cases, observers saw bodies turn up in rivers or dumped in ditches. Disposing of the evidence during this first period was done on an ad hoc basis and not as part of a well-planned or consistently implemented strategy. A great deal of evidence of the junta's atrocities was plainly available. Bodies were found in rivers and ditches as well as morgues, and images of mass detention centers like the Estadio Nacional splashed the headlines of the international media, feeding the growing condemnation of the Chilean regime. The disappearances, as a consistently implemented policy by one single organization, would in this context offer the junta what must have been an attractive refuge from international pressure: plausible deniability.[16] Without the firm evidence of bodies turning up in embarrassing places, the military could plead ignorance regarding the victims' whereabouts and deny responsibility for any wrongdoing.

During the months immediately after the coup, as we have seen, the military targeted broad sectors of the population in a somewhat haphazard way. Nevertheless, the group that suffered the most casualties during this time was the Socialist Party (PS). The armed forces, after all, had deposed a socialist president and a socialist-led government. Most of the socialist leaders were arrested or sent into exile, as were large numbers of party members. Repression against the PS continued until roughly 1975, but after 1973 the targets shifted. Indeed, in 1974 the MIR became the primary target, and in 1976 the Communist Party (PC).

We can infer from this pattern that instead of haphazardly targeting broad sectors of the population, the DINA proposed to target specifically only those groups perceived to pose serious threats to the regime. Doing this would benefit the regime in two ways. First, it would avoid unnecessary fallout from repressing people who might not have been particularly harmful to the regime in the first place. And second, it would mean more effectively targeting those groups that the DINA argued were the real enemies. This included the MIR in particular as well as the exiled left-wing political leaders who had begun to mobilize against the military regime.[17] Contreras's exaggeration of the dangers posed by the regime's enemies at home and abroad served his political ends of being awarded increased power and obtaining more material resources. There was no group, either inside Chile or outside, capable of forcibly deposing the military government. General Leigh of the air force noted subsequently that during this period the junta had been essentially captive to Contreras's intelligence reports on enemy operations and had had little way of assessing exactly how accurate these were (F. Varas 1979).[18]

It should by now have become apparent that the DINA did not simply arise as a "natural" development in the evolution of the regime and that Contreras or Pinochet did not simply impose it on the military leadership against their will. Instead, the junta allowed the DINA to gain increasingly official status and awarded it increasingly better resources to widen the scale and scope of its operations. Explaining why the junta would allow the DINA to accumulate power requires moving beyond the standard explanations for the creation of the DINA. As an outcome, it was neither natural nor necessary. The junta could have chosen to continue to carry out coercion through the preexisting military channels, without fundamentally altering the institutional topography of the regime and the Chilean military. There would have been costs to doing nothing, undoubtedly, but there were also costs, as sectors inside the military and political leadership had feared, to permitting the creation of a Chilean Gestapo.

In short, Manuel Contreras proposed to radically reorganize coercion. Crucial for this project was for the DINA to essentially become a powerful internal monitor. It would not only oversee how the other coercive agencies operated but also take over the bulk of operations itself. More narrowly targeted coercion, applied in a more systematically uniform manner, would require higher levels of internal monitoring. This required the creation of a new institution, since other efforts to increase internal monitoring from within preexisting channels had failed.

Moreover, we saw in the last chapter that while external monitoring during this initial period was low, some external monitoring—in the form of reports about prisoners and speculation about people killed— made attempts to improve secrecy an attractive alternative. How well did the DINA fulfill its promise? Do the observed measured levels of internal and external monitoring during this period correspond to what this explanation would predict? These questions are addressed in the next chapter.

FIVE

The DINA in Action (1974–77)

The DINA aimed to resolve a set of political and organizational problems that the dictatorship faced during the first few months after the coup. During this early period—the bloodiest of the dictatorship—detentions, torture, and summary executions were carried out in relatively public view, a practice that became increasingly costly in political terms for the regime. Compounding this problem, there were serious differences inside the regime concerning such basic questions as whether the crisis meant that the country was in a state of war, and such differences resulted in uneven patterns of repression across the country. The Arellano mission signaled that efforts to harmonize repression from within the existing institutional structure had largely failed. In this context, by taking over the bulk of repression, the DINA proposed to radically restructure how it was practiced. It would be applied in a more consistent and targeted fashion, and a new modus operandi—the disappearances—would provide the regime with much-needed plausible deniability for the killings it was committing. In return, the regime gave the DINA wide leeway to operate outside the standard military hierarchy, as well as to oversee and in some cases direct the activities of the other branches. In short, although these purposes were not described as such at the time, with the creation of the DINA the regime aimed to decrease external monitoring of its repression, as well as to increase the internal monitoring necessary to implement repression more evenly and consistently. Did the DINA achieve these goals? Unfortunately for the members of the junta, as this chapter will show, the DINA achieved only a marginal increase in internal monitoring and little overall reduction in levels of external monitoring. Indeed, the main instrument to try to achieve the latter (the disappearances) had the opposite effect, sparking a backlash against the regime by the general public, the domestic and international media, and foreign governments. The DINA's failure to achieve its goals contributed to its eventual demise.

The DINA Becomes Official

The DINA was formally constituted as an independent organization— separate from the army—by means of D.L. No. 521, in June 1974. Article 1 of this decree described the DINA as a "military body of technical professional nature, under the direct command of the junta. Its mission is to be that of gathering all information from around the nation and from different fields of activity in order to produce the intelligence needed for policy formulation and planning and for the adoption of those measures required for the protection of national security and the development of the country."

Even though the DINA was placed under the "direct command" of the junta, in practice this was not enforced. The rise of the DINA is intimately connected with Pinochet's consolidation of power in the regime,[1] and the relationship between Pinochet and Contreras was strong from the beginning. Colonel Contreras reported on a daily basis only to Pinochet and only indirectly to the junta. The *Informe Rettig* points out that the DINA removed itself from the scrutiny of the junta "so as to be protected from investigation or interference" (Chilean National Commission on Truth and Reconciliation 1993, 475).

Article 4 of D.L. 521 stipulated that the director of national intelligence could obtain, under penalty of law, any "reports or information" from any other state body or employee at any level deemed necessary to carry out his tasks. The same law also contained three articles (9, 10, and 11) published in an annex of the *Diario Oficial* with limited circulation.[2] Although the contents of the other articles were made public, Articles 9–11 effectively remained secret to all but a few top officials. An important clue to their contents, apart from how the DINA operated, was found in D.L. 1009, published in the *Diario Oficial* on May 8, 1975. Its first article stipulated the following: "During the state of siege, the specialized organizations that ensure the normal development of national activities and keep the constituted institutional structure, when they proceed—in the exercise of their faculties—to detain preventively those persons presumed guilty of putting the state's national security in danger, will be obliged to give notice of the detention, within forty-eight hours, to the members of the detainees' immediate family" (Rojas 1988; Chilean National Commission on Truth and Reconciliation 1993, 83).

The "organizations that ensure the normal development of national activities" included the DINA, but no mention had been made, prior to this law, of its ability to carry out detentions (Rojas 1988). Observers deduced that at least one of the secret articles must have allowed the DINA to detain prisoners. Later, it was learned that Article 9 had given the DINA wide leeway to coordinate the activities of the other military branches' intelligence services. Article 10 allowed it to detain prisoners, and Article 11 stipulated that the DINA was the legal corporate continuation of the previous DINA Commission (Rojas 1988; Chilean National Commission on Truth and Reconciliation 1993, 472).[3]

In short, the DINA was an agency with vast powers to carry out intelligence work under the very broad mandate of "the protection of national security and the development of the country." It could request information from all levels of the state at will and could carry out raids, arrests, and interrogations as it saw fit throughout the country.[4] According to the *Informe Rettig,* the DINA's activities included "controlling public records; establishing a network of collaborators and informers in government agencies; supervising, approving, and vetoing appointments and the granting of certain government benefits." Its agents were placed inside the state air and rail agencies, as well as inside the postal and phone services. The DINA was well funded (although its budget remained classified) but also set up its own companies and business partnerships to raise funds (Chilean National Commission on Truth and Reconciliation 1993, 473–75).

The DINA set up centers throughout the country, employing large numbers of people.[5] A large civilian staff worked at headquarters in administrative and analytical functions, and military personnel were appointed to managerial and operational functions. Military personnel came from all branches of the armed forces, including the Carabineros, and civilians came from far right-wing and nationalist groups (Chilean National Commission on Truth and Reconciliation 1993, 475).

The DINA became a complex organization. It was divided roughly into three hierarchical levels: the headquarters, the Metropolitan Intelligence Brigade (BIM), and various other groups or task forces. Intelligence and administrative functions were carried out in headquarters, while the BIM and its dependencies handled operations. The BIM consisted of at least four different groups, which included logistics, interrogations, transports, and guards of Villa Grimaldi, the former country house that served as the principal base of operations for the DINA's agents on the ground. The interrogation division was subdivided into at least four different groups, with names like "Caupolicán," "Lautaro," and "Purén," each one specialized in targeting specific groups. For example, Caupolicán was in charge of targeting the MIR, while Purén pursued other left-wing political organizations.

Different units were in charge of operations, government services, telecommunications and electronic intelligence, finance, propaganda or "psychological" warfare, economic research, and counterintelligence. Special sections also specialized on operations outside Chile, which will be discussed below.[6]

The DINA's Operations

A major signal of the shift brought about by the DINA was the sharp drop in the number of people detained and killed, illustrated in figures 5.1 and 5.2. Also, as noted previously, the DINA took over the bulk of coercive activities from the other branches of the armed forces and applied a different modus operandi with regard to those it did target. Table 5.1 illustrates this shift by comparing the number of disappearances during the last four months of 1973 (P1) and the period from 1974 to 1989 (P2).

The army and the Carabineros in particular carried out the majority of disappearances in 1973. The *Informe Rettig* distinguishes between two forms of disappearances during the early years of the dictatorship: "In the kind of disappearance most common after September 11, 1973, arrests seem to have been made throughout the country by different units of official forces, sometimes accompanied by civilians. These basically

Figure 5.1. Victims Killed per Year under the Regime, 1973–90

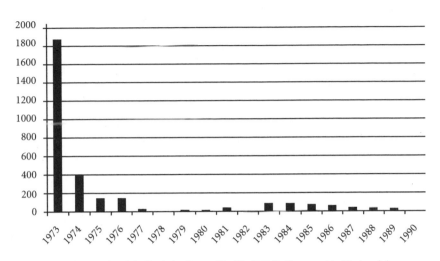

Source: Comisión Nacional de Verdad y Reconciliación (1991); Corporación Nacional de Reparación y Reconciliación (1996).

Figure 5.2. Detainees per Year under the Regime, 1973–90

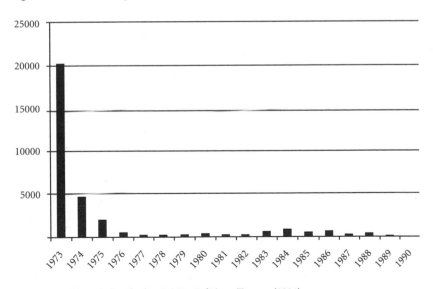

Source: Comisión Nacional sobre Prisión Política y Tortura (2004).

Table 5.1 Disappearances by Agency by Time Period

	P1 (Sept.–Dec. 1973)	P2 (1974–89)	Total
Army	125	21	146
Carabineros	248	45	293
Joint military and Carabineros	43	2	45
Joint military operations	54	5	59
Carabineros and armed civilians	17	14	31
Investigaciones	19	7	26
Air Force	11	7	18
Navy	3	2	5
DINA	0	324	324
SIM	0	13	13
State or security agents	11	19	30
Joint Command	0	26	26
CNI	0	9	9
Foreign armed forces and DINA	0	15	15
Armed civilians	3	0	3
Argentine armed forces	0	25	25
No information available	87	38	125
Total	**621**	**562**	**1193**

Source: Padilla Ballesteros (1995, 59).

Note: There is some disagreement as to the exact number of deaths and disappearances. Two state-sanctioned institutions have carried out investigations into these by collecting witness accounts and conducting their own independent research. The first was the National Commission on Truth and Reconciliation, which delivered its report (the Informe Rettig) in 1991. The second was its continuation, the National Corporation for Reparations and Reconciliation (CNRR), whose report was delivered in 1996. The Informe Rettig listed 2,298 victims and the CNRR a further 899 for a grand total of 3,197 victims officially recognized as such. Of these, 1,102 are listed as disappeared and 2,095 as executed. Padilla Ballesteros, in analyzing the disappearances, uses the state's data but adopts slightly broader criteria regarding who counts as a victim. The difference between Padilla's total number of disappearances and the state's is nevertheless not particularly significant for our purposes. Padilla counts 1,193 disappeared against the official state's total of 1,102.

consisted of a summary execution or murder of the victim and the disposal of the body (generally by throwing it into a river or burying it secretly) followed by a denial or false stories" (Chilean National Commission on Truth and Reconciliation 1993, 36). The purpose of the disappearance, in these cases, "was clearly to enable those carrying out the crime to avoid any kind of responsibility. Sometimes it was to hide the abuse the bodies had received either before or after death. But sometimes there was no imaginable reason, as for example, when the remains of those shot by firing squad in Pisagua were not turned over; they may or may not have been sentenced by war tribunals, but the authorities themselves had very openly spoken of the firing squads" (Chilean National Commission on Truth and Reconciliation 1993, 142). By contrast to this practice, the DINA generally operated in a much more consistently secretive and systematic manner than the other branches had done until then: "[The second form of] 'disappearance' was carried out primarily during the 1974–77 period, mainly but not exclusively, by the DINA. The Commission is convinced that behind most of these cases was a politically motivated and systematically implemented effort to exterminate particular categories of people" (Chilean National Commission on Truth and Reconciliation 1993, 36).

Prior to the DINA, the most dangerous period for a prisoner was the time immediately after arrest. During this period, prisoners were interrogated and often tortured, and this was the time when they were most likely to be killed.[7] After interrogations, the officers in charge could determine whether to release the prisoner or to hold him longer in case other information came up. Long-term prisoners received official status as such and were listed by the National Detainees Service (SENDET). Once prisoners received official status, for instance inside the National Stadium or one of the other concentration camps, outsiders could track them, relatives could visit and send them supplies, and relief agencies like the Red Cross could demand to have access and monitor their situation.

The DINA adopted a different pattern of operations, completely bypassing the functions and purpose of the SENDET, which functioned independently from the DINA. Taking fewer prisoners permitted a different and far less bureaucratic sort of treatment. The DINA did not report any details of its prisoners' captivity, and no outside contact was allowed. The result was that prisoners simply "disappeared," and relatives and observers had very little information regarding their whereabouts apart from witness accounts of where they might have been taken prisoner. In some cases, prisoners who were released revealed details of the whereabouts of other people they might have seen or had contact with while in captivity.[8] Overall, however, information about the DINA's operations was relatively hard to obtain.[9]

As was previously noted, there was great variation in the treatment of prisoners during the first few months after the coup.[10] In some cases people were rounded up and kept isolated under great duress, for instance in military barracks or detention centers, while in other cases prisoners were allowed many amenities such as regular visits and the freedom to organize their daily lives collectively with other prisoners. The DINA adopted the methods used by the most hard-line of the military's organizations. It did not hold large numbers of prisoners in large detention centers such as the Estadio Nacional and Estadio Chile or in concentration camps such as Chacabuco, Pisagua, or Ritoque. Instead, it kept prisoners in smaller, secretive locations such as Villa Grimaldi or various other sites throughout the country. Prisoners were often kept in small cells, blindfolded, and tied up; they were also subjected to regular tortures, and they enjoyed little or no contact with others.[11]

As the above descriptions suggest, the DINA did not simply hold prisoners. Rather, it mounted a campaign of repression against those it viewed as most directly threatening to national security. These included not simply members of the Chilean far left and the leadership in exile but also (as will be detailed below) left-wing opponents located throughout South America, in cooperation with the other authoritarian regimes in the region.

We can roughly infer the structure of the DINA's plans from the pattern of victims it targeted at different times. Table 5.2 indicates that during the first period (P1), from September to December 1973, the group with the most victims was the Socialist Party. Technically, the largest category is that for which there is no firm information as regards their political affiliation. Padilla Ballesteros (1995, 61–63) points out that lack of firm information does not necessarily mean that these were not leftist sympathizers. Most were arrested (and, we can suppose, also executed) by one of the security services. Though in 73 of the 369 overall cases there is no information as to which organization or group carried out the detention, in roughly two dozen cases the reasons for their arrest was not directly political and included criminal activities such as drug trafficking, assault, or theft.

During the last four months of 1973, 152 socialists were disappeared, by contrast to "only" 74 during the remaining seventeen years of the dictatorship (P2). The MIR and the PC suffered comparatively more casualties after 1973 and collectively sustained far more fatalities than the socialists did during either period. And the number of those without declared (or known) political affiliation was far higher before the DINA took charge (table 5.3).

Table 5.2 Disappearances by Political Affiliation by Time Period

	P1 (Sept.–Dec. 1973)	*P2 (1974–89)*	*Total*
PC (Communists)	87	158	245
PS (Socialists)	152	74	226
MIR (Movement of Revolutionary Left)	53	219	272
MAPU (United Movement of Popular Action)	10	10	20
PR (Radical Party)	9	3	12
PDC (Christian Democrats)	5	1	6
FPMR (Manuel Rodriguez Patriotic Front)	0	5	5
IC (Christian Left)	2	1	3
Other parties	30	5	35
No information	283	86	369
Total	631	562	1193

Source: Padilla Ballesteros (1995, 59).

Destroying the MIR became the biggest focus of domestic operations for the DINA in 1974 and 1975. After the coup, the MIR leadership went underground. Unlike the socialists and the communists, the MIR had always espoused, and organized for, an armed insurrection.[12] The MIR has its origins in the student movement of the 1960s strongly influenced by landmark events such as the Cuban Revolution as well as the wars of national liberation in Algeria and Vietnam. It was led by Miguel Enríquez, who embraced armed struggle from the beginning and who sharply criticized the "traditional left" (the communists) for believing

Table 5.3   Fatalities Attributed to Acts of State Repression, by Region and Party Affiliation, September 11 to December 31, 1973

Region	MIR	PC	PS	Other	N-M	Total	%
Tarapacá	1	2	13	1	8	25	2.1
Antofagasta	5	10	46	2	8	71	5.9
Atacama	5	2	11	0	1	19	1.6
Coquimbo	1	7	4	3	7	22	1.8
Valparaíso	4	10	12	5	10	41	3.4
Región Metropolitana (Santiago)	19	54	87	14	318	492	40.8
B. O'Higgins	0	4	2	0	2	8	0.7
Maule	9	3	19	2	29	62	5.1
Bío Bío	16	35	34	9	114	208	17.3
Araucanía	6	21	26	6	55	114	9.5
Los Lagos	27	16	31	5	49	128	10.6
Aysén	0	2	1	1	6	10	0.8
Magallanes and Ch. Antártica	0	1	2	0	2	5	0.4
Total	93	167	288	48	609	1205	100.0
%	7.7	13.9	23.9	4.0	50.5	100.0	

Source: Comisión Nacional de Verdad y Reconciliación (1991); Barros (1996).

that "it is necessary to perfect the [capitalist] regime in order to generate the forces that will destroy it. The MIR, on the other hand, believes that it is necessary . . . to implant immediately the bases for the construction of socialism. For them [the communists] one should not struggle directly against capitalism. For us the fundamental thing is to use violence to propel the working class in the city and the countryside."[13]

In early 1974, an intelligence report pointed out that the MIR, as well as the communists, remained in operation inside the country. Echoing these conclusions, Pinochet at this time argued, "The Communist Party is intact, and so is the MIR. Only the Socialists were disbanded."[14] The DINA assassinated Miguel Enríquez in May 1974, one of the few cases of a deliberately public assassination of a high-level opposition political leader (Cavallo Castro, Salazar Salvo, and Oscar Sepúlveda Pacheco 1989, 52–60; Chilean National Commission on Truth and Reconciliation 1993).

In July 1975 the DINA also mounted "Operación Colombo" against the MIR. A series of Argentine newspaper articles reported that 119 Chilean MIR members had killed each other in Argentine-based internecine battles while they were ostensibly engaged in terrorist actions against the Chilean regime. But the articles raised suspicions as to their authenticity because the newspapers that ran them—*LEA* in Argentina and *O'Dia* in Brazil—were not well known. (Indeed, they had published only one issue!) Moreover, the victims' names corresponded to persons the human rights community had already listed as disappeared. The opposition thus quickly spotted the entire operation as a DINA disinformation campaign. In response to the international outcry that followed, Pinochet called the incident an "international plot against Chile" by the forces of communism (Ahumada et al. 1989, 101–39; Constable and Valenzuela 1991, 153; CODEPU-DIT 1994; Padilla Ballesteros 1995, 40–41).[15]

Cóndor

By mid-1974 the DINA had begun to mount comprehensive operations not simply inside Chile but far beyond Chile's borders. This included pursuit of its enemies especially into Argentina but also as far away as Europe and the United States.[16] Indeed, the DINA intended for an integral part of the campaign against Marxism to be carried out beyond Chile's borders. Soon after setting up operations, Contreras convinced the government (essentially, Pinochet) that it was necessary to carry out a counterinsurgency campaign against those people who were acting against the military government from abroad. At the very least the objective was to neutralize out-of-the-country Chileans who were seen as possible threats. At best, it was hoped there would be a continent-wide concerted effort to counter the influence of the "Marxist international movement."[17]

In November 1973, Manuel Contreras met with Enrique Arancibia Clavel, a Chilean residing in Buenos Aires who was a fugitive from justice over the assassination of General René Schneider.[18] Other people implicated in the Schneider assassination also became involved at this time in the DINA's operations outside Chile. Some of these were residing in Argentina, and others had previously carried out sabotage activities against the Allende government in Chile. Immediately after setting up operations in the headquarters taken from the Communist Youth, the DINA established a "Foreign Department" under the command of Major Raúl Eduardo Iturriaga Neumann in December 1973 (Proyecto Internacional de Derechos Humanos 2008). Like Contreras, Iturriaga Neumann had gone through the U.S. Military School of the Americas training program. In 1973 he was second in command of the Black Berets Battalion.[19]

In November 1975, Manuel Contreras organized a meeting of the heads of the principal intelligence institutions in the dictatorships now in place throughout most of the Southern Cone.[20] The new campaign, known as Operación Cóndor and led in part by the DINA, aimed at a coordinated attack against Marxists and other key figures in the opposition to military rule.[21]

Although set up "formally" only in 1975, operations outside Chile had begun earlier. In September 1974, General Carlos Prats and his wife were killed by a car bomb in Buenos Aires.[22] In October 1975, a gunman in Rome seriously wounded Bernardo Leighton, former vice president during the Frei administration (1964–70) and a key opposition figure,

along with his wife. And in September 1976, Orlando Letelier and his assistant, Ronnie Moffitt, were killed by a car bomb as they approached
Sheridan Circle in Washington, D.C.[23] All three attacks shared similar
trademarks.[24] Prats and Letelier were killed in almost identical fashion:
by a car bomb. Leighton was the victim of a shooting, though subsequent
investigations, especially by Italian authorities, have linked many of the
perpetrators of the attack to the DINA. Moreover, all three acts reveal
that the DINA set up working relationships with various paramilitary
groups outside Chile, including anti-Castro groups in Miami and other
right-wing groups located throughout South America and in Europe
(Blixen 1994, 1997a, 1997b, 1998; Marchak 1999, 112–13).

Did the DINA Help the Regime Achieve Its Goals?

As the DINA took control, repression in Chile was carried out more uniformly and consistently than before. It was also more finely targeted
and generally applied more secretly. At the same time, through Operación Cóndor, the DINA oversaw the extension of the regime's repression beyond Chile's borders. But did the DINA help the regime resolve
the problems it faced during the early months after the coup? These
problems included poorly coordinated and unevenly applied repression
against large groups of people, for which the regime suffered embarrassing critiques, especially internationally. By creating the DINA, the regime hoped to reduce the political costs associated with repressing its
enemies. Although its goals were not described as such at the time, the
DINA was supposed to increase internal monitoring and to decrease
external monitoring; to centralize operations and to carry out repression more secretly; and to allow the regime plausible deniability for its
crimes.

Notwithstanding the changes the DINA brought about, in many
ways it failed to achieve these goals. For example, internal monitoring
increased, but only slightly. While the DINA became a central information clearinghouse for the regime's coercive activities, it failed to completely monopolize repression. Other coercive institutions remained, in
the other branches of the armed forces, operating with varying degrees

of independence from the DINA. Other than the Carabineros, the most important of these was the Comando Conjunto, directed by the air force. In other words, the DINA failed to bring the entire security and intelligence community into line behind a single organization that it could monitor and control.[25]

Lingering tensions remained with the other institutions, and competition with the Comando Conjunto in particular was at times violent. Sectors within the army's intelligence community (represented by individuals such as General Mena) never completely accepted the authority of Manuel Contreras, and they retained enough power to be able to pose a threat to his position at a later date.

Despite these rivalries, the DINA amassed a vast amount of power. It had no superior or oversight except Pinochet, and it used its formidable institutional capacity not simply to repress the regime's left-wing enemies and to direct coercion but also to monitor those sectors it suspected to be the regime's enemies from within the ruling circles. It even kept files on civilian supporters of the regime, being mistrustful of groups that Contreras feared had failed to build popular support for military rule. This level of intrusion even into supporters' lives provoked deep tensions between leading civilian conservatives and the DINA. In other words, one consequence of the DINA's power is precisely what we would expect from a simple increase in the levels of internal monitoring: Who would monitor the monitor? The DINA attained an unprecedented level of power, and controlling the DINA became a problem in its own right. As I show in the next chapter, the critiques against the DINA grew rapidly from within the regime's own circles, where increasing numbers of supporters and advisors argued that the DINA was an institution out of control.

In fact, the DINA succeeded in addressing only some of the problems it was designed to resolve, and even then it created a series of new ones. The DINA's efforts to carry out coercion in secret, and thereby to seek some degree of plausible deniability, did not always succeed. An increasingly sophisticated and safeguarded network of human rights lawyers, activists, and journalists, with increasingly comprehensive data and archives, kept track of the DINA's operations and made these findings public. Every time plausible deniability failed, the pressure on the regime increased.

At the same time, while the junta and the rest of the military leadership may have consented to the creation of the DINA in 1973, they did not wholeheartedly support it. The lingering tensions that the DINA was unable to resolve undermined its legitimacy as the prime coercive agency, particularly when some tensions threatened to spill over into political conflict inside the regime. In some ways, the DINA combined the worst of both worlds. It had both too much and too little power. It made internal enemies who resented its vast powers but was not able to completely get rid of them. The next chapter analyzes the efforts by the regime to address these and other new problems created by the DINA.

SIX

The Fall of the DINA
(1977–78)

A second shift in how the dictatorship organized its repressive agencies took place from 1977 to 1978. In August 1977, the regime replaced the DINA with a different institution, the Central Nacional de Informaciones (CNI). At first, the DINA team also led the CNI, with Contreras and his men still at the helm, but this team fell from power in April 1978, and their departure coincided with perhaps the most important political shift during the entire dictatorship.[1] The CNI adopted a new modus operandi, the number of victims fell sharply in 1978, operations abroad were curtailed, and there were practically no more disappearances during the rest of the regime. For the first time, also, civilians were appointed to the majority of cabinet positions, including the Ministry of the Interior (the leading cabinet position). As part of this change, the civilians gained control over the security apparatus led by the new CNI, now placed directly under the supervision of the minister of the interior. One of the first measures implemented by the new civilian-led cabinet was an amnesty for all human rights violations committed between 1973 and 1978. With this measure, the regime announced it was opening a new chapter and leaving behind the violence of the past.[2] Restrictions on civil liberties were also relaxed, a move that permitted new opposition groups to appear. What was behind this shift? Why was there a shift at all, and why did it include such a profound reorganization not simply of the repressive agencies but of the regime in general?

A Cosmetic Shift?

A common view regarding this shift is that the replacement of the DINA by the CNI was largely cosmetic—that the CNI was the continuation of the DINA by another name. At best, the regime played a subtle game of smoke and mirrors to appear to be addressing the problem of the human rights violations without changing much of substance.[3] It is true that the CNI was the DINA's legal successor and that both organizations shared many similarities. A point-by-point comparison of D.L. No. 521, which created the DINA, and D.L. No. 1828, which created the CNI, shows them to be extremely similar (Rojas 1988, 36–39). There was also a great deal of continuity between both institutions in terms of personnel and physical infrastructure. A large portion of the DINA's staff continued to work under the CNI, and the new organization continued to use many of the DINA's principal bases of operations.[4]

Yet despite these similarities and continuities, the differences between the two institutions were significant. For example, the DINA was an autonomous institution, but the CNI was placed under the jurisdiction of the Ministry of Defense, and it reported to the president through the Ministry of the Interior. Also, even though much of the DINA staff continued to work in the CNI, former DINA chief Manuel Contreras left precious few files for the new CNI. In addition, the cooperation of the DINA officers who remained was said to be "meager" (Cavallo Castro, Salazar Salvo, and Sepúlveda Pacheco 1989, 194).

At first, the CNI was also given fewer powers than the DINA. As noted in previous chapters, one of the three secret articles in D.L. No. 521 gave the DINA broad powers to carry out detentions. By contrast, the CNI's powers of arrests were more constrained. It enjoyed no secret powers, and it required a court order to carry out detentions (Frühling 2000). Nevertheless, the CNI made use of Article 1 of D.L. No. 1009, which gave it the power to make "preventive detentions" under states of emergency or siege. The CNI carried out thousands of arrests this way (Comisión Nacional sobre Prisión Política y Tortura 2004).[5]

The CNI's structure was also different from the DINA's. A general always headed it, and it maintained more bases of operations, throughout a larger part of the country, than its predecessor had.[6] The CNI inherited all the DINA's property and added several more bases of operations.[7] Available evidence suggests that it maintained a staff of about 2,200, half of whom were military and half civilian (de Luigi 1989, D1; Frühling 2000).

Another significant difference between the DINA and the CNI was the far narrower range of international operations under the latter. Mounting a broad-based international campaign against Marxism had been a central goal for Contreras from early on, and the DINA and Operación Cóndor were the instruments he used to achieve this. After Contreras's departure, there is little evidence of Cóndor continuing in a comprehensive way (Slack 1996; McSherry 2000). For instance, there were no more assassinations or attempts against opposition leaders such as the Prats, Letelier, and Leighton cases.[8] Instead, international operations under the CNI were restricted to using foreign embassies to infiltrate and spy on organizations in the community of Chilean exiles (Chilean National Commission on Truth and Reconciliation 1993, 637–38).

Perhaps the most striking difference between the two organizations is that while the DINA sought to exterminate the opposition (both in Chile and abroad), the CNI sought merely to contain and monitor it.[9] There was a sharp drop in the number of people killed during the time of the CNI's operations. Torture continued to be practiced but in a much more targeted fashion (Comisión Nacional de Verdad y Reconciliación 1991, 168; Frühling 2000, 541; Comisión Nacional sobre Prisión Política y Tortura 2004). Moreover, there was a sharp drop in the number of disappearances under the CNI. This practice had become the DINA's signature modus operandi, with hundreds of disappearances during 1974–77. After 1978, as table 5.2 shows, the number of disappearances dropped sharply to only a handful. The *Informe Rettig* notes that during Mena's period as CNI director (1977–80) the few disappearances that did take place were probably not attributable to the CNI (Comisión Nacional de Verdad y Reconciliación 1991).

In terms of the clearest outward signs of how coercion is practiced, in other words, the evidence simply does not support the claim that there was little difference between the DINA and the CNI. Instead of assuming that they were similar, we must explain the differences between them and the shift from one to the other.

Explaining the Shift

Many observers argue that the primary cause of the shift in 1977–78 (including the replacement of the DINA by the CNI) was international pressure against the regime. Human rights violations and acts of international terrorism (such as the Letelier-Moffitt assassination) resulted in demands against the regime, especially from the United States, to get rid of Contreras and the DINA. American officials pressured the Chilean regime as soon as it became clear that the DINA was implicated in the Letelier-Moffitt case, and Sigmund, for example, argues that "U.S. pressure was a major factor in the reorganization of the instruments of repression in Chile. The CNI was an improvement over the DINA, in that it did not resort to disappearance as an instrument of policy" (1993, 129). Moreover, according to Sigmund, U.S. pressure, particularly during the Carter administration in the aftermath of the Letelier case, resulted in the release of most political prisoners in 1976 and 1977 (129).[10]

Hawkins's review of the minutes of the junta's meetings also reveals a regime deeply concerned about its image abroad, seeking ways "to counter international critics of its human rights policies" rather than focus on its domestic critics (1996, 83–84). One way the government responded to these pressures was by replacing the DINA, the target of most international critiques, with the CNI (Hawkins 1994). In another variant of this idea, Huneeus (2000a, 162) also argues that U.S. pressures over the Letelier case left the regime with little choice but to replace the DINA with the CNI. Without U.S. pressure, the plan "would not have been implemented."

The timing of the shift certainly coincided with international pressures. U.S. officials were in Chile during the key periods in 1977 and 1978 when the shifts took place. In August 1977, during the visit of Assistant Secretary of State Terence Todman to Santiago, Pinochet announced the replacement of the DINA by the CNI, though with Manuel Contreras remaining as CNI director. In February 1978, U.S. investigators into the Letelier assassination presented Chile with Letters Rogatory officially requesting information on the case. The pictures of two DINA agents who had applied for U.S. visas in Paraguay using false passports and who were linked to the crime accompanied the request. Their pictures were printed in the U.S. press and also in Santiago's conservative and normally pro-Pinochet *El Mercurio,* the first time a DINA link to the Letelier assassination was publicly discussed among progovernment sectors in Chile (Dinges and Landau 1980, ch. 18; Sigmund 1993, 108–18).

The Carter administration also put heavy pressure on the Chileans to extradite Contreras in connection with the Letelier case. The Chilean Supreme Court refused this request,[11] but Michael Townley, the principal DINA agent responsible for implementing the plan, was eventually extradited. The Letelier case was specifically exempted from the Amnesty Decree of 1978, and this outcome can be very directly traced to arm-twisting by the Carter administration (Dinges and Landau 1980; Branch and Propper 1983; Sigmund 1993).

Beyond timing and specific outcomes such as the exemption for the Letelier case, however, international pressure alone is a poor explanation for the magnitude of the shift. International pressure against the regime specified both a broader and narrower range of goals than the reforms actually accomplished. On the one hand, there were repeated calls from a wide range of actors—from the UN General Assembly to multiple nongovernmental organizations—for a return to democracy and full respect for human rights. While the dictatorship was clearly concerned about its international image and took some steps to try to assuage the critiques against it,[12] international pressures continued until the end of the dictatorship (though with a hiatus during the early years of the Reagan administration).[13] This is a signal that the reforms of 1978 were about more than a straightforward response to the international community's concerns and pressure. If general international pressure (for instance, from the United Nations) were the regime's principal concern, there would have been a much clearer shift in the direction of the rule of law, respect for human rights, and democracy. Notwithstanding the regime's many attempts to convince the international community otherwise (e.g., by releasing some prisoners), it continued to tighten control over its coercive agencies and to violently repress its enemies. And it would be another twelve years before it transferred power back to democratically elected civilian authorities.

On the other hand, the United States placed a great deal of pressure on Chile to extradite Contreras and to cooperate with the resolution of the Letelier case. Yet the Chilean Supreme Court refused Contreras's extradition, although U.S. pressure did result in the exemption granted in the amnesty decree for the Letelier case, as well as in the extradition of Michael Townley. While these were significant results, they were less than what the United States wanted. In short, international pressure alone does not account for the magnitude of the shift that occurred.

A different set of explanations for the shift places more weight on domestic than on international factors. In one variant, the reforms were simply part of a long-range plan of "state terrorism." All military and police forces, including the DINA and CNI, "this last one being the legal successor of the first," implemented the plan (Padilla Ballesteros 1995, 43).[14] Apart from failing to distinguish the differences between the two institutions (which, as we have seen, were significant), this view presupposes that there was sufficient coherence at the top to implement such a plan from the first days of the regime to the last.[15] I have described in previous chapters the significant tensions and struggles at the top over fundamental issues such as which powers the regime had taken, how they would be divided, and what direction the regime would take. I discuss below the continuation of these uncertainties during the period of the shift from the DINA to the CNI. These uncertainties are too important to ignore in the development of the regime, and they cast doubt on explanations that presume an internally coherent and monolithic regime.[16]

An alternative explanation is that the reforms implemented in 1978 were driven by the consolidation of Pinochet's personal power. Remmer argues that Pinochet managed to personalize power and to build a "tyranny" by dividing and ruling. There were differences between the hard-liners and soft-liners (the *duros* and the *blandos*) in the regime, and Pinochet successfully played these sectors off against each other. "Even the organization of repression conformed to this tendency," she writes, "involving the Central Nacional de Informaciones (formerly DINA), the army, and rival police organizations. At various times certain elements of the governing coalition appeared to have won out at the expense of others; but Pinochet remained above the fray, where he was able to take advantage of divisions and conflicts" (Remmer 1991, 137–38). In a variant of this idea, the reforms came about because Pinochet simply made some compromises with the soft-line sectors. For example, Hawkins (1994) notes that the shift from the DINA to the CNI marked the rise in influence of soft-liners and the fall from power of the hard-liners, with a corresponding improvement in human rights practices.

Huneeus (2000a) presents a more nuanced version of this account. He argues that a core group of right-wing civilians gained extraordinary prominence under the new regime, especially after 1978. These were the previously mentioned *gremialistas,* conservative lawyers and economists from the Universidad Católica, led by Jaime Guzmán. Guzmán was critical of the mass movements and mobilizations of the 1960s and 1970s and felt that a radical transformation of the basic Chilean political institutions was necessary to prevent Marxism from returning to Chile. He realized that the military government presented the best opportunity to carry out such a transformation, the centerpiece of which would be a new constitution.[17]

Adopting a softer coercive policy was part and parcel of the institutionalization project. The leading pro-*gremialista* magazine, *Qué Pasa,* was generally supportive of the regime but took an increasingly critical stance against the DINA. The break took place in July 1975 after the case of the 119 MIR activists who had ostensibly disappeared in Argentina as a result of internecine fights (described in the previous chapter). *Qué Pasa* noted that the names corresponded to people listed as "detained-disappeared," making the DINA's responsibility for the murders all too clear. The magazine argued that such incidents damaged the regime by providing ammunition for its many enemies at home and abroad. Only by creating a clear and stable new political order could the regime put to rest the accusation of running a totalitarian police state (Huneeus 2000a, 284–91; 2000b).

The soft-liner and *gremialista* sectors themselves have presented a similar line of argument. Sergio Fernández, an ideological ally of Guzmán, became the first civilian interior minister in April 1978 and was given broad powers to implement sweeping reforms. He argues that his appointment was a victory over the hard-liners like Contreras and (in his view) the beginning of Chile's "transition to democracy" (Fernández 1994, 1998). One of his cabinet's first acts was to decree an amnesty (D.L. 2191) for all those who had been sentenced by military courts since the time of the coup.[18] Another was to lift the state of siege, which had been in place since 1973, as well as to ease the strict curfews. The most important reform was to oversee the implementation of a new constitution over the next two years (Fernández 1994).[19]

Jaime Guzmán, who became the chief architect of the 1980 Constitution and one of Contreras's principal rivals within the regime, lends support to these views. In a clear allusion to the DINA, he argued that the military regime during the first few years was a "bucking horse" that had to be tamed. The civilian-led administration under Fernández, presumably, largely succeeded in doing so (Guzmán Errázuriz 1992).[20] Guzmán also strongly believed that the junta should not be merely a hiatus between two periods of divisive partisan politics but instead should create a new institutional order (Huneeus 2000a, 343). Evidence of the softliners' complaints also supports the view that the DINA troubled them. Members of the Consejo del Estado—an important group of civilian and military advisors—protested in March 1977 that it was imperative to "moderate the actions of the DINA" given that its "violent measures" were compromising the government's image.[21] In May 1977, *El Mercurio* admitted that the DINA might have committed "criminal abuses."[22] Coming from the leading progovernment paper, this represented a significant critique.[23] In August 1977, when the DINA was replaced by the CNI, the same paper applauded the change and wrote, "No one can deny the serious possibility of grave errors and abuses of power [by the DINA]."[24] *Ercilla*, the country's principal conservative weekly magazine, noted in March 1978 that in "this muddy river [of coercion] it is imperative to touch bottom . . . in order to return to the tranquillity and prestige of the country."[25]

Critiques by civilians also echoed critiques from within the military itself, reinforced in part by the fact that the DINA, although led by a military officer, sidestepped standard military protocol. Contreras was a colonel, yet in practice his power was greater than that of any general except Pinochet.[26] The DINA remained outside the military hierarchy as an independent institution that answered only to the president.

Although some supporters of Contreras to this day claim that the Letelier murder was a CIA plot,[27] they are less exculpatory on other grounds. General (ret.) Fernando Arancibia, who was briefly the director of CNI immediately after Contreras, argued that the DINA had "successfully carried out a difficult task against subversion" but that its operations had often been "improvised" and marked by "excesses."[28] General (ret.) Odlanier Mena, a career intelligence officer and one of Contreras's most notorious critics,[29] argued that Contreras had essentially "confused intelligence with security," military parlance for stating that he believed the DINA was overstepping its jurisdiction and engaging in excessive brutality.[30]

Barros provides a different variant of the domestic politics explanation for the shift. While he supports the view that the push to institutionalize the regime played an important role in the 1978 reforms, he argues that the driving force behind this push was the need to settle rivalries among the four junta members over their precise division of powers. During 1977 and 1978, the junta engaged in tense debates over various proposals to regulate its structure and the division of powers between the executive and the legislative branches.[31] Pinochet floated several proposals that would have replaced the junta's unanimity rule with majority decision making, giving the president the deciding vote as well as giving the executive a series of other powers that could be exercised without consultation with the legislative branch as exercised by the junta (Barros 1996, 143–44). Air force commander Gustavo Leigh, in particular, strongly challenged Pinochet's drive to centralize power.[32] The tensions between Leigh and Pinochet were manifest at many levels, from deep disagreements inside the junta over the basic structure and purpose of the regime to the clashes of the DINA versus the SIFA and Comando Conjunto.

Guzmán also opposed Pinochet's efforts. He understood that a long-term military regime—the main outcome if Pinochet were to succeed in completely centralizing power—would be disastrous for the armed forces as well as the country as a whole. Experience in neighboring countries such as Argentina and Brazil suggested that political involvement risked undermining military professionalism, as the various branches of the armed forces fought with each other for resources and power (Barros

1996).[33] For soft-liners like Guzmán, Pinochet's efforts to accumulate power underscored the urgency of institutionalization.

Barros notes that Guzmán had to balance the projection of the regime into the future with the exigencies of rule in the present. He disagreed with a quick return to democracy, arguing that in the short run it was expedient to give maximum power to one person—Pinochet—in order "to get things done." But he was keenly aware of the pitfalls inherent in this practice: the regime would become personalized and not institutionalized and would risk the hazards of prolonged military involvement in politics. Even while Pinochet aimed to ensconce himself in power, Guzmán pressed for a new constitution to bind the regime and the entire country to a new and permanent set of political institutions beyond any one political sector's ability to alter (Barros 1996).[34] Beyond avoiding divisions inside the regime, Guzmán's principal aim was to avoid in Chile what had happened in Spain after Franco's death. The Spanish caudillo had built a highly personalistic regime but had failed to ground it in solid permanent institutions. After Franco's death in 1975, future governments found it relatively easy to transform the country's basic institutions and rapidly undo his regime's legacy (Maravall 1978; Huneeus 1985; Maravall and Santamaría 1986; Olmeda 1988; Agüero 1991; Linz, Stepan, and Gunther 1994). Thus having "recourse to sources of agreement beyond the junta for the first time functioned as a mechanism for bolstering the institutional order decreed from above and as a justification for introducing a limit upon the junta's unilateral exercise of constituent power" (Barros 2002, 208).

In this way, Huneeus's and Barros's explanations of how the CNI came to replace the DINA overlap and complement each other. The former emphasizes the *gremialista* push (led by Guzmán) to institutionalize the regime, and the latter argues that this push was made all the more urgent primarily by the intra-junta struggles. The civilians with a strong vision of the future found ready allies among the junta leadership keenly aware of the disastrous consequences of internal splits. All sectors wanted to capitalize on the potential of military rule to prevent a recurrence of the kind of political crisis that had led to the coup. None wanted a Marxist government to return to power. But the civilians, in particular, understood that the military regime itself also posed dangers that had to be avoided. On the one hand was the possibility of disintegration into internecine fights and even warfare among the different branches of the armed forces; on the other was the all-too-real possibility of the consolidation of one-man rule by Pinochet.[35]

Although these were different potential outcomes, each one was quite plausible. Pinochet ruled the army with an iron grip and ousted his chief rival inside the junta—Gustavo Leigh—on July 24, 1978, soon after the civilian-appointed cabinet took power.[36] But despite this victory over his most relentless rival inside the junta, Pinochet failed to achieve complete control over the junta, and the tensions leading to Leigh's ouster threatened to crack the regime even after his departure.[37]

Huneeus and Barros thus point to a more complex mechanism for the shift than simply a Pinochet power grab. This was the push to institutionalize the regime, which would not only prevent a return to Marxism in the future but also avoid the double pitfalls of collapse and one-man rule. The DINA's tensions with the rest of the armed forces provoked concerns about the regime's cohesion. Its tight nexus to Pinochet provoked concerns about the consolidation of personal rule. Replacing the DINA with the CNI—and restraining the regime's repression—accomplished the twin goals of appeasing the many critics of Contreras and the DINA at home and abroad and removing an important obstacle to the institutionalization of the regime.

While this is a powerful account, it provides at best a partial answer as to why the regime may have been interested in reorganizing coercion. It explains why the civilians who supported the regime wanted to do so (principally to avoid a personalization of power that would mortgage the kind of future regime they desired) and why their project found a ready audience inside sectors of the military seeking to avoid either a Pinochet power grab or a breakdown into internecine fighting within the armed forces. However, it does not provide a satisfactory answer to a crucial puzzle: why Pinochet would have supported institutionalizing the regime and why he would have agreed to reorganize coercion by breaking his connection with Contreras—an arrangement that had given him exclusive access to the most powerful and feared coercive institution in the country. Pinochet was the most powerful person in the country, and no reform of this magnitude could have taken place without his consent. Any explanation for the replacement of the DINA by the CNI must consider how the soft-liners managed to convince Pinochet to support the institutionalization of the regime and the reorganization of its repressive apparatus. As will be seen in the next chapter, Pinochet could have easily decided not to support these initiatives, thereby propelling the regime down a very different path than the one it actually took.

SEVEN

Options and Shifts

As shown in previous chapters, the regime created the DINA to resolve specific organizational problems, but the DINA did not completely take over and redirect coercion, and conflicts remained between the DINA and other coercive agencies (in particular the air force's intelligence agency [SIFA] and the Comando Conjunto), which undermined regime cohesion. Moreover, as the DINA ran increasingly amok, unconstrained by any other power inside the regime, it failed to deliver on the promise of plausible deniability. Risky and high-profile acts of international terrorism such as the Letelier assassination provoked U.S. retaliation over and above the growing international pressures caused by the human rights violations. Further, the DINA's excesses helped galvanize support both inside Chile and abroad for watchdog groups such as the Vicaría (see Appendix C), which increased external monitoring of the regime. Most seriously, the DINA and the reformist sectors inside the regime clashed repeatedly over all aspects of the DINA's operations. The DINA mistrusted the civilians and spied on them, and the civilians for their part understood that projecting the regime into the future required bringing the DINA under control (or taming the "bucking horse," in Guzmán's words). Put differently, the DINA did not deliver substantially higher levels of internal monitoring and failed as well to curb an increase in external monitoring of its activities. Instead of well-coordinated and highly secretive actions against the regime's enemies, the DINA's operations were often heavy-handed, clumsy, and visible.

In this context, what options were available to deal with the problems posed by the DINA? The regime's options essentially boiled down to either maintaining or altering the levels of internal and external monitoring.

With respect to internal monitoring, the options available to the junta principals were to decrease it, keep it the same, or increase it. One way to decrease internal monitoring would have been to get rid of the DINA altogether and to return the regime to the type of coercion employed during the first several months after the coup. The other branches of the armed forces and the Carabineros could have taken on a more active independent role, reporting to each of their superiors but not to the junta or Pinochet in a comprehensive way. Another option could have been to weaken the DINA substantially, abridging its information-gathering and reporting abilities. While in theory it would have been possible to adopt either course of action, in practice neither was likely. Both options would have returned the regime to a kind of organizational pattern similar to what existed during the first several months after the coup, with the attendant similar problems of coordination and control that prompted all the complaints against the regime discussed in chapter 3. Moreover, instead of providing the reformers with the necessary control they sought over the coercive forces, these options would have afforded them far less.

Keeping internal monitoring the same could likewise have been accomplished with or without the DINA and Contreras. The regime could have chosen to keep the DINA under Contreras, notwithstanding pressure against it from international sources and from critics inside the military and among civilian supporters. This alternative would no doubt have been attractive to many hard-line sectors within the regime. Pinochet himself may also have had an interest in keeping Contreras, given his direct and close relationship with the DINA's director. However, while in theory it would have been possible to do this, this option would not have resolved the problems of the DINA's tensions with the other branches, and it would not have given the reformers any greater leverage over coercion. Under these circumstances, the pressure to get rid of the DINA and Contreras increased the costs of this option.

Keeping the same level of internal monitoring as before but without the DINA could have been accomplished by having the agents in the different branches of the armed forces monitor each other and report to the top. Or Pinochet could have replaced the DINA and Contreras with another institution and leader that reported directly and exclusively to him;

this would likely have eased some of the domestic and international pressures against the regime for the DINA's excesses. But while many would have been happy to be rid of a source of internal conflict and international trouble, this option would not have appeased reformers who understood that they needed to play a greater role in controlling coercion in order to succeed at institutionalization. Indeed, neither decreasing internal monitoring nor keeping it the same would have addressed the DINA's problems, and at least one course of action risked a return to the previous state of affairs, the problems of which the DINA itself was designed in part to resolve.

The third broad alternative was to increase internal monitoring. Again, there are various ways the regime might have achieved this. One would simply have been for Pinochet and Contreras to stage what in essence would have been an internal coup, purging rival intelligence and coercive institutions. Doing this would have resolved one of the problems that the DINA had failed to address. The DINA was meant to take over the organization of coercion, but it did not achieve this goal. Getting rid of rivals like the Comando Conjunto and gaining complete control over coercion inside the different branches of the armed forces could have finally resolved this problem. As discussed in chapter 4, the level of internal monitoring inside the DINA (with Contreras as the principal) was relatively high. By getting rid of rival organizations over which it had little control, the DINA could simply have extended its operations to include the entire state coercive apparatus.

One important effect of such a coup would have been to allow Pinochet to consolidate his position as the unquestioned strongman in Chilean politics, with an iron grip over all major military and political institutions. By getting rid of rival coercive institutions, Pinochet and Contreras would have built a formidable power base. As we have seen, there is a great deal of evidence that Pinochet wanted to centralize power in this way, and, as indicated above, many observers refer to the 1978 shift in particular as an important step in the consolidation of Pinochet's personal power.

However, there is no doubt that such a purge would have been a costly option. The army was the dominant branch of the armed forces, but it did not completely overwhelm the navy, the air force, and the

Carabineros. This option would have required the army to risk a potentially serious armed conflict with the other branches. While Pinochet never openly discussed this possibility (according to public documents), it is important to keep in mind that such a move could have tilted the balance of power in a different direction.

Assuming for a moment that a Pinochet-Contreras coup would have been possible (and that there would have been little resistance from the other branches of the military), this option would still have left one major problem unresolved: it would have significantly increased Pinochet's dependence on Contreras and hence his own vulnerability. Pinochet therefore had to weigh carefully the benefits of relying on the DINA to consolidate power against the considerable costs this would have imposed on him.

One way to increase internal monitoring without incurring the costs of vulnerability would have been for Pinochet to place the DINA itself under stricter internal oversight. As it stood, while the DINA monitored operations in the rest of the state, Pinochet relied strictly on Contreras to monitor the DINA's operations. Changing this state of affairs could have been accomplished by placing the DINA under ministerial control, just as the CNI was placed, or by creating another regulatory or monitoring agency to oversee the actions of the DINA. This option was attractive to the junta and especially to the civilian reformers discussed above, for whom control over coercion was a necessary condition for institutionalization.

Even though Pinochet and Contreras enjoyed a close strategic alliance up to this point, events such as the revelations and political fallout of the Letelier case were a signal that the DINA was out of control, and they could have prompted Pinochet to place it under stricter oversight. However, this option would have had costs of its own. The most obvious of these would have been the deep resistance offered from within the DINA itself. Contreras no doubt would have strongly opposed and attempted to undermine any plans to place the DINA under any sort of oversight. This would have led to bitter divisions within the junta, creating serious problems of internal governability for Pinochet.

Indeed, there are strong reasons to believe that a higher level of internal monitoring was generally desirable and understood as such by the major players. This was part of what the DINA was intended to achieve but failed to do. However, different actors had very different trade-offs at stake in supporting each of the ways devised to increase internal monitoring. The starkest contrast was between Pinochet and the civilian reformers. Until this time Pinochet had relied heavily on Contreras to consolidate power, both by conducting the counterinsurgency campaign and by coercing the rest of the regime into line. On the face of it there was no obvious reason why this nexus should have been broken. Given the resistance to Pinochet's effort to consolidate personal power inside the junta, he might have calculated that the costs of relying too much on Contreras would have been a price worth paying for absolute control over the regime—provided, of course, that Contreras could deliver this extent of control. By contrast, the civilians were in a different position. They understood that controlling coercion was necessary for institutionalizing the regime. Some ways of implementing higher internal monitoring—such as terminating the DINA and replacing it with a new institution more accountable to civilian sectors—would have allowed them greater control. Other options, such as strengthening the Pinochet-Contreras nexus, would have achieved precisely the opposite effect.

Before analyzing the organizational reforms that actually took place in light of these alternatives, a second broad organizational dimension—external monitoring—must be considered. As we know, external monitoring involves many kinds of information gathering from many different sources (e.g., from the courts, the press, and/or other independent observers). The three broad alternatives related to this were straightforward: to do nothing, to decrease external monitoring, or to increase it.

Doing nothing meant simply continuing the situation where the courts had very weak oversight over coercion, the opposition press was driven underground, and a few human rights groups operated under the constant threat of government repression. This option would not have required any major institutional innovation, and it would have been unlikely to cause deep divisions inside the government beyond those that already existed. All things being equal, there is no reason why the regime could not have simply continued this strategy.

A different option would have been to impose, or revert to, far lower levels of external monitoring. Although external monitoring was already quite low, it was not completely nonexistent, and it would have been possible to go lower still. For example, the regime could have shut down the Vicaría (as it had previously shut down its predecessor, the Committee for Peace in Chile, or COPACHI) and prevented another similar organization from taking its place. This would have removed a troublesome critic that was an essential source of information for opposition campaigns, especially at the international level. However, the regime would have paid a huge political price at home and abroad for turning against an organization that formally belonged to and enjoyed the protection of the Catholic Church.[1]

Another related problem for the regime was that criticism of its coercive actions did not derive only from the opposition press. Increasingly, as mentioned earlier, such critiques also came from supportive magazines and newspapers, including *Qué Pasa* and *El Mercurio*. Despite—or perhaps because of—these sources' support for the regime, their critiques stung. Were the regime to have chosen to decrease external monitoring to silence its critics, it would likely have faced a daunting decision about what to do with critiques originating from within the ranks of its supporters. Censoring publications like *El Mercurio,* for example, would have seriously threatened the regime's crucial base of support among the country's elite.

The final option was to increase external monitoring. There were various alternatives, from allowing greater press freedoms, to lifting the restrictions on associations, to establishing clear Supreme Court oversight over the military courts.[2] These measures would have had the effect of increasing the pool of available information gatherers (and hence information) on the operations of the coercive institutions. The DINA (or any other coercive agency that took its place) would no doubt have strongly resisted any such efforts. In addition, while reformers within the regime might not necessarily have opposed this, there is little evidence that they favored an increase in external monitoring purely as a way to check the power of the coercive institutions. As suggested above, they would have resisted attempts to restrict *their* civil freedoms (for instance, by restrictions on such publications as *El Mercurio*). However, this did not necessarily extend to a defense for the protection of civil freedoms in general, for *all* groups and views. On the contrary, one of the reformers' basic goals was to permanently exclude left-wing groups and views from the Chilean political system.

The regime, of course, did not have complete control over external monitoring. Doing nothing would have meant that an organization like the Vicaría would continue to accumulate information, present it to the courts, and serve as the basis for critiques against the regime. These critiques, once in the public sphere, were available not only to the regime's enemies. As the examples of *El Mercurio* and *Qué Pasa* illustrate, they were also available to its supporters and could thus have an impact on the regime's image in such circles.

The regime was also worried about its image abroad and sent special envoys to the United Nations and to other countries to lobby on its behalf. However, there was no immediate or obvious reason to increase external monitoring to appease the regime's critics at home and abroad. There was also no pressure to increase it simply as a mechanism to allow greater information on coercion, nor is there evidence that the regime considered doing so. The path of least resistance for the regime concerning external monitoring would likely have been to do nothing.

In conclusion, the pressures on the regime were to leave external monitoring levels unchanged and to increase internal monitoring somewhat, with the attendant problem of choosing precisely which internal monitoring scheme best suited the situation.

Coercion after 1978

A comparison between two pairs of tables in the appendices, tables B.1 and B.2 and tables C.1 and C.2, shows an increase in both internal and external monitoring after 1978. We can infer that one important change was an increase in internal monitoring: in the information available to the principals on the CNI's own operations, and those of other organizations, from internal channels. For the moment, without complete access to the entire collection of the regime's archives, we cannot be completely certain about the extent of information availability. Nevertheless, it is possible to infer an increase on internal monitoring on the basis of several pieces of evidence. For instance, given that the CNI was more constrained than the DINA with regard to domestic operations, it is reasonable to infer that information on its operations was more readily available through established formal and informal military channels.[3] Moreover, the DINA relied more than the CNI on right-wing civilians and paramilitary groups.[4] These included many Cóndor operatives, such as local right-wing groups in Argentina, the United States, and Italy.[5] The CNI relied almost exclusively on its own personnel, recruited mainly from the different branches of the armed forces (especially the army). It was easier for principals to obtain information on the operations of an organization whose agents belonged to a known entity and to well-established structures under their own control than to organizations outside their direct control.[6] Consequently, we can surmise that the principals (not only Pinochet but also the cabinet and other members of the junta) received better internal information on agents' activities.

Internal monitoring also increased according to another criterion. Whereas Contreras had reported only to Pinochet, the head of the CNI reported to the president through his cabinet. Unlike the DINA, which was an independent institution, separate from the rest of the armed forces, the regime placed the CNI under the Ministry of Defense. This gave the CNI a status similar to that of the Carabineros. While not technically branches of the armed forces (which included the army, navy, and air force), both the CNI and the Carabineros were military institutions and were given status as such under the Ministry of Defense. (This status governed, for example, the jurisdiction of military courts over their actions, as well as their officer structure and career paths.) For day-to-day operational purposes, however, the Ministry of the Interior directed both. In other words, this change in status introduced at least two new internal oversight mechanisms over the CNI. This was a significant shift. It essentially meant that Pinochet gave up the monopoly control over coercion that he had enjoyed under the DINA.

With respect to the level of principals' trust in their agents, on the face of it there is no reason to assume that Pinochet (or the junta) fundamentally mistrusted the CNI, its leadership, or the other coercive agencies. However, at least two cases suggest otherwise. The first was the replacement of the CNI's first director, General Odlanier Mena, by hard-liner General Humberto Gordon. Pinochet removed Mena shortly after the guerrilla group MIR assassinated the director of the army's Intelligence School, Colonel Roger Vergara, on July 15, 1980.[7] The case sent shockwaves throughout the regime, and former DINA personnel (including Contreras) seriously criticized the CNI and Mena in particular for incompetence (Frühling 2000; Cavallo Castro, Salazar Salvo, and Sepúlveda Pacheco 1989, 303–8).

The second case was a serious dispute between the CNI and the Carabineros in 1985. The dispute followed the murder of three human rights workers who belonged to the Communist Party by Carabineros agents; because of the manner of their death, it has since become known as the "Degollados" ("Slit-Throat") case. The agents in question belonged to the Dirección de Comunicaciones de Carabineros (DICOMCAR), created in 1983 as that institution's intelligence and counterinsurgency agency in the aftermath of a wave of protests against the regime (Caucoto Pereira and Salazar Ardiles 1994). The DICOMCAR and the CNI cooperated on many cases, but the boundary between their spheres of jurisdiction was often unclear, and relations between them were tense (Maldonado 1990; Comisión Nacional de Verdad y Reconciliación 1991). After the murders, the CNI issued a report on the case and cooperated with the courts and even with human rights groups to bring the responsible officers to trial (see below). The result was a massive shakedown in the Carabineros, leading to the resignation of the top command, including its director, junta member General César Mendoza, along with four of his most senior officers. Apart from the case's deep political impact, the CNI's punishment of the Carabineros signaled deep mistrust between the two most important coercive institutions in the country. Consequently, there was probably little change in the regime's overall level of trust in the CNI as compared to the DINA.

Regarding inter- and intrabranch coordination, it is not entirely clear whether the CNI was more effective than the DINA. Under the DINA, tensions with agencies such as the air force and the Comando Conjunto lingered during a period of institutional confusion. The division of powers between Pinochet and the rest of the junta members (i.e., between the executive and the legislative powers) remained unresolved.

Compared to the DINA, the CNI operated in a period of far greater institutional clarity. The key struggles for power at the top (e.g., between Pinochet and Leigh) had been resolved, and the 1980 Constitution set the boundaries for politics for the duration of the regime. Yet lingering tensions persisted between the CNI and the Carabineros and increased especially after the 1983 wave of protests against the regime (resulting in the 1985 crisis mentioned above). In short, while overall the CNI performed better than the DINA with respect to coordination, given the generally stable institutional context it might have done better.

Last, regarding corruption, it is also not clear how much of an improvement the CNI was over the DINA, especially after 1980. Although apparently isolated, there were incidents of CNI agents engaged in bank robberies and other acts of personal corruption.[8]

In short, there was a moderate increase in internal monitoring with the shift from the DINA to the CNI.[9] With respect to external monitoring, however, some indicators remained more or less the same. Outsiders still had limited, if any, access to prisoners, and there was still no independent legislative oversight over the executive's coercive agencies. Nevertheless, with respect to other measures, we can observe an increase, and in some cases this increase was significant.

For example, the CNI leadership assumed a much more open public presence than Contreras had ever permitted. There had been virtually no public images of Contreras and no interviews or photographs of him in the newspapers. His identity was known, but little else was made public. In a sharp break from this practice, Mena called a meeting with church authorities to "present himself" soon after taking office.[10] Although the results of the meeting were less than fruitful, perhaps not surprisingly given the context, this type of public presence signaled a shift in the regime.[11] This initial meeting was the first of a series of contacts between the CNI and civil society groups.

Indeed, beginning in 1977, a series of new human rights groups began to appear, signaling an easing of the restrictions on associations that had been in place since 1973. One of these was the Servicio Paz y Justicia (SERPAJ), created at the end of 1977 to promote the defense of human rights in areas not covered by the Vicaría, such as education (Orellana and Hutchison 1991, 104). The largest and most important of the new organizations was the Chilean Human Rights Commission (Comisión Chilena de Derechos Humanos, or CChDH), created in 1978. The CChDH complemented the work of the Vicaría. It adopted a broader definition of human rights to include not only the rights to life and physical integrity but also the full range of civil, political, economic, and even cultural rights. The CChDH was led by high-profile political leaders and received support from various international organizations. A series of other groups would continue to appear throughout the 1980s (Frühling 1984, 1986; Orellana and Hutchison 1991). Although these groups operated under sometimes severe restrictions, their existence marked a major contrast to the early years of the dictatorship, when civil society was virtually shut down.

During the Degollados case, the head of the CChDH, Jaime Castillo, and General Humberto Gordon, Mena's successor, established regular and ongoing informal contact to share information and coordinate activities. The CChDH wrote a report implicating the Carabineros in the case and made it directly available to the CNI, which had arrived at a similar conclusion through its own investigations.[12] Most surprising, however, was a "hot line" established between the CNI and the CChDH— essentially between Castillo and Gordon—in the aftermath of the case. Both organizations maintained this link until 1989, when the CNI was finally disbanded.[13] The CChDH did not, of course, establish this link to furtively leak information to the CNI. Castillo stated simply, "We had to speak with those in charge. I am free and I have a right to be heard. We practiced democracy within the dictatorship."[14] Besides being another signal of the emergence of an interlocutor between the coercive agencies and outsiders, this sort of contact signals an increased trust in outsiders' information. It is unlikely that this sort of contact was a secret to the military leadership, or to Pinochet. It signals that the principals had enough trust in the reliability and validity of the information published by the CChDH to establish and maintain direct contact, a link that would have been unthinkable during the time of the DINA.[15]

The final notable change with respect to external monitoring was the behavior of some members of the courts. In April 1978, the government decreed an amnesty for all those charged by the military courts from the time of the coup until March 10, 1978.[16] Although some political prisoners were released under the law's benefits, the overwhelming majority of those who benefited from the decree were state agents.[17] Observers at the time rightly dismissed this law as an illegitimate blanket self-amnesty to nullify the regime's own crimes. In addition, in the overwhelming majority of cases that fell within this period (as most of the cases of the disappeared did), the attending civilian judge declared himself to lack jurisdiction *(incompetente)* and passed the case on to the military court. Given that the regime increased the jurisdiction of the military courts, this was the fate of the overwhelming majority of cases.

Notwithstanding all these obstacles, there were important and noteworthy exceptions. For example, in late 1978, fifteen bodies were discovered in an abandoned mine tract in the town of Lonquén, just south of Santiago (Pacheco 1979; Chilean National Commission on Truth and Reconciliation 1993, 238–40). The Supreme Court appointed a special judge for the case, whose investigation concluded that Carabineros agents had murdered the victims in October 1973. Because military personnel were involved, the judge passed the case on to the military courts, which invoked the amnesty decree and closed it.[18] Nevertheless, the case marked an important turning point. It showed for the first time that "horrific crimes had been committed by military personnel and then covered up by the government, and, moreover, that with a decided effort, the truth about such crimes could be discovered" (Hilbink 1999, 272).[19]

During the 1980s, other judges defied the injunctions of the Supreme Court and the regime and pursued cases of torture and abuse. For example, in October 1984, Judge José Benquis responded to a writ of habeas corpus *(recurso de amparo)* on behalf of Francisco Jara and Teresa Rosas, a married couple who were detained in their own home along with their maid, María Vásquez, by CNI agents. In an unprecedented move, Benquis went to the couple's home and demanded entry. After being refused by the CNI agents, he went to their superiors and eventually managed to free the detainees. The CNI agents, who had come in the night before, had also detained Vásquez's husband and had taken him away in custody. In one of the few cases of its successful use during the regime, Benquis presented a writ of habeas corpus and obtained the prisoner's release. The Supreme Court, moreover, issued a complaint to

Pinochet, who responded that no such further abuses would take place (Matus 1999, 149–51). The case is not significant because the promise was kept. It was not. It simply illustrates the kinds of actions that some judges took in exercising their powers, however limited, to oversee, and perhaps oppose, state coercion.

Judge René García Villegas, whose jurisdiction in Santiago in the 1980s covered the area where an important CNI detention center was located (in Borgoño Street), pursued the many accusations of torture and assassination that victims and their relatives issued.[20] Inevitably, the cases would end up in the military courts, where they would be closed. But Villegas persisted, taking on more cases and carrying out further investigations. The Supreme Court reprimanded García Villegas and eventually disbarred him, signaling the kind of pressures the institution brought to bear on dissident judges.[21]

In this sense, the amnesty decree was a double-edged sword. On the one hand, it forced the courts to close cases that fell between 1973 and 1978. On the other hand, it forced the regime to develop strategies to avoid legal prosecution after that time, given the absence of amnesty protection. These strategies included expanding jurisdiction of the military courts, as well as granting the executive new powers of detention during different states of emergency (Comisión Nacional de Verdad y Reconciliación 1991; Huneeus 2000a). In what was essentially a new political and legal space, some judges defied the strictures imposed by the court and the regime and went ahead with the prosecution of cases of human rights abuse that took place after 1978.

So began an increase in internal monitoring and a more substantial increase in external monitoring, as the comparison of tables B.1 and B.2 with tables C.1 and C.2 shows. The next section considers these results to suggest an explanation for the replacement of the DINA by the CNI.

Toward an Explanation

First, while the principal actors generally had an interest in increasing internal monitoring, each had substantially different trade-offs at stake in the different mechanisms to accomplish this increase. For example, it would have been possible to increase internal monitoring by making the DINA *more* powerful, but doing so would have gone against the interests of the civilian reformers. Alternatively, replacing the DINA with a new institution over which they could have greater supervision would have been in the interest of the reformers but not the hard-liners. The central figure in deciding which route was to be taken was Pinochet.

For all the criticisms leveled against Contreras, he and the DINA had been instrumental in helping Pinochet consolidate power, and the bond between the two men was strong. While Pinochet had to pay a price for keeping this relationship, he also accrued significant benefits by monopolizing control over the central coercive agency. Moreover, he paid a penalty for his ultimate decision to break his alliance with Contreras, particularly during a time of institutional uncertainty and lingering tensions with the rest of the junta members. Given these trade-offs, it is important to examine the replacement of the DINA by the CNI from the perspective of Pinochet and to ask why he allowed Contreras and the DINA to fall. How, in other words, did the reformers convince Pinochet to abdicate his monopoly control over coercion and to allow higher internal monitoring through greater overall (including civilian) supervision?

Guzmán and the other civilians advocating the institutionalization of the regime understood that controlling coercion was a necessary condition for their plans. However, the problem for the soft-liners was that the DINA, despite its blunders, remained powerful, particularly so long as Pinochet continued to see it as a central instrument for his rule and exercise of power. It is here that the international pressures, particularly over the Letelier case, presented an opportunity. Pressures on the regime accelerated the internal critiques against the DINA. The DINA's critics gained legitimacy and a political opening as previously silent observers now spoke up for the first time. Even *El Mercurio*, the country's leading newspaper and a staunch defender of the military regime, joined the fray to criticize the DINA and Contreras.

No single factor alone but rather a combination of factors explains the choice of higher internal monitoring through the CNI and greater civilian control. The reformers' institutionalization program explains why civilians sought to restrain and control coercion. International pressures explain some of the timing of the reforms, and probably encouraged the reformers who pressed to get rid of the DINA. The internal divisions among the military branches explain the overlapping interests between military insiders and civilians in institutionalizing the regime.

Yet important though these combined factors are, they miss the precise nature of the DINA's striking failures. The DINA was not created only to mount a counterinsurgency campaign and to centralize coercion. Even if the principals at the time did not say so, it was created to increase internal monitoring—to coordinate coercion efficiently and to prevent divisive internal disputes. But notwithstanding its power, the DINA failed to achieve substantially higher levels of internal monitoring. Although the DINA was powerful, it was ineffective. It did not accomplish what it was supposed to, and this must surely have weighed heavily on Pinochet's mind as he considered various parties' proposals over whether and how to reorganize coercion.

We know that Pinochet changed course. Although any explanation as to why must for the moment remain speculative without full access to all of the regime's archives, we can make better theoretically reasoned inferences using the available data. It is likely that Pinochet calculated that using Contreras to stage an internal coup in the face of the increasing critiques (inside the military and among civilians) would come at too high a cost. The risk of internecine fights was higher than the likelihood of achieving total power, but the central counterfactual that must be considered is this: had the DINA been even moderately more effective as an organization, it would undoubtedly have altered this balance. It would have provided Pinochet with significantly more benefits, which might have made its costs (such as the vulnerability of tying his fortunes so closely to those of the DINA) worth paying. The power balance was not so overwhelmingly tilted in one direction, or in favor of any single player, that there was no room for alternative paths. By convincing Pinochet to support their institutionalization project, the soft-liners effectively forced Pinochet to close off both the option of divisive internal disputes and that of his own permanent personal dictatorship. A more effective DINA would have been harder for Pinochet to break with and would have undermined the soft-liners' efforts.

In return for giving up permanent personal rule, Pinochet obtained a more secure position within a more clearly articulated institutional framework. The 1980 Constitution enshrined the division of powers between the executive and the legislative, with Pinochet occupying the former and the junta members (now with a separate army appointee to fill Pinochet's slot) the latter. While it forced Pinochet to accept a framework that limited his rule, it also put an end to the divisive squabbles that might have threatened the viability of the regime itself. Furthermore, Pinochet achieved the removal of his principal rival inside the junta—Gustavo Leigh, commander of the air force. It is plausible that Leigh's removal was a condition for Pinochet to support the "constitution project."[22]

Increasing external monitoring—or more accurately, easing the restrictions on the activities of external monitors—was part of the package of reforms that accompanied the shift from the DINA to the CNI. By loosening the reins on civil society, even slightly, the regime obtained a measure of reprieve from some of its critics. But as the surprising links between the CNI and the CChDH suggest, there was more to external monitoring than this. In limited but significant ways, at least some members of the regime understood that they could learn from external monitors such as the CChDH: for example, to obtain information about the operation of their own agents. The Degollados case illustrates the surprising new flows of information that emerged in the post-DINA period. These new relationships involved complex trade-offs for the regime. On the one hand, the authorities had more information available on their agents' behavior. On the other, independent institutions such as the Vicaría, SERPAJ, and the CChDH often strongly criticized the regime for its repressive activities. Indeed, such criticism was at the core of their purpose. The regime routinely harassed these organizations, sometimes with deadly force, and those who worked in them engaged in often heroic resistance against the regime in their determination to stay alive and continue their work. Yet it is also worth noting that shutting these organizations down altogether—besides provoking national and international outrage—would have forced the regime to rely once again on a narrower range of information sources, with all the expenses that this had involved under the DINA. In this sense, Castillo's claim to have "practiced democracy under the dictatorship" cuts both ways: while the dictatorship was far from democratic, after removing the DINA it was somewhat less authoritarian than before.

The analysis of how the DINA and the CNI were organized suggests costs and benefits to different patterns of organizing coercive force. The DINA was a powerful organization, but in many ways it was ineffective. It failed to substantially increase internal monitoring, and in significant ways it ran amok, defeating some of its own purposes. This pattern of operations suggests the constraints and opportunities available to Pinochet and others who had to decide what to do with the DINA. Instead of assuming that the DINA simply needed to be replaced (or ignoring the question of how or why it was replaced), asking why and how it was replaced sheds light on a critical turning point in the Chilean dictatorship. As we have seen, Pinochet decided to let Contreras and the DINA fall. While we may never know exactly what went through Pinochet's mind when he decided to replace the DINA, by reconstructing the constraints and opportunities available to him we can infer plausible reasons. Although the participants at the time did not refer to the DINA's manifest ineffectiveness in terms of internal and external monitoring, they understood all too well the consequences of its actions—and its failures.

Even these tentative conclusions are an antidote to accounts of this period that place too much emphasis on Pinochet's personal power, the inevitability of the reformers' project, or the power of international watchdogs. The power balance was not so tilted in one direction or another as to strongly determine outcomes. A small change in the DINA's operational structure might have propelled Pinochet, and the regime, down very different paths. Had the DINA been moderately more effective, it would have been easier for Pinochet to stick with it and risk taking absolute control. Had he succeeded, his regime might have ended only in December 2006, upon his death, as Franco's dictatorship in Spain terminated with the caudillo's death in 1975. On the other hand, had Pinochet tried but failed in his power grab, the dictatorship might have collapsed totally, much as the Argentine regime did in 1983, as a combined result of infighting and the defeat dealt against Argentine military might by Britain's forces in the Falkland Islands. Instead of celebrating the return of democracy in 1990, Chileans might have done so a decade earlier (Policzer 2007a, 2007b). In that scenario, they would have easily put Pinochet and the rest of the military leadership on trial for crimes against humanity, as their neighbors did in Argentina in 1983.

Ruling often brutally for seventeen years qualifies Pinochet as a "bad man," as at least one obituary noted (*Economist* 2006). Yet he might have been a worse dictator had he failed to restrain repression by replacing the DINA with the CNI or had he followed more closely in Franco's footsteps and stayed in power until his death.

PART III

EIGHT

The Politics of Organizing Coercion

A common justification for authoritarian rule is the promise to "get rid of politics" by replacing corrupt, ineffective, or quarrelsome politicians with a more disciplined military, party, or bureaucratic cadre. This book throws such a notion into doubt by showing that even in authoritarian regimes, organizing coercion is a distinctly and unavoidably political problem of governance. Rulers have to build coercive institutions by selecting from among a discrete set of organizational alternatives and by grappling with the different trade-offs they impose. Weber's fundamental insight about coercion in politics can thus be turned in on itself: not only is coercion at the center of politics, but the choices and conflicts involved in organizing coercion show that politics is also at the center of coercion. Rather than getting rid of politics, authoritarian rulers simply exchange one set of political choices and conflicts for another.

The typology in this book maps a heretofore understudied political and policy space and provides a new language to analyze the conflicts that take place within it. In the case of Chile, this analysis sheds new light on the rise and fall of repression during the military regime, especially during the period of greatest institutional flux, between 1973 and 1978. While we still lack a complete picture of the events during this time, this book makes clear the need to move beyond the debate over whether this period signaled the triumph of the soft-liners or the consolidation of Pinochet's personal power. Each of these accounts contains elements of truth, but each also ignores fundamental aspects of the problems faced by decision makers at the time and fails to ask crucial questions.

In 1973–74, the two crucial questions were: Why would the junta agree to the creation of a repressive agency—the DINA—that would undermine its own power, and how did the DINA manage to convince the military leadership to allow it to take over the task of repression? Understanding the problems of near-blind coercion and the benefits of increasing internal monitoring is not a sufficient explanation for the creation of the DINA, but it is a necessary one. In much the same way, the crucial questions in 1977–78 were these: Why would Pinochet agree to dismantle the DINA, an agency that had allowed him to centralize power, and how did the soft-liners manage to convince him to drop his allegiance to it? The DINA's organizational fiascos (its failure to significantly increase internal monitoring and its resulting tendency to run amok, as well as its failure to decrease external monitoring and its resulting failure to deliver on the promise of plausible deniability) are also not a sufficient explanation for its fall, but it is necessary to consider them.

This analysis brings contingency into the history of this period, an element that receives insufficient attention in the standard accounts. It makes clear that neither the rise nor the fall of the DINA was preordained. In 1973–74 the regime could have continued to muddle through with near-blind coercion, or it could have chosen to increase internal monitoring by reorganizing each of the armed forces and improving interforce communication and coordination. Undoubtedly there would have been problems with each of these alternatives, but these would not have been significantly higher than the problems imposed on the regime by creating the DINA. And while reorganizing coercion to address the failures of the DINA was crucial to institutionalizing the regime, the regime would have taken a radically different path had Pinochet chosen to strengthen his bond with the hard-liners and Contreras instead of breaking it. The real costs for Pinochet of backing the soft-liners—such as his more narrowly circumscribed powers—were not overwhelmingly outweighed by the potential benefits of a more clearly institutionalized regime, such as putting an end to the intra-junta rivalries.

At the same time, the significance of the information on the regime's crimes compiled by human rights watchdogs is presented here in a new light. This information played a role in curbing the dictatorship's repression, but it did so in a more contingent manner—with more contradictory results—than is often assumed. As suggested above, replacing the

DINA with the CNI was not a foregone conclusion, and Pinochet might have decided to back Contreras instead of the reformers. Moreover, the information provided by external monitors demonstrating the DINA's many failures was one of the factors that led Pinochet to break his alliance with Contreras. In this sense, this information helped the regime restrain its coercive apparatus, but it also helped Pinochet and the rest of the regime increase their control over it. The CNI continued to commit human rights violations, but in a more restrained fashion than the DINA. This restraint was crucial to the reformers' project of institutionalizing the regime in order to project it into the future. In doing this, the regime avoided the path of a permanent personal dictatorship by Pinochet, as well as the path of internecine conflicts among the different branches of the armed forces and—very likely—the collapse of the regime. In one case, the dictatorship would have ended only upon Pinochet's death, in 2006. In the other case it would have very likely ended far earlier than it did.

Human rights organizations often operate as if there were a direct and linear relationship between the information they publicize to "name and shame" a particular government (or armed group) and any apparent drop in human rights violations. Curbing such violations is the purpose of publicizing them. Some governments may not pay attention to the information that watchdogs provide or may not care about their reputation. But others, like the Chilean dictatorship—even while denouncing the international community's human rights critiques against it—both paid attention to this information and cared enough about its international reputation to at least take some action about the abuses it was committing. Yet even here the information provided by external monitors did not affect the regime in a direct and linear way. It was refracted through the prism of the dictatorship's internal political dynamics, which might have led the regime down a different path than the one it actually took. Moreover, even though violence decreased in Chile, the dictatorship used the external monitors' information to correct its institutional mistakes and replace the DINA with the CNI. This may have decreased repression, but it also permitted the dictatorship to regroup and to strengthen its institutional basis. While this was not a direct consequence of the watchdogs' information, it is also important to understand the indirect ways in which external monitoring can affect a regime.

The Coercion Problem in Comparative Perspective

This book has focused on the case of Chile, but the typology it develops can be applied more generally. All authoritarian regimes face the coercion problem; they have to build coercive organizations by choosing from among a limited set of alternatives, each with its own set of trade-offs. In this section I show how three other authoritarian regimes—Argentina during the "Proceso de Reorganización Nacional" (1976–82), East Germany, and South Africa under apartheid—dealt with the coercion problem. The organizational problems in each case were different than in Chile, as were the directions each regime took, but in each case we can use the same framework to describe how coercion was organized, as well as the trade-offs that each type of organization imposed.

Argentina

The Argentine military came to power in a coup against the government of Isabel Perón on March 24, 1976. Perón had been in power since her husband—Juan Perón, the populist leader who returned from exile to power in 1973—had died in 1974. Juan Perón's return had come in the midst of a growing guerrilla insurgency from a series of groups, the most serious of which included the Ejército Revolucionario del Pueblo (or Montoneros), from the left wing of his own Partido Justicialista. The armed forces had previously held power from 1966–73, but they stepped aside and held elections (which the Peronistas were likely to win) in the hope that Perón in power would be better able to halt the growth of the guerrillas and the insurgencies. Instead, guerrilla activity grew under Perón. After Perón's death his wife countered the guerrillas through a series of secret and shady alliances with military and paramilitary groups such as the Alianza Argentina Anticomunista (Triple A).[1]

The military justified its takeover as a restoration of order in the face of a growing guerrilla threat and virtual civil war. The military claimed that it was fighting a "Dirty War" against a well-organized, secretive, and violent opponent. However, according to the best estimates, the guerrillas numbered some two thousand at the height of their power (Frontalini and Caiati 1984, 63; Brysk 1994, 197). The military's claims to have fought a "war" are thus largely self-serving and exculpatory. Andersen (1993) systematically rebuts the claim and shows that even at the peak of their power the guerrillas never posed a serious military threat to the armed forces, which were about a hundred times more numerous.[2] The evidence thus suggests that "the guerrilla threat . . . was not the only, nor even the most important, reason for the coup" (McSherry 1997, 78). Army commander-in-chief Jorge Videla had stated that the guerrillas had by and large been defeated by 1975 (Mignone 1991, 53, quoted in McSherry 1997, 78). Instead of relinquishing power at that point, however, the armed forces took power to implement a major reorganization of the country and to "change the mentality of Argentines" (McSherry 1997, 79).[3]

Coercion in Argentina during the Proceso was most similar to that in Chile before the DINA but was far closer to pure blind coercion. First, as Appendix D's table D.1 shows, external monitoring was lower then than at any period in Chile. For example, unlike in Chile, the Argentine military took over the judicial branch, the independent Argentine media were weaker than in Chile, and while there were human rights organizations, they were also weaker than their Chilean counterparts, especially because they lacked the protection of the church, which in Argentina sided with the military regime.

Internal monitoring levels were also very low. The Argentine dictatorship oversaw a hydra-headed repressive apparatus with shadowy connections to a highly decentralized network of different military and paramilitary organizations. The roots of this lie in the fact that there is no clearly dominant branch within the Argentine armed forces.[4] In Argentina, unlike countries such as Chile or Brazil, where the army has unquestioned predominance over the other branches, the navy is a serious rival for power against the army. As a result and probably to avoid a major power struggle among the different branches, when they took power the army, navy, and air force divided the country into geographically separate areas over which each branch enjoyed virtually complete control (Stepan 1988, 25).[5] Moreover, although the junta set the broad outlines of repression, in practice there was a great deal of autonomy within each branch concerning which enemies to target and in what ways. Brysk writes, "Each service, each military zone, each concentration camp, and even each task force had considerable latitude in deciding whom to detain, whether and how much to torture them, whether to officialize, release, or execute them, and how to dispose of their children and property. . . . As one who was a political prisoner at the time (and subsequently, a Peronist legislator) put it: 'In those days, the country was feudalized; there were guys decorated by the First Corps, kidnapped in the Second, killed by the Third, and vindicated by the Fifth'" (1994, 39).[6]

This kind of organizational decentralization was also believed to be a fundamental strategy of counterinsurgency: the fight against an enemy decentralized in clandestine cells was thought to require similar kinds of organization. The junta relied extensively on highly autonomous task forces (*grupos de tarea*) within the armed forces to carry out detentions, tortures, and assassinations. Paramilitary groups such as the Triple A had begun operations before the coup, but the military replaced the activities of the Triple A with its own task forces, often teams of five to fifteen members from the military, the police, and civilian groups that operated in secret (McSherry 1997, 93). Decentralized agents both within the military and among outside groups who collaborated with it had wide discretion, and coordination among different institutions and organizations was often poor. The absence of a central information clearinghouse in Argentina (e.g., of any organization equivalent to the DINA or CNI) and comparatively higher levels of corruption, among other indicators, also suggest low levels of internal monitoring.

This pattern of organizing coercion remained remarkably stable during the dictatorship. Increasing external monitoring is inherently problematic for authoritarian regimes. Accepting legitimate independent actors involves restrictions on the powers and scope of the government. It would take a severe crisis to force the government to consider trading off limitations on its power for increased accountability of its coercive institutions. In Argentina, the junta might have responded to rising popular discontent by increasing external monitoring but chose instead to attempt to divert attention away from these problems by stirring up nationalist sentiment through the invasion of the Malvinas/Falkland Islands. If the military regime had somehow managed to survive, it is likely that the staggering defeat that resulted would have prompted calls for political reform and opening—external monitoring by different names. Instead, external monitoring was imposed only with the collapse of the military regime and the transition to a democracy with a separation of powers and respect for basic rights and liberties. Had the war been fought (and lost) earlier, the shift might also have happened earlier.

Somewhat more puzzling is why the Argentine generals did not increase internal monitoring. The explanation is most likely rooted in the decision at the time of the coup to radically divide power among the three branches of the armed forces. This initial division, which was far more extreme than anything attempted in Chile, made it very difficult to later create a single all-powerful coordinating or overseeing institution. Any such attempts would have faced the hurdle of interservice competition for control of a new agency of obvious political importance (Stepan 1988, 24–25).

East Germany

The new East German state was formally declared in November 1949, and the Socialist Unity Party of Germany (SED, or Sozialistische Einheistpartei auf Deutschland) imposed a strictly Stalinist model of social and political control that had emerged in the postwar years. East Germany was a case of almost pure bureaucratic coercion. There was no external monitoring to speak of. A Politbüro and a Zentralkomitee (ZK) were established by the cadre of party executives to ensure political control and to allow Moscow supervision of its new satellite. A new Ministry of Security (MfS) was created in February 1950. This State Security

Service (Staatssicherheit or Stasi) aimed to centralize control over coercion and intelligence throughout the country. The coercive apparatus was crucial to the party's control.

The failure of the Stasi to predict a serious uprising in 1953 led to the fall of its head, Ernst Wollweber, who had neither Moscow's nor the SED's confidence (Fulbrook 1995, 33–34; Childs and Popplewell 1996, 54–65).[7] Wollweber was replaced by Erich Mielke, a Moscow-educated admirer of Felix Dzerzhinskii (the founder of the Soviet Union's Cheka).[8] Mielke remained in charge of the Stasi until the breakup of the GDR[9] and imposed a hierarchical "Chekist" structure on the agency (Childs and Popplewell 1996, 81). Under his command, especially given his deep Soviet ties, the Stasi established extremely close relationships with the KGB in the Soviet Union.

Mielke also used his position to turn the Stasi into the leading coercive institution, especially after the 1960s. It became more powerful than any other coercive force, reporting on all agents and operations. Also, the functions of domestic and foreign intelligence were carried out not by separate and independent agencies (as for, instance, in the United States or the United Kingdom) but by different branches of the Stasi. And, particularly through a rapidly growing and massive file system on the GDR's citizens, the Stasi acted as the crucial vetting mechanism for career advancement and for keeping social control (Rosenzweig and Le Forestier 1992). The Stasi also employed a massive number of agents, either officially or as informers, and served as the crucial link through which Moscow exercised control over the GDR. As explained in Appendix D, East Germany achieved high levels of internal monitoring. As in Argentina, there was very little variation in this pattern of organizing coercion after the Stasi under Mielke established its predominance in the 1960s. Fundamental change came only after 1989, when the collapse of the Berlin Wall led to the end of the GDR altogether.

South Africa

Apartheid in South Africa was a repressive authoritarian regime that denied suffrage to blacks,[10] the bulk of the population, while a white minority retained complete political and economic control and enjoyed the protection of their basic civil and political liberties.[11] In South Africa under apartheid, unlike Argentina or East Germany, the organization of coercion underwent several shifts and maintained far higher levels of external monitoring. In this way, South Africa resembled Chile. All the various shifts in levels and techniques of coercion will not be described here; rather, the focus will be on coercion especially after the Soweto uprisings of 1975.

The apartheid regime exhibited low to moderate levels of external monitoring. Given the fusion of powers in a parliamentary system, the ruling Afrikaner-led National Party (NP), which put apartheid into practice during its forty-six years in power (1948–94), retained an iron grip on both the executive and the legislative branches during its reign. Consequently, there was no equivalent to effective legislative oversight over coercion. There remained a vibrant civil society, however. As noted above, whites enjoyed full civil rights, and white opposition movements challenged the government. While many black organizations (such as the African National Congress [ANC]) were driven underground, they remained active and continuously challenged the regime's coercive practices. While the judiciary remained independent, it tended to favor the executive (until the 1980s, when there were some rulings against it, in reaction to the regime's increasing recourse to extralegal means to uphold apartheid).

Far more problematic for the regime was the independence of the media. The National Party tried to control the press, something that according to Hachten, Giffard, and Hachten was "not easy to do because freedom of the press is a long-established value in South African society. Even right-wing Afrikaners give it lip service. . . . Further, the opposition English press, financed as it is by major financial and mining interests, represents significant economic power. And, finally, the Nationalists recognize that South Africa's claim to the 'freest press in Africa' is one of its few assets in world opinion" (1984, 76).

Censorship of various forms was an essential tool of governance for the NP, however.[12] Through the Publications Act of 1974 (and its predecessor the Publications and Entertainments Act of 1963), the government asserted control over all media. The act included extremely vague and broad grounds for banning and censoring material. "Anything that might cause 'ill-feeling' among the different races is reason for finding an utterance or object 'undesirable.' T-shirt slogans, key-ring emblems, films, audiotapes, videotapes, song lyrics, plays, cabaret skits, even government broadcast material, are all subject to banning, just as much as the obviously threatening political speeches, books, socially critical novels, and works of scholarship. There are stretches of blank pages in locally published encyclopedias" (Phelan 1987, 8).

Nevertheless, the NP faced continuous strong challenges to its coercive practices from the press. For example, the NP denied responsibility in the 1977 death of Black Consciousness leader Steve Biko, held under police custody. When Police Minister Kruger suggested that Biko had died as a result of a self-imposed "hunger strike," the English-language press responded with strong critiques (Woods 1991, 246–56). An inquest into the death ruled that Biko died of head injuries but found no evidence to attribute the death "to any act or omission amounting to a criminal offense on the part of any person" (396).

The relationship with the main black opposition shifted in the mid-1980s, however. At this time the NP began to hold secret talks with the ANC leadership, including Nelson Mandela, after it became clear that apartheid could be maintained only by increasing levels of repression, which the bulk of the white community was not prepared to accept. During this time such external monitoring mechanisms as the press, the courts, and outside (opposition) groups gained in power and made more of an impact inside the government.

Regarding internal monitoring, the apartheid regime responded to the Soweto uprisings in 1975 by centralizing its security forces and essentially imposing a higher level of internal monitoring. The police and security establishment was caught unprepared for the levels of violence marked by the Soweto uprising. A 1977 South African Defense Force (SADF) white paper called for a new "total national strategy" against the insurgency in what was described as a "state of war" against a guerrilla army (Stanbridge 1980, 93–94; Seegers 1996, 151–52; Truth and Reconciliation Commission 1999, 26–27). Defense Minister P. W. Botha argued that the shift to mass violence marked by Soweto also required a much more comprehensive response than the South African Police (SAP) alone were able to provide. "What [the SADF] had learnt in the preceeding *[sic]* years of coexistence with the SAP was that military decisions had to be linked with non-military ones. It enhanced efficiency, if only by reducing rivalries" (Seegers 1996, 161–62). A series of coordinating committees were created to oversee operations carried out jointly between the SADF and the SAP as well as the National Intelligence Service and the Department of Foreign Affairs. Seegers notes that this "was going beyond coordinating information; its interest was in coordinating the implementation of policy" (163).[13]

Such coordination suggests high levels of internal monitoring on several criteria. However, this was contradicted by other developments. For example, in the 1980s in particular the security establishment responded to increased opposition violence through a series of covert (Third Force) operations that relied on groups within the black communities to strike against the ANC and other opposition black groups. The South African Truth and Reconciliation Commission notes, furthermore, that during this time the SADF took on an increasingly predominant role as the leading coercive institution in the state and that "violence was met with greater violence and the security forces themselves became involved in extra-judicial killings, acts of arson and sabotage and other reprisals" (Truth and Reconciliation Commission 1999, 38).

In short, the Argentine example came closest to blind coercion, the GDR was closest to bureaucratic coercion, and South Africa (like Chile after 1978) occupied a position somewhere in the center of the matrix. These comparisons are summarized graphically (along with the organization of coercion in the different periods in Chile) in table 2.4 (in chapter 2).

Consequences

Chapter 2 discussed the different trade-offs in the ways of organizing coercion. All things being equal, lower levels of internal monitoring are likely to result in more intra- and interorganizational coordination problems and a higher likelihood that agents will deviate from their assigned task. Although rulers (principals) are less likely to have accurate information, and hence direct control, over agents' actions without high internal monitoring, there may be times when rulers want to simply let their agents loose to do as they will.[14] Higher levels of internal monitoring, by contrast, give the principal more precise information on his agents and hence more direct control. While this has obvious advantages, it means more work, such as hiring and training a staff and writing reports. It can also make the principal more accountable for his agents' actions or more dependent on (and hence vulnerable to) any specialized internal monitor.

Low levels of external monitoring are likely to give coercive institutions maximum freedom from independent outside observers, with the attendant benefits of high discretion. Principals and agents may find it desirable to operate with this freedom, but on the other hand, more actors providing oversight means more available information and hence more feedback channels.

We can use the Chilean case along with those of Argentina, East Germany, and South Africa, to compare the trade-offs and consequences of different organizational types. These comparisons are speculative. I have not controlled for important differences in the cases, such as ideology or the existence of an armed opposition. They are intended to show the kinds of hypotheses that a comparison of the organization of coercion could be used to test.

For example, the more discretion agents on the ground have to apply coercion, the more likely their actions are to deviate from their principal's policies or from the strictures of outside observers such as the courts or groups in society at large. The more discretion agents have, and the freer they are from outside oversight, the more differences there are likely to be among different agents' application of coercion, and hence the more broadly targeted it is likely to be.

Our cases support this prediction. Coercion was targeted very imprecisely (and hence broadly) in Chile in 1973, and targeting became more precise and narrower as both internal and external monitoring increased. In East Germany, coercion was targeted very precisely to specific individuals that the SED deemed enemies, though the Stasi's reach meant that virtually the entire population was subjected to its snooping. In South Africa, there were fluctuations in targeting. At some points there was massive application of force—for example, in response to protest. In other cases specialized forces were effective in pinpointing specific targets. This pattern is consistent with South Africa's position in the middle of the organizational matrix. With respect to Argentina, targeting was probably narrower than might be expected given quasi-blind coercion. Coercion was not applied to broad sectors of the population but targeted to specific sectors of the opposition. One explanation is that Argentina was not a pure case of blind coercion but rather had some degree of internal monitoring. Another may be a learning effect from neighboring countries such as Chile, which by the time the Argentine generals came to power had adopted a far more targeted (and secretive) modus operandi.

Another consequence of the organization of coercion is the sheer number of people killed. All things being equal, it follows that as agents have more discretion (less internal monitoring) and less oversight from outside sources (external monitoring) there are likely to be more victims. Again, our cases support this prediction. Argentina, the closest to pure blind coercion, had the highest number of victims, while East Germany, with the highest level of internal monitoring, had relatively few victims.[15] In Chile, the number of victims dropped as the levels of internal and external monitoring increased. And in South Africa, the number of people killed increased as the NP pursued its "total national strategy" (against what it perceived was a coordinated guerrilla onslaught). This effort increased internal monitoring in the SADF and SAP but reduced it elsewhere through reliance on independent coercive agents. It also reduced external monitoring—for example, through increased press restrictions. (As we saw above, the efforts to reduce external monitoring, in particular, met with resistance and raised the costs of repression.)

How coercion is organized and implemented is also likely to have an impact on regime stability and on the possibilities and types of regime transition. All four of our cases are authoritarian regimes that eventually underwent a transition to democracy. A brief comparison, however, reveals two broad modes of regime transition. The Argentine and East German dictatorships (for quite different reasons in each case) essentially collapsed and were replaced by new democratic regimes. In Chile and South Africa, by contrast, regime and opposition negotiated a transition to democracy. No doubt many political factors account for this difference, such as the kinds of policies pursued by the regime against the opposition, the decision whether to undertake broad political reform, the existence of a viable opposition, and its decision eventually to negotiate with the regime instead of fighting it. Nevertheless, it is striking that Argentina and East Germany shared similar low levels of external monitoring, while in Chile and South Africa external monitoring was higher. The analysis of the 1977–78 shift in Chile showed that not all of the external monitoring factors could be explained strictly as a function of the broader political developments, such as the reforms to institutionalize the regime.

Principals in authoritarian regimes have a great deal of control over many aspects of external monitoring. For example, they can decide how much freedom and discretion to provide independent bodies such as judiciaries and the media. But external monitoring is also carried out in various ways by a wide range of actors, many of them beyond the principal's or the regime's direct control. Organizations and individuals can dodge a regime's strictures and collect information on its operations. In this way external monitoring may be seen as a double-edged sword for authoritarian regimes. More actors and institutions providing oversight impose limitations on the principal's control over the organization of coercion. Yet these new actors also provide an opportunity to capitalize on new networks and contacts. The opening and closing of these spaces is not directly under the control of the principal, yet a savvy principal can learn to navigate these openings and capitalize on their opportunities.

This suggests the need to pay closer attention to the impact of the organization of coercion on liberalization in authoritarian regimes. The literature on regime transition focuses on the *last* stages of authoritarianism, immediately prior to the transition to democracy.[16] As we have seen, however, some authoritarian regimes restrain their repressive forces before the transition to democracy while others do not, and we have seen that the organization of coercion is not completely reducible to broader political trends and factors. Indeed, this observation turns many of the recent debates about "authoritarian enclaves" in newly democratic regimes on their head (Mainwaring, Valenzuela, and O'Donnell 1992; O'Donnell 1993; Mainwaring 1994). The politics of organizing coercion—especially external monitoring—may in some cases result in a "democratic enclave," however precarious or limited, within an authoritarian regime. The effect of different organizational options and strategies on regime liberalization is fertile ground for further research.

The last major consequence of the organization of coercion follows from targeting, number of victims, and regime stability. It is the likelihood that perpetrators of state crimes will eventually be brought to justice after the end of an authoritarian regime. Here again our cases offer fruitful comparisons. In the collapsed regimes (Argentina and East Germany), the incoming regime was essentially the winner in a winner-take-all game and hence was more likely to be able to impose its agenda after the transition. In 1990, the incoming democratic Chilean regime had the least capacity to bring the perpetrators of state crimes to justice. In South Africa, the government of national unity between the NP and the ANC worked out a formula to maximize the information about the human rights violations by encouraging perpetrators to testify in exchange for an amnesty. All of the factors discussed above that shaped the direction of the authoritarian regime, in other words, also affected the possibilities of justice after the end of the regime.

Internal and external monitoring are also likely to have a more direct and independent impact on the possibilities of justice, notwithstanding broader political factors such as regime stability and type of transition. Accountability is premised on information. Hence, higher levels of monitoring—either internal or external—are a necessary factor to bring perpetrators of crimes to justice. In South Africa, for example, most of the agents who availed themselves of the amnesty provision were those for whom there would otherwise have been enough information to prosecute. The agents were given a clear choice: to confess and receive amnesty or to face the full force of the law. By definition, this means that agents on whom there was little information—such as those who acted outside the direct control of the SADF and the SAP—did not have the same incentives to confess or the same reasons to worry about being put on trial.

Moreover, even though there were no trials in Chile immediately after the end of the military regime, external monitoring by human rights groups eventually made it possible to bring some perpetrators to trial. Pinochet's London arrest in October of 1998, as well as his subsequent prosecution in both England and in Chile, was made possible thanks to the wealth of information on state crimes that was accumulated by human rights groups in Chile from the earliest days of the dictatorship. It was this information that permitted stubborn prosecutors (such as those in Spain) to keep trying.

Shining a Light on a Necessary Evil

The cases in this book show how the typologies discussed here can be applied more generally. Bureaucratic coercion in East Germany was a different sort of animal from blind coercion in Argentina, and each of these cases also differed from the experiments with increased external monitoring in Chile and South Africa. The framework in this book helps us make sense of these differences in a systematic way through categories that are mutually exclusive and jointly exhaustive. These cases are a starting point for further research. Most of the elements presented here can and should be disaggregated further and more systematically. This includes further disaggregating across time (more organizational shifts), space (more cases), and institutions (different police and military organizations).

Regime type is another variable that needs to be examined more systematically. For example, the framework presented in this book applies to democratic and authoritarian regimes alike, whereas this book has concentrated on the latter. Notwithstanding the liberalization in Chile and South Africa, in none of the cases are the levels of external monitoring especially high. Future research should focus more systematically on analyzing the relationship between the organization of coercion and regime type. What kinds of coercive organizations are most likely in what kinds of regimes? Which are most effective? What consequences do different organizational forms have on different regimes?

Another variable is the relative weight and importance of various monitoring options. This book analyzes the organization of coercion through the various criteria associated with internal and external monitoring. However, it is likely that not all of the criteria carry the same weight across different times and places. For example, access to prisoners may be a relatively minor aspect of external monitoring, and there could be good reasons for giving different criteria different weights. Moreover, in some places such factors as information clearinghouses or legislative oversight may be far more significant than in others.

Further work should also distinguish between state and nonstate actors. Although we have been discussing essentially state coercion until this point, there is no reason why the basic framework in this book could not be used to analyze nonstate armed groups as well. Indeed, preliminary research on this question suggests that, from an organizational perspective, states and nonstate groups are not dichotomous. Nonstate armed groups are likely to lie in any space on the organizational matrix presented here, although they are unlikely to have very high levels of external monitoring (Policzer 2006). These groups are important players in many of the world's conflict zones, from Colombia to the Congo. A more systematic understanding of the trade-offs and consequences of how they organize coercion would address blind spots in literatures as diverse as those on democratization and realist international relations, which tend to focus overwhelmingly on states.

Coercive institutions are a necessary evil of politics, but unfortunately, as a rule, they tend to be secretive. A great deal of information about these institutions is always likely to lie in the shadows beyond the well-lit areas and to be patchy and imperfect as a result. Nevertheless, social science is in the business of shining lights in these dim areas by making inferences based on what we do know about that which we do not know for certain. Systematic, theoretically driven frameworks and models are crucial to increasing the leverage of the available information. That is the spirit in which this book is written.

At a different level, this book is also guided by the conviction that it is necessary to understand how coercive institutions work in order to bring them under better democratic control. Regimes whose coercive institutions are controlled by tyrants have not receded into the annals of history. Their durability and pervasiveness make our task an urgent one.

Appendix A

Monitoring Indicators, September–December 1973

Internal Monitoring

Table A.1 shows levels of the seven indicators of internal monitoring for the period of September–December 1973. Rationales for each code are given below.

Table A.1   Internal Monitoring (September–December 1973)

	Low	Medium	High
PROCESS			
Internal reporting by agents to superiors on their activities (IM1)		X	
Monitors' briefings on agents' operations to principals (IM2)		X	
Information clearinghouse (IM3)		X	
Number of monitors divided by number of agents (IM4)	X		
OUTCOME			
Principal's trust in agents (IM5)		X	
Intra- and interbranch coordination (IM6)		X	
Corruption and coercion for personal ends (IM7)		X	

Upon seizing power, the junta used Article 75 of the Code of Military Justice (Código de Justicia Militar) to delegate broad powers to local division commanders. This included not only administrative powers but also the power to carry out military tribunals and to pass sentence (Chilean National Commission on Truth and Reconciliation 1993, 131). There were few established procedures, and there was a great deal of variation in the application of coercion. Some local commanders took a harder line than others did. In some places commanders imposed strict discipline, while in others (especially in more remote regions) local police and soldiers were less constrained and could enact personal revenge.

As a result, there was a great deal of variation in terms of how prisoners were treated. Some sectors of the military acted as though they were fighting a war against a serious and well-armed enemy (which was largely a fabrication) and took a decidedly hard-line stance against all opposition. General Alejandro Medina, whose duty as leader of the Black Berets Battalion within the army was to conduct house-to-house raids through working-class neighborhoods, defended hard-line measures by stating, "No one likes to have his house raided. But if there are rats inside, you accept that someone comes in and gets them out" (Constable and Valenzuela 1991, 20). Medina believed that "the country was in a state of war at least until November 1973." His combat souvenir is a beret that received a bullet hole through it while he was wearing it. "I am alive," he said in characteristic bluster, "thanks to those dummies' bad aim".[1] But not all sectors within the military shared this view. In the provinces, in particular, which had not experienced the same types of sporadic armed resistance and sense of war found in Santiago, relations between military commanders and the local authorities from the Allende government often continued in much the same way as before the coup. Where there were prisoners, many local commanders adhered strictly to military procedure in terms of treatment and due legal process for the military tribunals.

In these circumstances, the level of internal reports by agents to superiors was probably in the middle range. There was no doubt a great deal of reporting, and the junta appears to have had a reasonably good idea of broad patterns such as the number of prisoners and casualties. But the great variation in the administration of coercion during this time suggests that reporting on many aspects of coercion was patchy, ad hoc, and in many cases unreliable. As a result, I have coded IM1 = Medium.

Regarding IM2, the *Informe Rettig* reports that the commission could not "determine exactly what role was played by the different intelligence services of the armed forces and police in the provinces during this period or how that role was coordinated with that of the officers [in charge]" (Chilean National Commission on Truth and Reconciliation 1993, 131). While this could mean that the various intelligence agencies reported accurately and consistently on their branches' operations, this appears unlikely. The reason is that internal reporting was not the mandate of the intelligence services. (Reporting on enemy activities was.) As a result, also, I have conservatively coded the monitors' reporting to their superiors as reflective of medium levels of internal monitoring (IM2 = Medium), given the chaotic situation and the lack of clarity over division of powers.

The principal clearinghouse for information about prisoners was the Servicio Nacional de Detenidos (SENDET). The SENDET was created in November 1973 to administer the prison camps. The SENDET was usually the first place where relatives of those who had been detained looked for information (often without success). But there are several reasons why the SENDET failed to act as a comprehensive clearinghouse.

The most important is that it dealt only with the status of prisoners, and coercion did not amount simply to holding prisoners. The SENDET could provide no information on the scores of victims who, for example, had been rounded up and summarily executed, nor the agents who had undertaken these executions. In many rural areas, for example, local commanders permitted such summary operations. Also, the SENDET lacked the power to carry out independent investigations. It depended essentially on self-reports by the different branches on how many prisoners they held and on their status. Victims' relatives reported repeated frustrations during this time in their failure to get accurate information on their relatives' whereabouts. Consequently, I have coded IM3 = Medium.

During this period each service essentially carried out its own internal monitoring, but there was no specialized overarching monitor for all the services. The number of agents exceeded the number of monitors or overseers (IM4 = Low).

The available evidence suggests that at the very top, and notwithstanding official proclamations, the various junta members (the principals) deeply mistrusted one another. The confusion over powers and the division of labor between the various branches created a situation that could be exploited. In this book I have documented the struggles between Pinochet and the rest of the junta members over the extent of his power accumulation. Although each junta member probably trusted his own services' reports, there is little evidence of interbranch trust. I have split the difference and coded this as reflective of a medium level of internal monitoring (IM5 = Medium).

In many ways there was a great deal of coordination among the leaders of the junta. The four branches of the armed forces acted in unison to overthrow the Allende government and, notwithstanding their deep internal divisions and confusions, were coordinating their actions to run the government. But it is difficult to isolate a single coercive modus operandi during this time that applied to all branches.

The military issued *bandos,* official public announcements with the character of edicts that contained lists of names of people it was looking for. (The best description and analysis of the political and legal aspects of the *bandos* is Garretón Merino, Garretón Merino, and Garretón Merino [1998]). In many cases, these persons presented themselves to the Carabineros or army bases voluntarily. Sometimes they were released, but often they were detained on the spot. During the first couple of weeks in particular, before the extent of the repression became clear, many people believed that the military was simply "restoring order" after deposing the Allende government. Although it seems remarkable in retrospect, at that time many thought that their best chances for survival lay in cooperating fully with the new authorities, even to the point of voluntarily presenting themselves when their name showed up on a list or in a *bando.*

The country's two main police forces, Carabineros de Chile and Investigaciones de Chile, also carried out searches, for instance within the shantytowns *(poblaciones)* of Santiago, once the victim's identity and whereabouts had been established. Houses and offices were ransacked in search for people and information. In other cases, the police would respond to tip-offs by neighbors or coworkers about people who had a known affiliation to the Allende government, were members in one of the left-wing parties, or had occupied high positions in trade unions or state enterprises.

Both institutions operate throughout the country, often with considerable overlap, even though they are sharply distinct. The Carabineros is a uniformed police force. When it was created in 1927 it formed part of the armed forces, on par with the army, navy, and air force and under the control of the Ministry of Defense. President Alessandri changed its status in 1960, placing it under the control of the Ministry of the Interior and removing its parity with the other branches of the military. With the coup, the junta (which included Carabineros General Cesar Mendoza, who took over the command of the institution during the coup by jumping over seventeen senior officers) restored the police force's status on a par with the other branches of the armed forces. Investigaciones is a civilian police force and has always been under the control of the Ministry of the Interior (Frühling, Portales, and Varas 1982; Maldonado 1990; Mery Figueroa 1996).

Sometimes the Carabineros would act in coordination with the other branches of the armed forces, such as the army and the air force, to carry out more massive search and detention raids in particular *poblaciones:* for instance, to search for supposed weapons caches. Typically, all the men would be rounded up and detained in a local field or guarded compound, and a smaller group within this would be selected and carried out to a military or police center, where they would be kept for several hours or even days. During this time there would be questioning, rough beatings, and tortures. The majority of these prisoners were subsequently released, and the remainder would be either detained or taken to isolated spots, usually on the outskirts of Santiago, and executed. The bodies would usually be taken to the morgues or in some cases hastily dumped in fields, ditches, or even Santiago's Mapocho River (Comisión Nacional de Verdad y Reconciliación 1991, 38, 109–11).

Consequently, while the level of coordination within and among the various branches was high at times, the high degree of suspicion and independence that remained merits coding this as medium (IM6 = Medium).

In many cases coercion was not carried out strictly for the political purposes dictated by the junta. While there is little evidence of personal corruption (partly because of the regime's lack of transparency and accountability), many summary executions were carried out in revenge for local disputes, especially in some parts of the countryside. However, deficiencies in coordination and the monitoring mechanisms enabled agents to sometimes act in their own interests—often contrary to the interests of the principal. For example, in November 1978 the bodies of one local massacre, in the town of Lonquén, near Santiago, were found. The victims were local farmers without political affiliation. Carabineros agents had killed them shortly after the coup in what appears to have probably been a local dispute (Pacheco 1979; Chilean National Commission on Truth and Reconciliation 1993, 238–40).

Although the regime had a reputation for not being corrupt, this myth was destroyed in 2004 by U.S. Senate investigations demonstrating that Pinochet had illegally diverted millions of dollars into his personal accounts (*Economist* 2004; for full report, see U.S. Senate, Committee on Homeland Security 2005). However, this type of corruption appeared later in the regime and was not a factor during this early period, especially in the coercive agencies. For example, there is no indication that any members of the armed forces or the secret police undertook raids, to repossess properties, as occurred in Argentina.

Thus, while there were some cases of personal corruption, corruption was not considered a primary modus operandi in coercive campaigns, and the overall levels were lower than one might expect, especially when compared with other authoritarian regimes. IM7 was consequently scored as Medium.

External Monitoring

Table A.2 shows levels of the eight indicators of external monitoring during the period September–December 1973. Rationales for each code are given below.

Table A.2   External Monitoring (September–December 1973)

	Low	Medium	High
Interlocutor or ombudsman for outside groups (EM1)		X	
Outsiders' access to prisoners (EM2)		X	
Principal's trust in monitor's reports (EM3)	X		
Unofficial human rights agencies (EM4)		X	
Independent media (EM5)	X		
Legislative oversight (EM6)	X		
Judicial independence (EM7)	X		
Freedom-of-information laws (EM8)	X		

I have coded EM1 = Medium for this period. Although the pattern of detention varied across regions and across the different armed forces branches, the Servicio Nacional de Detenidos (SENDET) served as a tool to provide a measure of external monitoring. As mentioned previously, it largely failed to act as a comprehensive clearinghouse of information on all aspects of the organization of coercion. To that extent, it did not provide the new regime with a significant source of internal monitoring. As a mechanism for external monitoring, however, it served as a link to outsiders. Relatives could sometimes obtain some information on their relative's whereabouts through the SENDET. Indeed, with all its limitations the SENDET was the only link outsiders had to the coercive forces.

Typically, a detention would proceed through several stages. After an arrest, a victim would be held incommunicado for an undetermined period of time. This first stage was by far the most dangerous, during which the bulk of the assassinations and tortures were bound to take place. Prisoners were kept in secret for as long as the authorities determined necessary. Afterward, if the person was still alive, he or she could simply be released. Or, more likely, he or she could be placed in one of the many long-term detention camps that began to appear during this period. Under this status, a higher degree of external monitoring was possible. The Red Cross monitored the detention centers such as the Estadio Nacional (National Stadium), as did various other national and international organizations. It was possible for relatives to visit prisoners and to deliver food and clothing. (I experienced some of this firsthand during my father's political imprisonment. I have also conducted informal interviews with many former prisoners at different times.)

While the military sought to maximize its discretionary powers regarding coercion, with respect to some kinds of prisoners outsiders were able to achieve a measure of control and oversight. Detention centers were set up in army, navy, and air force bases, as well as in Carabineros and Investigaciones stations and jails. The bulk of these centers were in Santiago and Valparaíso (Chile's second-largest city), but there were numerous others throughout the country. Carabineros stations (Comisarías) were normally a transit point toward other more permanent detention centers, either in military bases or in other, more hastily improvised centers. Images of the scores of prisoners in the sports stadiums (in particular the Estadio Nacional) traveled around the world. Family members would gather outside these centers in their attempts to obtain updates on their relatives' whereabouts. I have coded EM2 = Medium.

The main reports from external monitors were the *recursos de amparo,* which were gathered by human rights monitors and the Catholic Church. While these reports ultimately posed problems for the regime, which denounced them as communist propaganda, there is no evidence that the principals (the junta) had any direct confidence in their validity during this period. Over time, however, this record would become the best source of information on the regime's coercive operations, with sometimes surprising consequences. Consequently, EM3 = Low.

One consequence of the opposition's strategy to pursue the *recursos de amparo* was the gradual development of an increasingly larger and more systematic database under the auspices of the Catholic Church. In consort with human rights agencies, individuals were able to continue pressuring the regime for information regarding detainees. Information gathered on the coercive operations served as an important nexus for the opposition and helped mobilize resources against the regime. Organizations as varied as Amnesty International and the Organization of American States made use of this information as the basis for numerous reports on human rights violations in the country. Thus EM4 = Medium.

EM5 = Low because the opposition press was shut down immediately after the junta came to power. The only media that continued to function were outlets either directly controlled by the regime or posing little or no opposition to the regime's governance. Similarly, EM6 = Low because Congress was disbanded immediately after the junta came to power, and legislation was drafted by decree of the junta. And EM7 = Low because even though the judiciary was allowed to remain independent by the military, it failed to pose much of a challenge to the junta's exercise of power with regard to coercion. The junta also moved to deliberately constrain the judiciary's jurisdiction with regard to coercion.

In October 1977 the junta modified the Code of Military Justice to allow the delegation of all authority to local field commanders, including heading the courts of military justice (Consejos de Guerra) and passing sentences. Shortly after the first Consejos de Guerra began operations, lawyers began to present *recursos de queja* in complaint of irregularities. In November the Supreme Court ruled that it lacked jurisdiction over the military courts, setting a precedent that would be followed for much of the regime. The independence of the military courts became entrenched in the 1980 Constitution (Barros 1996, 78; Barros 2002). Gonzalo Prieto, the first justice minister under the junta, suggested at the time that the Court's "self-limitation" may have been a calculated "hedging to avoid sharing responsibility for the military court abuses and infractions during the emergency."[2]

Chilean military courts prior to the coup had jurisdiction not only over military personnel but also over civilians. After the coup, the jurisdiction of the military courts was expanded such that the majority of cases having to do with state coercion came before the military and not the civilian courts. The jurisdiction of military courts also grew as a result of legislation specifying a series of new political crimes that the military courts were mandated to enforce. These new crimes included, among others, membership in a political party (D.L. No. 77), "political disobedience" and clandestine entry into the country (D.L. No. 81), and adherence to doctrines "propagating violence" (Law 18.314); (Derechos Chile 2002).

This also set in motion a pattern that would be repeated throughout the regime. Lawyers acting on behalf of victims and their relatives began increasingly to present their cases in front of the courts. They made use of the *recurso de amparo,* and during the course of the regime thousands of *recursos* were filed with the courts. The overwhelming majority went unheeded (Frühling 2000).

The courts would typically request information on the case from the executive. But given the military's and the executive's extensive jurisdiction under the state of siege, the court had little power to pursue the request. The minister of the interior, for example, might declare that the person had been "arrested pursuant to faculties conferred by the state of siege," and this was enough for the court to put an end to the *recurso* (Barros 1996, 86).

In short, there were severe restrictions on the extent to which the judiciary could make use of its independence to oversee the executive's use of coercion. Some of these limitations were self-imposed, and some were imposed by the new regime itself as it sought to implement coercion with a maximum degree of discretion. Hilbink (1999) argues that the judiciary's rigid hierarchy and its "extreme legalism" contributed to its capitulation to the new regime. But for these reasons, with respect to judicial jurisdiction the level of external monitoring was low.

Last, EM8 = Low because there were no freedom-of-information laws through which outsiders could formally request information about detainees or the actions of the junta.

Appendix B

Monitoring Indicators, 1974–78

Internal Monitoring

Table B.1 shows levels of the seven indicators of internal monitoring during the period 1974–78. Rationales for each code are given below.

Here, the question arises of who exactly the principal is. As we have seen, the DINA was technically dependent on the junta but in practice

Table B.1   Internal Monitoring, 1974–78

	Low	Medium	High
PROCESS			
Internal reporting by agents to superiors on their activities		X	
Monitors' briefings on agents' operations to principals		X	
Information clearinghouse			X
Number of monitors divided by number of agents	X		
OUTCOME			
Principal's self-reported trust in agents		X	
Intra- and interbranch coordination		X	
Corruption and coercion for personal ends		X	

160

answered only to Pinochet. Moreover, there is some dispute, to this day, about who the head of the DINA actually was. There is no doubt that Manuel Contreras was the executive head of the organization and that he ran it from day to day, but what about Pinochet? Did his status as president and commander in chief of the armed forces mean that he was the head of the DINA? From a principal-agent perspective, how should we understand the complex relationship between the junta, Pinochet, and Contreras?

I will not presume to come to a final settled answer regarding who was the final principal. Instead, we can use the principal-agent framework to analyze the complexity of the relationship between the junta, Pinochet, and Contreras. What were the levels of IM for each of these principals?

For Contreras, all available evidence suggests that he had a very firm and tight control over the DINA. We do not yet know the kinds of databases and records the DINA kept on its agents' operations, but we can speculate. First, it is unlikely that such databases, if they exist at all, were as extensive as, for instance, those of the East German Stasi or even the KGB in the Soviet Union. No archives of such magnitude have been found or, I suspect, are likely to be found. On the other hand, it is likely that some records of some sort were kept. The DINA was a complex hierarchical institution, with extensive operations both inside and outside Chile's borders. It is improbable that this level of coordination could have been achieved without a reasonably sophisticated bureaucracy to coordinate such things as communications and the allocation of resources.

It is also unlikely that such records, if they exist, would contain detailed information on the full spectrum of the DINA agents' operations. For instance, it would be highly surprising, given the DINA's well-known propensity for secrecy, to find records of specific tortures applied and assassinations committed.[1] Instead, records would be likely to serve a coordination purpose: to show requisition forms, purchases, calls, letters, and so forth. But overall there is no evidence in any of the thousands of internal documents of the DINA and the junta that Contreras was unaware of what his agents did or that they engaged in actions that he did not know or did not permit. It seems reasonable, in other words, to expect that the levels of reporting of agents to Contreras were quite high.

Moreover, although the evidence is questionable at best, we can infer from this that he must have had a reasonably high degree of trust in his main agents. This would follow from the fact that he had a great deal of control over how to shape the agency and that the group that formed the core of the DINA had worked together for some time inside the army.[2] Familiarity, we can assume, breeds trust.

With regard to Pinochet, the scores would be a little different. If Contreras is the agent and Pinochet is the principal, we can assume that he must have had a great deal of trust in Contreras, for many of the same reasons I suggested above. Pinochet knew Contreras well, since Contreras was his student in the War Academy. And all indications are that he supported Contreras and lobbied on his behalf to convince the other junta members to support the creation of the DINA. Moreover, there is no doubt that once the DINA was in operation Pinochet placed a great deal of trust in Contreras, relying almost exclusively on him and the DINA for intelligence information. By most accounts, Contreras and Pinochet held regular daily briefings. We can only speculate as to the contents of these briefings, but we know that there were regular and frequent opportunities for Pinochet to receive and to request information from Contreras on the DINA's operations.

There is no indication that Pinochet received regular reports directly from midlevel DINA commanders. His knowledge of DINA agents' operations was filtered through Contreras. We do not know how well Contreras reported on the DINA's plans and operations. And indeed, there are some indications that Contreras's reports may have been partial or inaccurate. This remains a matter of dispute. For instance, while it seems unlikely that the DINA would engage in acts of international terrorism without Pinochet's approval, we do not know exactly how much detailed information Pinochet received on the DINA's operations outside Chile. Did Pinochet know about and approve all the working relationships that the DINA built with foreign right-wing terrorist and paramilitary groups? Or did he simply give Contreras a virtual carte blanche to operate the DINA as he wished so long as it produced results by "neutralizing" the regime's enemies? Although there is a great deal of assertive speculation about it, at this point we do not have the evidence to tell the complete story of the relationship between Pinochet and Contreras or about the level of detail that Pinochet knew of the DINA's operations.[3]

The third extension of this relationship is the junta. The junta also relied on Contreras's reports about the DINA's activities. But unlike Pinochet, the junta does not appear to have had regular and frequent access to Contreras. We can infer that the quality of information and reporting that the junta received on the DINA's operations was far less than that of the information and reporting Pinochet received. Also, we know that at least one member of the junta—Commander Leigh—had profound reservations about the DINA and that the air force's intelligence agency (the SIFA) fostered its own secretive counterinsurgency organization, the Comando Conjunto (CC).[4] Leigh also pulled his men out from the DINA when, as he describes it, he saw that they were given only administrative tasks and were not included in the main operational plans (F. Varas 1979).

The SIFA and the CC competed with the DINA on several fronts over counterinsurgency operations. Colonel Horacio Otaíza, one of the key counterinsurgency leaders in the air force affiliated with the CC, and others were convinced that the DINA, and especially Contreras, displayed a high degree of incompetence regarding intelligence (González and Contreras 1991, 35). The SIFA and the CC deployed a highly effective operation against the MIR in 1974, which included arresting almost half of the people who formed the MIR's central committee. The effectiveness of the operation proved deeply embarrassing for the DINA (González and Contreras 1991, 31–32).

The DINA responded harshly to its rival's actions. Colonel Otaíza was killed in an airplane accident under mysterious circumstances on July 31, 1975. The air force suspected DINA involvement, and DINA agents, fearing a counterstrike against Contreras, arrested one of the top CC officers and forced the dismissal of another (González and Contreras 1991, 99–100).

The dispute between the DINA and the CC was a serious cleavage inside the regime that threatened to spill over from mere disputes over operations and prisoner control to internecine bloodshed. Inside the army also, many sectors resented the DINA's broad powers, though there is less evidence of the kinds of serious clashes that existed with the CC. But overall, these tensions suggested that the level of trust between the junta and military leadership and the DINA was low, certainly compared to that between Pinochet and the DINA.

In short, there was a difference in trust and in the levels of self-reported information available between the DINA and the different principals, especially between Contreras and the rest. I have split the difference and coded IM1 and IM5 = Medium.

With regard to the other internal monitoring criteria, the clashes with the SIFA and the CC posed difficulties for the DINA's monitoring of the other coercive agencies. The disputes that flared up (in 1974 and 1975) were essentially resolved by dictate in November 1975 through a secret order from the Ministries of the Interior and Defense that made the DINA the only organization allowed to detain and question prisoners and to keep secret detention centers (González and Contreras 1991, 206).[5] Nevertheless, tensions with the other agencies remained. Briefings on other agents' operations are therefore coded as IM2 = Medium.

The DINA was known to have kept extensive records on others, with informants throughout various state agencies and elsewhere. The people the DINA watched ranged from opposition individuals and groups to members of the regime itself (Chilean National Commission on Truth and Reconciliation 1993).[6] I have therefore coded IM3 = High.

Even though the DINA had taken over the bulk of coercion, other coercive agencies remained. And because the DINA was now the principal monitoring agency, the ratio of overseers to agents reflected a low level of internal monitoring; therefore, IM4 = Low.

The level of intra- and interbranch coordination under the DINA was higher than in the previous period, but problems remained (IM6 = Medium). As we have seen, the DINA was given broad authority to direct and coordinate intelligence gathering and security operations across the services. It could request information from any branch of the state and could direct operations counting on the support not simply of the other branches of the armed forces but of the entire state apparatus, including the postal service, telephone company, airline, railway, and so on.

With regard to corruption and common crime (or coercion for personal revenge), the DINA agents do not appear to have acted primarily for personal monetary gain, although there is some evidence of this (IM7 = Medium). The DINA used various companies and financial dealings to finance its operations, but victims were not selected according to their spoils.[7] Indeed, most DINA victims came from modest backgrounds.

We can also infer that internal sanctions for not following orders would have been relatively high inside the DINA. The DINA used its broad powers to advance the careers of allies within the other branches of the armed forces and to curtail those of its enemies, in some cases by simply assassinating them.[8] It is reasonable to expect that internal sanctions within the DINA were at least as severe as those inside of the individual branches of the armed forces. The fact that there is little evidence of these sanctions having been applied suggests that the DINA was most likely effective at enforcing discipline within its organization and that its personnel generally agreed to follow the policies set down by its leadership.

External Monitoring

Table B.2 shows levels of the eight indicators of external monitoring during the period 1974–78. Rationales for each code are given below.

During the DINA period, the levels of external monitoring remained more or less unchanged from what they had been previously. Indeed, there is no evidence that the principals placed any more trust in outsiders' reports (EM3 = Low). There was also neither legislative nor judicial oversight over coercion (EM6 and EM7 = Low), and there certainly was nothing close to freedom-of-information laws (EM8 = Low).

The first substantial shift from the previous period was the absence of an interlocutor to outside groups (EM1 = Low). Whereas the SENDET, with all its faults, had served as a nexus of sorts to victims' relatives and outside observers, under the DINA there was no such representation or access. Indeed, the DINA's entire policy of plausible deniability rested on denying such access and on erecting a formidable barrier

Table B.2   External Monitoring, 1974–78

	Low	Medium	High
Interlocutor or ombudsman for outside groups (EM1)	X		
Outsiders' access to prisoners (EM2)	X		
Principal's trust in monitor's reports (EM3)	X		
Unofficial human rights agencies (EM4)		X	
Independent media (EM5)	X		
Legislative oversight (EM6)	X		
Judicial jurisdiction (EM7)	X		
Freedom-of-information laws (EM8)	X		

between outsiders and the coercive agents. Exemplifying the tone of this policy, Contreras never made public appearances, and newspapers were forced to recycle one or two stock photographs of him.

Related to this was prisoner access. Outsiders continued to have access to the prisoners who had been taken earlier and who were already being held in the major camps such as Chacabuco, Ritoque, and Cuatro Álamos; but as we have seen, the DINA adopted a radically new modus operandi with regard to its prisoners. No outsiders were ever allowed access to the DINA's prison camps. These held fewer people and operated in relative secrecy. For this reason, on this criterion the level of EM decreased under the DINA (EM2 = Low).

One of the most substantial shifts was that human rights organizations were becoming increasingly sophisticated (EM4 = Medium). Shortly after the coup, the Comité Pro Paz (COPACHI) was formed as an interfaith organization that included members from all major religions in the country. Lawyers affiliated with COPACHI began to present *recursos de amparo* with greater frequency on behalf of those who had been detained by the security forces. The team of lawyers working with

COPACHI grew in size, and presenting the *recursos de amparo* required that they develop increasingly sophisticated archives and databases.

COPACHI staff collected information from witnesses, friends and relatives, and released prisoners. In doing this, they had few precedents to follow regarding how to set up and operate human rights databases. Peruvian activists, for example, had earlier begun to gather information on "events" such as protests, strikes, or specific attacks. While this is one possibility, it did not serve the needs of lawyers working to present *recursos de amparo*. Presenting appeals to the courts on behalf of individual victims required detailed information on individual cases and not on broadly gauged human rights "events."[9]

When the DINA began taking prisoners, in early 1974, COPACHI's lawyers responded by presenting more *recursos de amparo*. Overwhelmingly, the courts failed to respond to these.[10] But an important consequence of presenting these en masse was the gradual accumulation of an increasingly comprehensive and systematic database on human rights violations in Chile. Indeed, over time this would become the single most important source of information on the coercive history of the regime (Frühling 1984, 1986).

COPACHI's efforts met with resistance from the regime. In 1975 three of its main lawyers, including the former Christian Democrat senator Jaime Castillo Velasco, were forced into exile after protesting the DINA's attack against a large group of MIR members in Argentina. Finally, in December 1975, it was forced to close down.

These were serious setbacks, but they forced a shift in organization and strategy. COPACHI had been a coalition of primarily religious organizations that shared the common goal of providing services for the large number of prisoners and disappeared. The forcible closure of COPACHI demonstrated to its members that they needed to operate under greater institutional protection. The head of the Chilean Catholic Church, Raúl Cardenal Silva Henríquez, proposed that the work COPACHI had been carrying out be transferred to the church itself. In January 1976, less than a month after COPACHI was closed, the church opened the new Vicaría de la Solidaridad as an integral part of its corporate structure, and with the correspondingly greater protection this afforded the human rights lawyers and workers.[11]

Another effect of the systematic accumulation of information by the human rights community was the appearance of increasingly regular reports on the Chilean situation. COPACHI, and later the Vicaría, published monthly reports on the human rights violations, and these circulated widely inside Chile and abroad. The protection afforded by the Vicaría, in particular, also drew journalists and others who used its information to publish articles outside the largely proregime media.

Moreover, there was growing discontent with the DINA even in the proregime media (*Qué Pasa* magazine) during this time. *Qué Pasa* began to publish articles critical of the DINA (especially during 1975–77), suggesting that its thuggishness undermined regime support. Even moderate supporters of the junta began to view its heavy-handedness as contemptible and meriting censure. These critiques grew as there began to be increasing evidence linking the DINA to the September 1976 Letelier assassination and also after Contreras began to criticize the *gremialista* groups affiliated with the regime. The *gremialistas* were lawyers and economists based at the Universidad Católica who had been involved in student politics and in anti-Allende demonstrations. Their de facto political leader was Jaime Guzmán, a deeply religious disciple of former conservative president Jorge Alessandri (1958–64). Contreras suggested that these groups largely failed to build popular support for the regime.

One problem for the regime during this period was that while repressing the opposition groups during this time was not especially difficult (e.g., the COPACHI was shut down and other vocal critics were exiled, not to mention the hundreds of disappearances), shutting down *supporters'* media organizations was much more costly. The regime depended on political and economic support from civilian right-wing sectors, and these relied on the regime to implement their agenda for political and economic reforms (Huneeus 2000a).

Shutting down a conservative proregime magazine would have seriously compromised the relationship between these sectors and the political leadership. For these reasons, it is appropriate to score an increase not only in the human rights agencies, but also with regard to independent media; therefore, EM5 = Medium.

Appendix C

Monitoring Indicators after 1978

Internal Monitoring

Table C.1 shows levels of the seven indicators of internal monitoring for the period after 1978. Rationales for each code are given below.

We can infer that one important change after 1978 was an increase in overall information to the principals on the CNI's own operations

Table C.1 Internal Monitoring, 1978–90

	Low	*Medium*	*High*
PROCESS			
Internal reporting by agents to superiors on their activities (IM1)			X
Monitors' briefings on agents' operations to principals (IM2)			X
Information clearinghouse (IM3)		?	
Number of monitors divided by number of agents (IM4)		X	
OUTCOME			
Principal's self-reported trust in agents (IM5)		X	
Intra- and interbranch coordination (IM6)		X	
Corruption and coercion for personal ends (IM7)		X	

and on those of other organizations. For the moment, without complete access to the entire collection of the regime's archives, we cannot be completely certain about the full extent of information availability. Nevertheless, we can infer an improvement based on several pieces of evidence. For instance, given that the CNI was more constrained than the DINA with regard to domestic operations, it is reasonable to infer that information on its operations was more readily available through established (formal and informal military) channels. Moreover, the DINA relied more than the CNI on right-wing civilians and paramilitary groups. These included many of the Cóndor operatives, such as local right-wing groups in Argentina, the United States, and Italy.

The CNI relied almost exclusively on its own personnel, recruited mainly from the different branches of the armed forces (especially the army). It was easier for principals to obtain information on the operations of an organization whose agents belonged to a known entity and to well-established structures under their own control than on operations of organizations outside their direct control. Consequently, we can gather that the principals (not only Pinochet but also the cabinet and the junta) received better information from the coercive agents on their operations, as well as better reporting on other agents' actions. Therefore, IM1 and IM2 = High.

In one respect, the full extent of which is hard to gauge at this point without an ability to delve inside the DINA's and the CNI's archives, it is possible that internal monitoring decreased with the CNI. Although the CNI inherited the bulk of the DINA's personnel and physical infrastructure, Contreras took what appears to have been a great deal of information with him (in the form of archives). How many archives or how valuable is not clear. Nevertheless, this suggests a reason why at least with respect to its capacity as information clearinghouse the CNI might have been less effective than the DINA. I have therefore coded this with a question mark (IM3 = Medium?).

Internal monitoring increased according to another criterion, however. Unlike the DINA, which was an independent institution, separate from the rest of the armed forces, the regime placed the CNI under the Ministry of Defense. Whereas Contreras had reported only to Pinochet, the head of the CNI reported to the president through the Ministry of the Interior. This gave the CNI a status similar to that of the Carabineros. While it was not technically a branch of the armed forces, both were military institutions and were given status as such under the Ministry of Defense. This status governed, for example, the jurisdiction of military courts over their actions and their career or officer structure. For day-to-day operational purposes, however, the Ministry of the Interior directed both. In other words, this change in status introduced at least two new internal oversight mechanisms over the CNI (thus IM4 = Medium). This was a significant shift that meant essentially that Pinochet gave up the monopoly control over coercion he had enjoyed under the DINA. Even though the DINA was technically under the jurisdiction of the junta, in practice Manuel Contreras reported exclusively to Pinochet.

With respect to trust, on the face of it there is no reason to assume that Pinochet (or the junta) fundamentally mistrusted the CNI, its leadership, or the other coercive agencies. However, at least two cases suggest otherwise. The first was the replacement of Mena by the more hard-line General Humberto Gordon. Pinochet removed Mena shortly after the MIR assassinated the director of the army's Intelligence School, Colonel Roger Vergara, on July 15, 1980. The case sent shockwaves throughout the regime, and former DINA personnel (including Contreras) seriously criticized the CNI and Mena in particular for incompetence (Frühling 2000).

The second case was a serious dispute between the CNI and the Carabineros in 1985. The dispute followed the infamous murder by-Carabineros agents of three human rights workers who belonged to the Communist Party. Because the victims' throats had been slit, it has become known as the Degollados ("Slit-Throat") case. The agents belonged to the Dirección de Comunicaciones de Carabineros (DICOMCAR), created in 1983 as that institution's intelligence and counterinsurgency agency in the aftermath of a wave of protests against the regime (Caucoto Pereira and Salazar Ardiles 1994). The DICOMCAR and the CNI cooperated on many cases, but the boundaries between their spheres of jurisdiction were often unclear, and relations between the two were tense (Maldonado 1990; Comisión Nacional de Verdad y Reconciliación 1991).

After the murders, the CNI issued a report on the case and cooperated with the courts and even with human rights groups to bring the responsible officers to trial. The result was a massive shakedown in the Carabineros, leading to the resignation of the top command, including its director, junta member General César Mendoza, along with four of his most senior officers. Apart from the case's deep political impact, the CNI's punishment of the Carabineros signaled deep mistrust between the two most important coercive institutions in the country. Consequently, I have coded IM5 = Medium.

Regarding inter- and intrabranch coordination, it is not entirely clear whether the CNI was more effective than the DINA. Under the DINA, tensions with agencies such as the air force's Comando Conjunto (CC) lingered during a period of institutional confusion. The division of powers between Pinochet and the rest of the junta members (and between the executive and the legislative powers) remained unresolved. Compared to the DINA, the CNI operated in a period of far greater institutional clarity. The key struggles for power at the top (e.g., between Pinochet and Leigh) had been resolved, and the 1980 Constitution set the boundaries for politics for the duration of the regime. Yet there remained lingering tensions over primacy between the CNI and the Carabineros, which increased especially after the 1983 wave of protests against the regime (resulting in the 1985 crisis mentioned above). For this reason, with respect to coordination I have coded the CNI's performance as medium (IM6 = Medium). Overall it performed better than the DINA in this respect, but given the more stable broad institutional context it was reasonable to expect greater coordination.

Last, regarding corruption, it is also not clear how much of an improvement the CNI was over the DINA, especially after 1980. There were incidents, although apparently isolated, of CNI agents engaged in bank robberies and other acts of personal corruption. Therefore, IM7 = Medium.

External Monitoring

Table C.2 shows levels of the eight indicators of external monitoring for the period after 1978. Rationales for each code are given below.

Table C.2   External Monitoring, 1978–90

	Low	Medium	High
Interlocutor or ombudsman for outside groups (EM1)		X	
Outsiders' access to prisoners (EM2)	X		
Principal's trust in monitor's reports (EM3)		X	
Unofficial human rights agencies (EM4)			X
Independent media (EM5)			X
Legislative oversight (EM6)	X		
Judicial jurisdiction (EM7)		X	
Freedom-of-information laws (EM8)	X		

After 1978 external as well as internal monitoring increased. Some measures of external monitoring remained more or less the same. Outsiders still had very little if any official access to prisoners (EM2 = Low). There was still no real independent legislative oversight with respect to coercion (EM6 = Low). There was no change with respect to freedom-of-information laws (EM8 = Low). However, with respect to other measures we can see differences, and in some cases they are significant.

For example, the CNI leadership assumed a much more open public presence than Contreras had ever done. There had been virtually no public images of Contreras or any interviews or photographs of him in the newspapers. His identity was known but little else. In a sharp break from this practice, soon after taking office Mena called a meeting with church authorities to "present himself." Although the results of the meeting were less than fruitful, perhaps not surprisingly given the context, this type of public presence signaled a shift in the regime. Therefore, I have coded EM1 = Medium.

Indeed, this initial meeting was the first of a series of contacts that would later become far more direct. During the Degollados case, the head of the Chilean Human Rights Commission (Comisión Chilena de Derechos Humanos, or CChDH), Jaime Castillo, and General Humberto Gordon, Mena's successor, established a regular and ongoing informal contact to share information and coordinate activities. The CChDH wrote a report implicating the Carabineros in the case and made it directly available to the CNI, which had arrived at a similar conclusion through its own investigations. Most surprising, however, was a "hot line" established between the CNI and the CChDH—essentially between Castillo and Gordon—in the aftermath of the case. Both organizations maintained this link until 1989, when the CNI was finally disbanded.[1] The CChDH, of course, did not establish this link to furtively leak information to the CNI. Castillo stated simply, "We had to speak with those in charge. I am free and I have a right to be heard. We practiced democracy within the dictatorship."[2] Besides being another signal of the emergence of an interlocutor between the coercive agencies and outsiders, this sort of contact signals an increased trust in outsiders' information. It is unlikely that this sort of contact was a secret to the military leadership or to Pinochet. It signals that the principals had enough trust in the reliability and validity of the information published by the CChDH to establish and maintain direct contact. Therefore, EM3 = Medium.

An important shift was the appearance of a series of new human rights groups during this time. One of these was the Servicio Paz y Justicia (SERPAJ), created at the end of 1977 to promote the defense of human rights in areas not covered by the Vicaría, such as education (Orellana and Hutchison 1991, 104). The largest and most important of the new organizations was the CChDH, created in 1978. The CChDH complemented the work of the Vicaría. It adopted a broader definition of human rights that included not only the rights to life and physical integrity but also the full range of civil, political, economic, and even cultural rights. The CChDH was led by high-profile political leaders and received support especially from various international organizations. A series of other groups would continue to appear throughout the 1980s (Frühling 1984, 1986; Orellana and Hutchison 1991, 103). Although these groups often suffered severe restrictions, their appearance was a major departure with respect to the previous period. Thus EM4 = High.

The media also gradually gained independence after this time, with the appearance of new magazines and newspapers (such as *APSI* magazine, which began circulation in 1976), many of which were critical of the regime. Last, another notable change with respect to external monitoring was the behavior of some members of the courts. After 1978, the Supreme Court and the judiciary did not experience any fundamental structural changes. Also, in April 1978, in one of its first acts, the new civilian-led administration decreed an amnesty for all those charged by the military courts from the time of the coup until March 10, 1978. The government announced that its purpose, now that a new "peace and order" prevailed, was to "leave hatreds behind" (República de Chile, *D.O.*, April 19, 1978, quoted in Constable and Valenzuela 1991, 129).

Although some political prisoners were released under the law's benefits, the overwhelming majority of those who benefited from the law were state agents.[3] Observers at the time quite rightly dismissed this law as an illegitimate blanket self-amnesty for the regime's own crimes. To this day, human rights lawyers are fighting in court to overturn it or, as a second-best strategy, to exploit potential loopholes.[4] In addition, in the overwhelming majority of cases that fell within this period (as most of the cases of the disappeared did) the attending civilian judge declared himself without jurisdiction *(incompetente)* and passed the case on to the military court. Given that the regime increased the jurisdiction of the military courts, this was the fate of the overwhelming majority of cases.

Nevertheless, the amnesty decree forced the regime to develop strategies to avoid legal prosecution after that time, given the absence of amnesty protection. These strategies included expanding jurisdiction of the military courts, as well as granting the executive new powers of detention during different states of emergency (Comisión Nacional de Verdad y Reconciliación 1991; Huneeus 2000a). In what was essentially a new political and legal space, some judges defied the strictures imposed by the court and the regime and went ahead with the prosecution of cases of human rights abuse that took place after 1978. For these reasons, I have coded EM7 = Medium.

Appendix D

Cross-Country Comparisons on Monitoring Indicators

Argentina

Coercion in Argentina during the Proceso was most similar to that in Chile before the DINA but was far closer to pure blind coercion. First, as table D.1 shows, external monitoring was lower than at any period in Chile. When the military took power in 1976 in Argentina, unlike Chile, where the judiciary remained at least nominally independent, it took

Table D.1 External Monitoring in Argentina

	Low	Medium	High
Interlocutor or ombudsman for outside groups (EM1)	X		
Outsiders' access to prisoners (EM2)	X		
Principal's trust in monitor's reports (EM3)	X		
Unofficial human rights agencies (EM4)		X	
Independent media (EM5)	X		
Legislative oversight (EM6)	X		
Judicial jurisdiction (EM7)	X		
Freedom-of-information laws (EM8)	X		

complete control of all three branches of the state (EM6, EM7 = Low). There was no interlocutor to outside groups (EM1 = Low), and outsiders had no access to prisoners (EM2 = Low). There was a far weaker independent media than in Chile (EM5 = Low),[1] and there were no freedom-of-information laws to speak of (EM8 = Low).

There were several human rights organizations, some of which, such as the Asamblea Permanente de Derechos Humanos (APDH), had existed for a long time. These organizations provided a measure of external monitoring, but far less so than in Chile. First, they lacked the protection of the Argentine Church, which supported the dictatorship. Second, they made less use of the *recurso de amparo* as a strategy for challenging the state's detentions and consequently developed far less comprehensive archives (EM4 = Medium). There is no indication that the principals inside the regime trusted these organizations' reports. On the contrary, the human rights groups operated under constant threat of harassment, detention, or closure (EM3 = Low).

Internal monitoring (table D.2) was also low in Argentina. As a result of the wide discretion given to radically decentralized agents both within the military and in outside groups, very little information was available to principals on the details of agents' operations (IM1, IM2 = Low), and coordination among the different institutions and organizations, as Brysk (1994) notes, was often poor (IM6 = Low).

There was also no equivalent to the DINA or CNI as an information clearinghouse. The closest institution that could have served this function in Argentina was the State Intelligence Service (Servicio de Inteligencia del Estado, or SIDE). But this institution lacked the power and scope to systematically monitor all coercive agencies. Moreover, the SIDE had been created under the Perón government, which meant that it lacked prestige and legitimacy in some sectors of the military (Stepan 1988, 24–25), and was relatively ineffective as a clearinghouse. At most, each branch monitored its own divisions and in particular its own intelligence agencies (Pion-Berlin 1989, 102–4). Thus IM3 = Low. As a result, also, the ratio of monitors to agents also reflected low internal monitoring; therefore IM4 = Low.

How much trust principals had in agents is hard to gauge in any military institution prone to secrecy. But I have coded it with a question

Table D.2   Internal Monitoring in Argentina

	Low	Medium	High
PROCESS			
Internal reporting by agents to superiors on their activities (IM1)	X		
Monitors' briefings on agents' operations to principals (IM2)	X		
Information clearinghouse (IM3)	X		
Number of monitors divided by number of agents (IM4)	X		
OUTCOME			
Principal's self-reported trust in agents (IM5)	?		
Intra- and interbranch coordination (IM6)	X		
Corruption and coercion for personal ends (IM7)	X		

mark as IM5 = Low? The reason is the relatively unspecialized manner in which coercion was organized. Each branch of the armed forces took part in repression, and all branches rotated their agents to ensure a pact of silence by widespread guilt (Brysk 1994, 39; Roniger and Sznajder 1999, 20–21). A chilling account of this rotation is provided by Horacio Verbitsky's interview of Captain (ret.) Francisco Scilingo.

Scilingo took part in missions to kill opponents by throwing them from a plane, alive and drugged, into the open ocean. His was the first public confession of this practice. He states that the majority in the navy took part in the flights and that this rotation was a deliberate policy, a kind of "communion," something "that had to be done." He noted, "The whole country had been on rotation. Maybe one guy might have been able to avoid it, but only rarely *[en forma anecdótica]*. It was not one little group: it was the entire navy [that took part]" (Verbitsky 1995, 31–32). This kind of rotation among the agents of coercion can thus serve the purpose of accentuating the differences between the agents and the victims by preventing any possible formation of affective bonds and by emphasizing the differences between "us" and "them."[2] It also serves to build loyalty by ensuring that everyone's hands are dirty.[3] I have taken this as an indicator of basic mistrust by principals in their agents.

Finally, corruption was far more common in Argentina than Chile. For example, taking possession of a victim's property was often an important incentive for agents to take part in repression.[4] Thus IM7 = Low.

East Germany

In East Germany, all EM criteria (table D.3) are low. There were no independent organizations or institutions in civil society, separation of powers, independent media, or other institutions that would have provided external monitoring.

Table D.3   External Monitoring in East Germany

	Low	Medium	High
Interlocutor or ombudsman for outside groups (EM1)	X		
Outsiders' access to prisoners (EM2)	X		
Principal's trust in monitor's reports (EM3)	X		
Unofficial human rights agencies (EM4)	X		
Independent media (EM5)	X		
Legislative oversight (EM6)	X		
Judicial jurisdiction (EM7)	X		
Freedom-of-information laws (EM8)	X		

As for internal monitoring (table D.4), because of the Stasi's "Chekist" structure, its massive system of oversight and file keeping on citizens and all branches of the states, IM1, IM2, IM3, and IM6 = High. There were two kinds of agents who worked for the Stasi: officers and informants. The former were full-time employees directly employed by the Stasi. The number of full-time officials had grown from 52,700 in 1973, to 81,500 in 1981, to roughly 100,000 by the time of the breakdown, including some 11,000 MfS special guards regiments. This represented roughly one MfS agent per 165 inhabitants in 1989. By contrast, official statistics showed one medical practitioner per 450 inhabitants in 1988 (Childs and Popplewell 1996, 82).

The number of informers *(Inoffizielle Mitarbeiter)*[5] was far larger and had grown especially in the 1970s. Conservative estimates are that by the mid-1990s there were some 174,000 informers (Childs and

Table D.4   Internal Monitoring in East Germany

	Low	Medium	High
PROCESS			
Internal reporting by agents to superiors on their activities (IM1)			X
Monitors' briefings on agents' operations to principals (IM2)			X
Information clearinghouse (IM3)			X
Number of monitors divided by number of agents (IM4)			X
OUTCOME			
Principal's self-reported trust in agents (IM5)			X
Intra- and interbranch coordination (IM6)			X
Corruption and coercion for personal ends (IM7)		?	

Popplewell 1996, 82–86; Garton Ash 1997, 84; Koehler 1999, 8). By this measure, in a country of sixteen million, this meant that one out of every fifty people had a connection with the Stasi.[6] Thus IM4 = High.

The Stasi under Mielke was crucial to Moscow's control over the GDR. In 1970, Mielke's support was instrumental in removing GDR President Ulbricht from the top leadership of the SED, after Moscow felt that Ulbricht had established too close a relationship with West Germany's Willy Brandt under the sway of the latter's *ostpolitik* (Childs 1966; Fulbrook 1995, 36; Koehler 1999, 65–75).[7] His lieutenant, Erich Honecker, who remained in power until 1989, replaced Ulbricht. Under Honecker, Mielke continued to expand the size and reach of the Stasi, turning it into the premiere coercive institution in the country (Childs 1983, 1985). Thus IM5 = High.

The Stasi was the antithesis of a small and highly specialized institution. As these figures suggest, the level of specialization was very low as regards informants and somewhat higher as regards the full-time employees. The Stasi's broad reach was crucial to establishing control over the population. Not only were its agents literally everywhere, but cooperation with the Stasi had a corrupting effect on the population (Rosenberg 1995). Consequently, I have coded IM7 = Medium?, with the question mark indicating the countereffects of corruption.

South Africa

With regard to external monitoring (table D.5), there was no effective legislative oversight over coercion (EM6 = Low) or freedom-of-information laws (EM8 = Low). The vibrant civil society, however, results in EM4 = Medium.

The judiciary remained independent, although the executive, "through scarcely disguised manipulation of the composition and quorum requirements of the appellate division," often forced its policies through (Corder 1987, 98). In practice, until the 1980s the courts tended to rule in favor of the executive, even though such an outcome was not an "intentionally biased or prejudiced policy" (99). However, as the government resorted increasingly to extralegal means to maintain apartheid

Table D.5   External Monitoring in South Africa

	Low	Medium	High
Interlocutor or ombudsman for outside groups (EM1)	X		
Outsiders' access to prisoners (EM2)	X		
Principal's trust in monitor's reports (EM3)		X	
Unofficial human rights agencies (EM4)		X	
Independent media (EM5)		X	
Legislative oversight (EM6)	X		
Judicial jurisdiction (EM7)		X	
Freedom-of-information laws (EM8)	X		

in the 1980s, the courts often ruled against the government and in favor of individual applicants. As a result, EM7 = Medium.

With regard to the media, I have coded EM5 = High because of the media's independence and willingness to challenge the apartheid regime. The absence of an interlocutor to outside forces (as exemplified by the Biko case) indicates EM1 = Low. The Biko case also exemplifies the fact that outsiders had relatively little access to prisoners held by the security forces (EM2 = Low). It also indicates the tense relationship to outsiders' reports on its coercive practices. While accusations from the black press or other groups were likely to be dismissed, those from the liberal white press—representing a constituency whose support the government courted—were more likely to have an impact. Therefore, EM3 = Medium.[8]

With regard to internal monitoring (table D.6), part of the state operated with high internal monitoring on some criteria (IM1, IM2, IM3, IM5, IM6). But this was counterbalanced by reliance on coercive agents over which the government had accordingly less direct control and by the Truth and Reconciliation Commission's suggestion of the blurred boundaries between both groups' activities. I have split the difference and coded IM1, IM2, IM3, IM5, IM6 = Medium. Given the reliance on such outside agents, also, IM4 = Low. There is little evidence of corruption for personal ends in the main security forces, but for the same reasons as above I have coded IM7 = Medium.

Table D.6   Internal Monitoring in South Africa

	Low	*Medium*	*High*
PROCESS			
Internal reporting by agents to superiors on their activities (IM1)		X	
Monitors' briefings on agents' operations to principals (IM2)		X	
Information clearinghouse (IM3)		X	
Number of monitors divided by number of agents (IM4)	X		
OUTCOME			
Principal's self-reported trust in agents (IM5)		X	
Intra- and interbranch coordination (IM6)		X	
Corruption and coercion for personal ends (IM7)		X	

Notes

ONE   The Dark Spaces of Politics

The chapter epigraph is cited in Mannix (1986).

1. Graham Allison and Philip Zelikow's classic study of the Cuban Missile Crisis (1999) is an example of this kind of approach.

2. This is an idea that traces its roots to Plato's proposition to entrust rule to a well-trained "philosopher king."

3. The framework thus permits nominal and ordinal comparisons, which can be used to build systematic historical narratives (Mahoney 1999a).

4. Others have documented the ways in which watchdog or "advocacy" groups can pressure authoritarian regimes by publicizing their abuses (Keck and Sikkink 1998). This book dovetails with that work.

5. On mechanisms, see (Elster 1989), Bennett (1999), Hedström and Swedberg (1998), and Tilly (2000a, 2000b).

6. For various perspectives on counterfactual analysis, see Lebow (2001), Tetlock and Belkin (1996), and Stalnaker (1996).

7. This is the "external validity" problem (Kirk and Miller 1986, 9–52; Kritzer 1996).

8. Although it has no direct translation, the *recurso de amparo* is a legal instrument akin to a writ of habeas corpus.

TWO   The Coercion Problem

1. Tilly's recent work (2000) has been more directly concerned with organizational problems.

2. Wilson (1989) points out that agency problems are more likely to appear in political than in economic institutions. First, the output of the agency is likely to be more vague. Instead of producing car parts, for instance, a government agent may be charged with the "welfare" of a given group. Second, government agents are likely to have many principals, some-

times with confusing or contradictory jurisdictions. And third, government agents are likely to have their own political preferences.

3. The distinction can also refer to ex-ante versus ex-post monitoring by the same organization, such as a congressional committee. In police patrol monitoring, members of Congress actively pursue (ex-ante) information on agencies' performance, while in fire alarm monitoring they wait for information on an agency's behavior (e.g., a misdeed or a transgression) to reach them from other sources.

4. Rosberg (1995), in an analysis of the appearance of independent courts under Nasser's authoritarian regime in Egypt, adopts the same framework as McCubbins and Weingast (1984) but with his own terminology. Police patrols are centralized monitors, and fire alarms are decentralized monitors. In my view, there are subtle but important differences between internal and external monitoring and the degree of their centralization that Rosberg's terminology fails to capture.

5. I have drawn widely on various contemporary and classic works in political economy and sociology (in the theory of the firm, organization theory, and the sociology of information) in devising these criteria. For both internal and external monitoring, these include Mill ([1859] 1955), Coase (1937), Barnard (1938), Blau (1955), Crozier (1964, 1973), Williamson (1975), Aoki (1984), Crawford and Sobel (1982), Cross and Israelit (2000), Johnson and Libecap (1994), Krehbiel (1991), Sabel (1993), Stinchcombe (1990), Wilson (1989), and of course Weber (1946). The criteria are not faithful applications of any particular work. Instead, I have taken what appear to be useful concepts and have applied them to the problem of the organization of coercion as I have seen fit, and I have devised my own where this seemed appropriate.

6. In most cases, the principal is the chief executive, given that coercion is normally carried out through the executive branch. There can, of course, sometimes be competing principals (when there are struggles over who controls the executive).

7. Indeed, this is a standard distinction between analytical and operative functions in intelligence agencies (Smith 1983; Zegart 1999; Rudgers 2000). The problem of who monitors the monitor, discussed later in the chapter, is inherent in internal monitoring as an information-gathering strategy only. But it is made all the more significant (in the sense of high stakes) when monitors have not only the power to gather information but coercive capacities as well.

8. For example, Argentine President Juan Perón, and especially his wife Evita, would routinely hold audiences where the people lined up to speak with them directly.

9. However, the operations of external monitors such as Human Rights Watch or Amnesty International are not always directly proportionate to the level of coercive activity (Bob 2005).

10. There can, of course, be extraterritorial challenges, such as from foreign militaries or from breakaway regions not under the executive's control. These may be politically significant, but they are beyond the scope of this analysis, which focuses on the organization of coercion as it pertains to executive control within a given territory.

11. In chapter 8 I discuss how this matrix may be used to analyze other sorts of regimes and discuss the problem of the relationship between the organization of coercion and regime type.

12. This problem is complicated further by the increasing inefficiency in information flow as the number of bureaucratic layers increases (Crozier 1964).

13. O'Rourke (2000) uses the same phrase to denote a somewhat different phenomenon, where external monitors monitor each other.

THREE   The Overthrow and Turmoil

1. For an analysis of the political events that led to the coup, the classic source remains Valenzuela (1978). See also M. A. Garretón Merino (1989), González (2000), de Vylder (1976), and Sigmund (1977). For analyses of the political history of the Chilean armed forces, see Arriagada Herrera (1986) and A. Varas (1987).

2. The junta disbanded Congress through Decree Law (D.L.) No. 27, issued September 24. A few days later the Constitutional Tribunal, whose main purpose was to resolve conflicts between the executive and legislative branches of government, was also dissolved. The junta, in D.L. 50, stated that the tribunal was superfluous given that such conflicts could no longer "occur since Congress is disbanded" (Chilean National Commission on Truth and Reconciliation 1993, 58). The parties that had supported the Allende government mostly went underground after the coup, and all were formally disbanded on October 13, 1973, through Decree Law (D.L.) 77. D.L. No. 78, issued on October 17, suspended the activities of all other parties, declaring them "in recess" (Chilean National Commission on Truth and Reconciliation 1993, 58). D.L. No. 1697 of 1977 banned all political organizations altogether, from either the left or the right wing (Chilean National Commission on Truth and Reconciliation 1993, 58). The State Comptroller's Office (Contraloría) remained in operation but was taken over by the military. The judiciary was the only branch of the state that remained in operation and was

allowed, in theory, to remain independent. In the next chapter I discuss why and how in practice the judiciary capitulated to the new regime and failed to check its use of coercion. The only independent social institution that was allowed to continue to function was the church. As we will see in subsequent chapters, the participation of the church would later prove crucial to the mobilization of the opposition against the regime.

3. Television channels 9 and 13, belonging to the University of Chile and to the Catholic University, were quickly taken over by the military when they took control of each university. The government-run newspaper *La Nación* was taken over by military forces on the day of the coup. It resumed publication a few weeks later. The junta closed down the communist-run newspaper *El Siglo,* the pro-Allende *Puro Chile,* and the socialist-run *Noticias de Ultima Hora.* The conservative dailies *El Mercurio* and *La Tercera de la Hora,* long opposed to Allende, continued to publish without interruption. The weekly newsmagazine *Qué Pasa,* run by probusiness interests that supported the coup, also continued to publish without interruption. The magazine *Ercilla,* affiliated with the Christian Democratic Party (PDC), managed to continue publishing independently until 1977, when it was bought by a proregime business group (Sigmund 1977; González 2000; Huneeus 2000a).

4. The junta decreed a state of siege on the day of the coup through D.L. No. 3. D.L. No. 5, on September, 22, 1973, stipulated that the state of siege should be understood as "a state or time of war." The state of siege was renewed every six months until March 1978, when it was replaced by a "state of emergency" (Chilean National Commission on Truth and Reconciliation 1993, 58).

5. From the War Academy, the army had drawn up a plan of action in July 1973 that called for an overthrow of the government on September 14 (Whelan 1993, 450).

6. Admiral Sergio Huidobro, one of the key coup strategists, later wrote how in Santiago, which saw the fiercest resistance, "control over the city was achieved within a matter of hours" (Huidobro 1989, 269).

7. Although Chile was popularly known as the "Britain" of Latin America because of its ostensibly long and uninterrupted democratic tradition, this reputation is an inaccurate reflection of its history. The early independence years ushered in a period of civil war (1810–14). This was followed by a restoration of Spanish dictatorship through the Lima Viceroyalty (1814–17), the dictatorship of independence leader General Bernardo O'Higgins (1817–23), and a period of political uncertainty and institutional chaos (1823–30), leading finally to the creation of a the "Portalian State," an authoritarian republic of strong executive rule (1830–91). In the 1891 Civil War, essentially a fight between supporters of the executive and legislative

branches of government, the army supported the executive while the navy supported the legislature, which prevailed. From 1891 to 1924, a "Parliamentary Republic" ruled the country, but from 1924 to 1932 the army became involved again in politics, staging coups on two separate occasions and running the country during a four-month period in 1924. The end of this period saw the reimposition of an executive-led system. Political involvement made a deep impression on many sectors of the military. As a whole the different branches of the military were happy at the end of this period to return to the barracks. But the events of the 1920s meant that by the sixties and seventies, within living memory of many people, there had been a time when the military had been deeply involved in politics (Arriagada Herrera 1986; North 1986; Nunn 1994, 1997).

8. Cited in Arriagada Herrera (1985, 44–45). One of those involved in the plot against Schneider, Enrique Arancibia Clavel, would later become one of the top agents under the DINA. Arancibia went into exile in November 1970 and returned to Chile after the coup. He was arrested in Buenos Aires in 1996 and condemned in 2004 for his role in the assassination in Buenos Aires of Schneider's successor, General Carlos Prats, and his wife Sofía Cuthbert. See "Sentencia en el caso Enrique Lautaro Arancibia Clavel que confirma la imprescriptibilidad de los crímenes contra la humanidad," August 24, 2004, www.derechos.org/nizkor/arg/doc/arancibia1.html.

9. On the U.S. role, and especially that of Henry Kissinger, in the Schneider assassination, see Hitchens (2001a, 2001b).

10. This event should not be confused with the Tacnazo, the uprising led by General Roberto Viaux in October 1969, mentioned earlier.

11. General Fernando Arancibia, a major during 1973 and brother of Enrique Arancibia (a key DINA agent implicated in the assassinations of Generals Schneider and Prats), stated that "Prats was in the game of the Unidad Popular. He lost touch *[se desentendió]* with the thinking of his own people!" (interview, October 26, 1995). Prats never understood why his fellow soldiers, who for the most part did not come from the upper classes of Chilean society, would want to defend the interests of a minority of the Chilean population, albeit the minority with the balance of economic power. He asked, in an interview after the coup, "Why are those, whom I know so well, modest products of the middle class, in the service of the Pirañas *[sic]* or the Edwards?" (Harrington and González 1987, 184). The name Piraña, for all its evocative power, is most likely a typo or a mistake in transcription, since it is not the name of any prominent Chilean family. Most likely Prats said (or meant) Piñera, which, like the Edwards family, is one of the most prominent upper-class families in the country.

12. By Federico Willoughby, a close collaborator of the military government and a coup plotter as a leader of the right-wing armed movement, Patria y Libertad, quoted in Verdugo (1989, 14). Arellano was a leading anticommunist who had close contacts with the Christian Democratic Party (PDC), having been an *edecán* (aide-de-camp) under the Frei administration. General Oscar Bonilla, later to become the first minister of the interior under the junta, was another leading coup plotter, in part thanks to his contacts inside the PDC, having also been an *edecán* under Frei.

13. See also Arellano Iturriaga (1985) and F. Varas (1979).

14. Federico Willoughby, quoted in Verdugo (1989, 12).

15. A year-end report in the newspaper *La Nación* canvassed the opinions of several of the country's leading personalities on the event they thought the most important during the previous year. Pinochet surprisingly responded that surely it was the president's trip to the United Nations a few months earlier. The reasons, he argued, were that it meant

> an insistence that those countries struggling for their development be heard, understood, and supported by those countries that for many reasons have reached a level of development that allows their people material and emotional welfare; a demonstration that direct contact among governors, no matter what their ideologies, produces an effective and wide understanding that benefits those governed; an opening for effective cooperation and support not only with the country visited but also with international organisms and with numerous nations regardless of their ideological differences, which so often in history prove to be only transitory; an appreciable reduction of internal tensions, which are so damaging to the country's citizens. (*La Nación*, December 31, 1972)

16. Recently declassified U.S. government documents reveal that Pinochet had been in contact with, and paid by, the CIA as far back as 1972. While these documents suggest that Pinochet's involvement in coup plans may have begun earlier than previously thought, the jury is still out. It is possible that the CIA established contacts with Pinochet, but the relationship between these contacts and Pinochet's participation in the plans that actually took place remains unclear. Moreover, even if such contacts had taken place, they would not prove much, given that most senior officers were probably contacted. It would also be consistent with Pinochet's ability to play many different sectors off against each other (demonstrated once in power) that he had the capacity to maintain contacts with a range of different sectors, including Allende himself. For a list of recently declassified documentation on

Chile, see the Chile Documentation Project at the National Security Archive's Web site, www.gwu.edu/~nsarchiv/latin_america/chile.htm.

17. The navy was the institution that most actively pursued the idea of a coup, and it is likely that Carvajal, appointed defense chief of staff in January of 1973, was the key instigator. See, for example, Cavallo Castro, Salazar Salvo, and Sepúlveda Pacheco (1989, 126). See also Carvajal's memoirs (Carvajal 1993).

18. The transcript of these communications was originally published by María Olivia Monckeberg and Fernando Paulsen in *Análisis*, December 24–30, 1985 (Cavallo Castro, Salazar Salvo, and Sepúlveda Pacheco 1989, 135). There are various possible ways to interpret these communications. The most radical is that they reveal clear proof that the military as a whole sought to exterminate the opposition right from the beginning of the takeover. This seems a stretch, in my view, given that key actors like Pinochet jumped on board the coup at the last possible moment. A more plausible interpretation is that Pinochet's evident cruelty in these communications is a sign of his relatively weak position within the team that plotted and carried out the coup. Pinochet's tone throughout the exchanges differs sharply from the rest of the commanders. Whereas Carvajal and Leigh, the two principal interlocutors, are models of military professionalism and coolness in battle, Pinochet repeatedly interjects with exhortations about the need to show a firm hand and not give the enemy an inch more than necessary. It might be read as a "more papist than the pope" tone, in which he tries to ingratiate himself with the officers, like Carvajal, who really represented the center of power at the time. See also Carvajal (n.d., 87–112).

19. Although the Carabineros also have the manpower and infrastructure to cover the entire national territory, they lack the firepower of the army and have not always been considered part of the armed forces. Indeed, at the time of the coup, the Carabineros were actually under the command of the Ministry of the Interior rather than the Ministry of Defense and were technically not part of the armed forces. After the coup their status was changed: they came under the command of the Ministry of Defense and became the fourth branch of the armed forces.

20. In Brazil, Uruguay, and Peru, where reforms had been inspired by the French *armée*, military officers were also influenced by its anticommunism.

21. Also paraphrased in Arriagada Herrera (1986, 186).

22. Trinquier (n.d., 36–38) cited in Arriagada Herrera (1986, 199). See also Trinquier (1980).

23. The events in the Balkans during the 1990s—where groups of soldiers went on a rampage against civilian populations—might seem to con-

tradict this analysis. However, closer scrutiny reveals that highly trained specialized units committed the worst atrocities and that many common soldiers either stood aside or were themselves coerced into committing brutalities (see, e.g., Human Rights Watch 2000). Today, many common soldiers complain about the difficulty of watching while atrocities were being committed. While some of these complaints may be self-serving rationalizations, they are consistent with what we know about this kind of activity. Notwithstanding Arendt's claims about the "banality" of evil, such acts lie at the limits of human experience.

24. See also Chevigny (1999) and Pinheiro (1999).

25. Weiss Fagen argues that blurring the boundaries between military and police work had been taking place long before the coups, as a result of the doctrines of counterinsurgency and national security exported from Western Europe and the United States. She concludes that as a result, "the military overthrew the existing governments largely to permit greater institutional independence and freedom of action than was possible under civilian rule" (1992, 55). However, Weiss Fagen's explanation suffers from the standard problem of functionalist explanations: reading history backwards. Institutional reorganization did take place after the coups, but that does not mean that the coup was carried out to implement it. Instead, it is more appropriate to understand the kinds of reorganizations that took place as the result of new regimes that faced discrete and often unanticipated problems in how to rule, particularly how to organize coercion.

26. One of the first key decisions confronting the military was what to do with Allende. The official position, proclaimed by the junta on the day of the coup, was that Allende committed suicide. Although the opposition to the military dictatorship in Chile long doubted this story, the *Informe Rettig* later confirmed this version of events. The essential basis of this story is the declaration by "Allende's doctor," Patricio Guijón, who saw the president's body soon after General Palacios's troops stormed the Moneda Palace. Guijón heard shots in Allende's office, apparently, and went in to find the president holding the AK-47 given to him by Fidel Castro, which he had apparently fired directly under his chin. Former Allende aide Luis Vega recounts a different version of events. Vega had been a legal aide in the Ministry of the Interior and a member of Allende's security organization, the GAP (Grupo de Amigos del Presidente), and maintained numerous contacts inside the government as well as in the military. He recounts that on the day of the coup the main plan of action, "Plan Hércules," was led by Pinochet. At the same time, a second plan, "Plan Alfa," conceived to orchestrate Allende's "suicide," was crafted and implemented by Leigh, Merino, and Carvajal but without the knowledge of Pinochet. This would explain why during the radio

communications between Pinochet and Carvajal, before it became clear that Allende had perished, Pinochet at first ordered that Allende be taken out of the country. The actual assassination would have been carried out by personnel under the direction of General Ernesto Baeza soon after the storming of the palace. The key witness to the events, Dr. Enrique Paris, a close aide of Allende's, died a few days later in the Estadio Nacional. Vega was in prison with Dr. Guijón, whom he describes as a person who was "correct, serene, intelligent, and cultured" but not a Unidad Popular supporter or Allende's "personal physician," as he has been widely described; nor did he witness Allende's death firsthand. His entire testimony is based on his having seen the body after the death (Vega n.d., 283–91).

27. Although many Latin American constitutions explicitly gave the military this responsibility, the Chilean 1925 Constitution, in force at the time, did not. The Chilean military notably did not make any reference to specific articles of the constitution that allowed them to take power. In this sense, the coup may properly be labeled "unconstitutional" (Barros 2002). However, the belief that the military ought to intervene in politics was widely held and was consistent with a historical standard throughout Latin America (Loveman 1993, 1999).

28. Rillón had written *Ramón* Pinochet instead of *Augusto* (Cavallo Castro, Salazar Salvo, and Sepúlveda Pacheco 1989).

29. *Diario Oficial [D.O.],* September 18, 1973.

30. Actas de las Sesiones de la Honorable Junta de Gobierno, Santiago, 1973–89, No. 14, November 16, 1973.

31. D.L. No. 128, *D.O.,* November 16, 1973.

32. Actas de las Sesiones de la Honorable Junta de Gobierno, Santiago, 1973–89, No. 19, October 10, 1973.

33. The armed forces from the very beginning refused to use the word *coup* for the coup of September 11. Instead, they said they had staged a *pronunciamiento militar,* a military reaction to the chaos under the Unidad Popular.

34. *La Tercera,* April 8, 1997.

35. Actas de las Sesiones de la Honorable Junta de Gobierno, Santiago, 1973–89, No. 19, October 10, 1973.

36. See Ahumada et al. (1989, 386). The nature of this meeting has recently become the subject of debate. Journalists reported that according to ex-junta member and ex-Carabineros director General César Mendoza, Aylwin entered the meeting "with a smile that I found surprising, given that there were still shots being heard in the streets." He said Aylwin simply presented himself and declared that he and the Christian Democrats were thankful to the junta for having rid the country of the Marxist yoke. Aylwin, on the other

hand, recalled that the purpose and nature of the meeting was simply to "clear up the political recess" in the country and to express his party's concern about the human rights abuses being committed. According to Aylwin, Merino's revolver was the clearest indicator of the junta's intentions. The minutes of the meeting conclude by noting, "The president of the Christian Democracy ended by pleading that any charges against personnel of his party be made known to the Directive [of the PDC] in order to clear it up suitably, given that they realize that there is interest in making them seem to have attitudes contrary to those of the government" (Actas de las Sesiones de la Honorable Junta de Gobierno, Santiago, 1973–89, No. 19, October 10, 1973).

37. The main reason for the prominence of the army and the Carabineros is that these are the only branches of the armed forces with an institutional presence throughout the country. The navy and air force have bases far less widespread. The navy assumed control of public order in the province of Valparaíso (where it had its main headquarters), and the air force in the province of Llanquihue, where it had a strong presence. The rest of the county was effectively under the control of the army and the Carabineros (Comisión Nacional de Verdad y Reconciliación 1991).

38. This is especially noteworthy when compared to regimes such as Zaire under Mobutu or Haiti under the Duvaliers.

39. According to various interviews conducted by the author with former Chacabuco prisoners, the other purpose appears to have been to allow the Estadio Nacional to be used as a soccer stadium for a World Cup qualifying match.

40. Sergio Arellano Iturriaga, Arellano Stark's son, confirms that in October 1973 his father had received the "order to look over various trials [procesos] under way in the provinces." See Arellano Iturriaga (1985, 62), cited in Ahumada et al. (1989, 368).

41. Jaña also noted that despite the difference in rank he could talk to Arellano in this tone (e.g., "more timely orders" and "I don't know what war you are talking about") because Arellano at one point had been his student. Jaña also recounts his experiences on film in Ancelovici (1990). Plan Zeta was the name of an alleged plan by Allende and his followers to stage a self-coup that would allow them to purge their enemies inside the government and the armed forces.

42. Arellano himself has maintained that he is innocent of the crimes attributed to him and that other officers who traveled with him (specifically army colonel Sergio Arredondo) acted without his knowledge. Apart from the fact that this version clearly contradicts the military's official statements regarding the deaths, it is belied by numerous other declarations by witnesses and participants.

43. See also Ahumada et al. (1989, 357–60, 370, n. 353). Lagos's sworn testimony is reproduced in *APSI*, no. 188, December 14–28, 1987.

44. Pinochet himself has been linked to the crimes. Lagos reported to Pinochet on all the deaths that had taken place under his command. These were divided into the ones for which he was directly responsible and those (the majority) for which Arellano was responsible. Pinochet refused to sign this document, suggesting that Lagos simply lump all the deaths together in one column, which would essentially have meant that on paper he would take primary responsibility. Lagos did not do this and kept the original report, with Pinochet's corrections on the margins. In January 2001 he presented this document to Judge Juan Guzmán, at that time carrying out the Chilean investigation into the Arellano case (González 2001a, 2001b). Judge Guzmán indicted Pinochet as a coauthor of the crimes in December 2000, but in 2002 the Penal Chamber of the Supreme Court dismissed the case against him on medical grounds, citing his condition of "dementia." Dr. Luis Fornazzari, a Chilean-Canadian neurologist, dissented from the dementia diagnosis (Memoria y Justicia 2001). For more on the mission and its legal history, see Memoria y Justicia (2002).

45. The mission included major Pedro Espinoza, Marcelo Moren, and Lieutenant Armando Fernández Larios, all of whom would later become key DINA agents. Espinoza is currently serving a sentence, along with Manuel Contreras, for the assassination of Orlando Letelier, a crime in which Larios is also implicated.

46. General (ret.) Odlanier Mena, interview, *La Tercera*, March 12, 1998.

47. See also Verdugo (1989).

48. See Acta No.17. This reflects what was surely an exaggerated estimation prior to the coup of the size and strength of the opposition that the military would face once it took power. Even if the military was wrong about how well armed an opposition it would have to fight, the fears themselves were real. Barros argues that "the verbal violence of the months preceding the coup, with calls for a revolutionary resolution to the crisis, or, at a minimum, the armed defense of the government in the event of a coup, distorted military estimations of expected armed resistance. The fraudulence and irresponsibility of this revolutionary grandstanding was exposed on 11 September 1973 as the armed forces rapidly controlled the internal security situation and demonstrated the military preparedness of the Left to be negligible" (Barros 1996, 95).

49. Actas de las Sesiones de la Honorable Junta de Gobierno, Santiago, 1973–89, No. 17, October 18, 1973, items 1977 and 1913.

50. A little-understood and poorly documented episode in the dictator-ship's history is the very real danger of war that existed with Peru during the mid-1970s. The border tensions with Argentina in the late 1970s led to more public clashes, ending with papal mediation. The tensions with Peru re-mained secretive but no less threatening to the new regime. Future research once military archives are opened will map out the extent of the threats and the manner in which they influenced decision making on both sides of the border.

51. General Joaquín Lagos, for instance, was removed from his com-mand in Antofagasta several months later, in February 1974, by which time the DINA was already in full operation (Ahumada et al. 1989, 360).

52. The Comisión DINA was an informal group of officers that oper-ated in the days and weeks after the coup (originally as the "Grupo DINA"), which would later become formally established as the DINA (Comisión Na-cional de Verdad y Reconciliación 1991, pt. 2, ch. 1).

53. José Zalaquett, interview, September 16, 1996, Santiago, Chile.

54. Ibid.

55. Barros argues that the 1980 Constitution was essentially a mecha-nism to regulate power relationships among the junta members. It was not a vehicle for the accumulation of power by Pinochet (Barros 1996).

FOUR   The Rise of the DINA (1973–74)

1. See both the report of the Rettig Commission on Truth and Reconciliation, which documents cases of assassinations and disappearances, and the report of the Valech Commission on Political Imprisonment and Torture (Comisión Nacional de Verdad y Reconciliación 1991; Comisión Nacional sobre Prisión Política y Tortura 2004).

2. For classic statements of this view of authoritarianism, see Machia-velli (1950) and Friedrich and Brzezinski ([1956] 1965).

3. O'Shaughnessy adopts another version of this argument:

General Augusto Pinochet's use of overwhelming force to propel him and his comrades-in-arms into full control of the country was followed by the formulation of a medium-term strategy which would destroy any challenge to his own rule from inside or outside the country. His strat-egy was to a large extent planned by his former pupil Colonel Manuel Contreras Sepúlveda, known to his intimates as "Mamo." Apart from his wife and his mother Contreras was to be the person who had the most influence on Pinochet. . . . With the coup, Pinochet and his co-conspirators had undoubtedly stolen the initiative. There was no real organized resistance to the new regime in Chile. At home, the Junta had less to worry about from its political enemies than from opponents and rivals within the armed forces in particular the army. Similarly, outside the country the danger to his position came less from foreign enemies than from Chileans who might set up a government-in-exile. . . . The instrument chosen to deal with rivals within the armed forces and the exile community was the Directorate of National Intelligence, the DINA (2000, 64–65).

4. In Argentina, by contrast, junta members maintained a rotating presidency.

5. See, for example, M. Salazar Salvo (1995).

6. Pinochet's main enemy within the military—air force commander General Gustavo Leigh—fell from power *after* the DINA was replaced by the CNI, and his fall was not really a result of actions by the intelligence community.

7. Although the junta's power over legislation was reduced later in the regime, the unanimity rule was never dropped (Barros 1996, 2002).

8. The unanimity rule was essential to preserving the equal balance of power inside the junta and indeed to cobbling together the coup coalition in the first place.

9. The army had the Servicio de Inteligencia Militar (SIM), the air force the Servicio de Inteligencia de la Fuerza Aérea (SIFA), the navy the Servicio de Inteligencia Naval (SIN), and the national police the Servicio de Inteligencia de Carabineros (SICAR).

10. On Manuel Contreras, see M. Salazar Salvo (1995). On Fort Benning, which would later become the School of the Americas, see Gill (2004).

11. By and large, the staff came from the different military intelligence organizations, as well as from the Carabineros and "Investigaciones" and from civilian right-wing groups such as Patria y Libertad (Dinges and Landau 1980; Ahumada et al. 1989, ch. 16; Cavallo Castro, Salazar Salvo, and Sepúlveda Pacheco 1989, chs. 5 and 14). Some of the principal centers were Londres 38 (pictured on the cover of this book), Villa Grimaldi, and the center on José Domingo Cañas Street. All would become notorious as locations where tortures, murders, and disappearances were carried out.

12. Actas de las Sesiones de la Honorable Junta de Gobierno, Santiago, 1973–89, No. 33, November 12, 1973.

13. General (ret.) Odlanier Mena, interview, October 7, 1996, Santiago, Chile; Ensalaco (1999, 56). The *Informe Rettig* observes that although many

officers shared the DINA group's anticommunism and desire to mount an effective campaign of counterinsurgency, "the Commission knows that a good number of officials did not agree with the group, its activities, or its justifications, at least in 1973 and 1974, and expressed their disagreement to their superiors on a number of occasions both orally and in writing" (Chilean National Commission on Truth and Reconciliation 1993, 62).

14. A great amount of information on the behind-the-scenes decision making during the dictatorship has come to light recently. The archives of the junta's minutes, the only available written record of the history of the junta's meetings, represent an invaluable resource that greatly advances our understanding of the Chilean regime. But even these minutes often record items only by the most general of references. Little information is available in many cases on the precise nature of the debates among the different actors.

15. The minutes of the junta's meeting on November 5, 1973, record the junta's decision to forbid the visits by "unofficial" international organizations such as Amnesty International. The minutes read: "It should be decided whether to continue with these veritable inspection reviews, which in the end provide negative results and which are indirectly an intrusion into the country's internal politics. The junta decides to definitively terminate these visits" (Honorable Junta de Gobierno, Santiago, 1973–89, No. 28, November 25, 1973). A short time later, during the meeting of November 19, 1973, the junta approved the allocation of US$1 million to "maintain the propaganda campaign abroad, through the Ministry of Foreign Affairs" (Honorable Junta de Gobierno, Santiago, 1973–89, No. 37, November 19, 1973).

16. This was the conclusion the *Informe Rettig* reached, as well as the hypothesis of many in the human rights community in Chile during the dictatorship (José Zalaquett, interview, September 16, 1996, Santiago, Chile, September 16).

17. As I show later, beginning in 1974 the DINA staged a campaign of extermination against the MIR, the only political organization to have attempted any sort of armed resistance against the dictatorship during this period. The DINA also began to stage a series of international operations that included formal agreements and institutional arrangements with the other military dictatorships in the Southern Cone region to share prisoners and information—an arrangement known as Operación Cóndor—and to organize missions to assassinate prominent Chilean political leaders in exile.

18. Opposition groups were crucial, however, in mobilizing public opinion against the regime and in blocking access to resources such as international loans, especially after Carter assumed power and pursued a more aggressive human rights agenda.

FIVE   The DINA in Action (1974–77)

1. D.L. No. 527, Article 7, also decreed in June 1974, named the president of the junta (Pinochet) the "supreme commander of the nation." This essentially ended the principle of a rotating presidency, under which the junta had at first announced it would operate. Pinochet was not named president because at the time there was profound resistance to this from within the junta. Naming a president would have meant essentially accepting that the junta would be not simply a transitional regime but one that would hold power for a long time. This was the source of great conflict inside the junta, with some members (Leigh) opposed to being in power for a long time. By the end of 1974, however (through D.L. No. 806), Pinochet did take the title of president of the republic. Even though this represented the climax of his consolidation of power, it is important to note that Pinochet was not given a key power that civilian Chilean presidents had always enjoyed: the power to designate and remove the heads of the armed forces (Arriagada Herrera 1988, 139). The military president of a military government, in other words, lacked the power to interfere in the internal affairs of the other branches of the armed forces. Moreover, neither D.L. No. 527 nor D.L. No. 806 did away with the unanimity rule of voting inside the junta. Even with Pinochet as president, the junta retained the unanimity rule, and Pinochet lacked the power to overrule it. This was far less than Pinochet originally wanted, as evidenced by analysis of drafts of proposed versions of D.L. No. 527 found in the minutes of Pinochet's advisory body, the Junta Assistant Committee (COAJ). For an informative discussion and analysis of this crucial period in the division of powers between the junta and the newly created presidency, see Barros (1996, 29–39; 2001).

2. By tradition in Chile, laws do not take effect until they are published in the *Diario Oficial*. Because Articles 9–11 were intended to be secret, the junta got around the publication requirement by publishing these in an annex of the *Diario Oficial* with very limited circulation. This is an example of the kind of pressure to properly use formal legal mechanisms that the Comptroller's Office brought to bear on the junta. The decision to publish the articles probably represents a compromise between the junta's natural desires for secrecy and the comptroller's worries that decrees needed to be formally legal.

3. Also José Zalaquett, interview, September 16, 1996, Santiago, Chile.

4. The only secret police institution in the Southern Cone more powerful than the DINA in terms of scope and depth of activities was Brazil's Na-

tional Information Service (SNI). Unlike the DINA, the SNI also set up its own intelligence academy, which allowed it to control the state bureaucracy to a far greater extent than the DINA (Stepan 1988).

5. The number of people working for the DINA is difficult to determine. According to one estimate, by 1977 the DINA probably employed up to ten thousand people directly, with two or three times as many people as paid informants (S. Collier and Sater 1996, 360). The Vicaría de la Solidaridad, the principal human rights organization that had emerged at the time, in 1975 stated that according to "indirect information and rumors," they believed the staff to number between three thousand and nine thousand.

6. For more on the DINA's structure, see Kornbluh (2003, esp. 164–99).

7. The great variation in the treatment of prisoners meant that those taken by institutions such as the Air Force Intelligence Service (SIFA) were far more likely to be severely tortured or summarily executed than those taken by Investigaciones, the civilian police force.

8. The true extent and purpose of the DINA's operations was not immediately obvious, and many prisoners in places such as the Estadio Chile report that they greeted the DINA's appearance with relief. Instead of having to be interrogated by a multiplicity of institutions (such as "Investigaciones," the Carabineros, the SIM, and SICAR), under the DINA all interrogations would be centralized in one place. Potentially, this meant less time in prison waiting for one's case to move through the various institutions' bureaucracies (author's interviews with former Estadio Chile and Chacabuco prisoners).

9. Padilla writes that relatives or friends' "lack of information on the victims made it impossible to know exactly who carried out the detention. From the beginning of 1974 until August 1977, many testimonies blame security agents and other such groups, when in fact the detentions were carried out, as would be shown later, by DINA agents" (Padilla Ballesteros 1995, 52).

10. This was implied in an April 1974 CIA report comparing how the DINA and other Chilean armed forces agencies treated prisoners (Central Intelligence Agency 1974).

11. The large detention centers continued to operate, run mostly by the army and the Carabineros, though after 1974 few new prisoners were held there. By mid-1975 most of the army-run concentration camps and detention centers were closed, and very few political prisoners remained whose condition it was possible for outsiders to monitor.

12. The Chilean Communist Party had traditionally rejected violence in the pursuit of revolution, but they broke with this policy in 1980 as a result

of a shift in doctrine at the international level in response to the rise of authoritarian regimes throughout Latin America.

13. *Punto Final*, no. 53, April 23, 1968, quoted in Sigmund (1977, 69).

14. Pinochet Ugarte (1974) quoted in Cavallo Castro, Salazar Salvo, and Sepúlveda Pacheco (1989).

15. International criticism against the DINA had already begun to reverberate at the top of the Chilean government before this incident. A CIA memo dated January 30, 1975, noted, "Several army generals have [deleted] approached President Augusto Pinochet and presented corroborated accounts of torture and mistreatment of detainees by the; [sic] DINA. They have also presented proofs of amateur tactics on the part of DINA officials in the course of the latters [sic] intelligence collecting activities. A number of high ranking army officers agree that DINA's methods of operation have done a great deal to tarnish Chile's international image" (Central Intelligence Agency 1975).

16. Recently declassified documents have lent weight to previous speculations that the U.S. government knew in detail about Cóndor. The evidence also suggests that U.S. forces to some extent cooperated with the operation (Martorell 1999; Marquis and Schemo 2000; McSherry 2000, 2005; Schemo 2001; Kornbluh 2003; Dinges 2004).

17. In August 1975, U.S. ambassador to Chile David Popper cabled the State Department regarding information over Cóndor planned assassinations. He noted, "Cooperation among southern cone national intelligence agencies is handled by the Directorate of National Intelligence (DINA), apparently without much reference to anyone else. It is quite possible, even probable, that Pinochet has no knowledge whatever of Operation Cóndor, particularly of its more questionable aspects." David Popper, Telegram to Secretary of State, Washington, D.C., August 7, 1975, www.gwu.edu/~nsarchiv/NSAEBB/NSAEBB125/condor07.pdf.

18. Clavel is currently serving a life sentence in Argentina for the assassination of General Carlos Prats in Buenos Aires; see Kornbluh (2003); Associated Press (2004).

19. Currently, he is a fugitive from justice after having been sentenced in Chile and Italy for a number of crimes committed during the dictatorship (Délano 2007; *La Nación* 2007).

20. A copy of the invitation to the meeting exists in Asunción's "Archivo del Terror" (the archives of the Asunción Police Department, discovered in 1992). Dated October 1975, it states, "Colonel CONTRERAS requests that Genal [sic] BRITES [Chief of Asunción Police Force] honor him with his presence, in the company of some of his advisors, because he hopes that this meeting may be the foundation of an excellent coordination and better ac-

tivity to benefit the national security of our respective countries." The meeting took place in Santiago from November 25 to December 1, 1975. An internal report by Mr. Brites in response to the invitation, also in the archive, suggests that coordination between the Chilean and the Paraguayan intelligence agencies lacked some basic pieces of information. Brites writes: "It is surprising that they did not consult with us prior to sending this. The Capital's police force does not operate at the national level." See Folio 47 DI, Centro de Documentación y Archivo para la Defensa de los Derechos Humanos, Asunción, Paraguay). Uruguayan journalist Samuel Blixen, a leading expert on Operación Cóndor, found a letter from Manuel Contreras to Pinochet in the Paraguayan archive. In the letter, dated September 16, 1975, Contreras requests US$600,000 to pay for an "increase in DINA personnel affiliated to foreign embassies." The letter details that two agents would be assigned to each of the embassies in Peru, Brazil, and Argentina; one agent would be assigned to each embassy in Venezuela, Costa Rica, Belgium, and Italy. Contreras also argues that the money would go toward covering the "additional expenses for the neutralization of the principal adversaries of the [military] junta abroad, especially in Mexico, Argentina, Costa Rica, United States, and France, and Italy." On January 21, 1999, he presented the letter to Spanish Judge Baltasar Garzón in relation to the latter's ongoing case against Pinochet. See *El País*, January 22, 1999. See also Blixen (1994, 1996, 1997a, 1997b, 1998), Blixen and Bergalli (1998), Calloni (1994), and Cuya (1996). Paraguay officially joined Operación Cóndor in July 1976. For an overview of human rights violations in Paraguay, see Simon (1992). For a testimonial account of Paraguay's role in Operación Cóndor, see Meilinger de Sannemann (1993).

21. It would ostensibly be implemented in three phases. Phase 1 covered storage of prisoners and exchange of information on the enemy. Phase 2 included joint operations between Cóndor member countries within those same countries, and phase 3 aimed at creating jointly operated teams from member countries that could strike at enemies anywhere in the world. For examples of intelligence exchanges and two-country operations, see Comisión Nacional de Verdad y Reconciliación (1991), CONADEP ([1984] 1995), Meilinger de Sannemann (1993), and Martorell (1999). It is likely that the Letelier assassination was intended as part of phase 3.

22. For an in-depth investigative account of the case, see Harrington and González (1987).

23. FBI agent Robert Scherrer indicated shortly after the assassination that it was very likely a Cóndor operation. His declassified report, "FBI, Operation Condor Cable, September 28, 1976," can be found at www.gwu.edu/~nsarchiv/NSAEBB/NSAEBB8/ch23-01.htm.

24. It is probably not a coincidence that these crimes took place at roughly the same time of year. September 18 is Chile's Independence Day, September 19 is Armed Forces Day, and the entire month of September is known as *el mes de la patria*. National elections traditionally took place on September 4, and the coup took place on September 11. Michael Townley suggested that he was pressured to ensure that Letelier would be killed during the month of September for symbolic purposes (Dinges and Landau 1980).

25. It might have been possible to achieve higher internal monitoring without centralizing coercion under an organization like the DINA, but efforts in this direction (such as the Arellano mission) were tried without success. The DINA's principal mission was to streamline coercion by increasing internal monitoring through centralization, but it failed to deliver on this.

SIX   The Fall of the DINA (1977–78)

1. The 1980 Constitution marked a fundamental institutional shift, but the events of 1977–78 were a critical precondition, without which the constitution would have been unlikely (Huneeus 2000a, 2000b; Barros 2002).

2. In a speech delivered on national television and radio on June 15, 1978, Interior Minister Sergio Fernández declared that the amnesty "constitutes an eloquent testimony of the spirit of national reconciliation that inspires the government . . . and [shows] that the most acute stage of the internal emergency that we are living through can today be considered happily over." (See transcript in Guzmán archives, 01260, DEH 78.01, Fundación Jaime Guzmán, Santiago, Chile).

3. Leslie Bethell, for example, suggests that the DINA and the CNI were virtually identical: "General Pinochet's centralization of power owed a great deal to [his] control over the DINA (later renamed the Central Nacional de Informaciones [CNI] in an attempt to introduce some cosmetic changes). . . . The newly named CNI essentially performed the same functions as the old DINA" (1993, 187–88).

4. These included Villa Grimaldi and the building in Jose Domingo Cañas, both of which were used as detention and torture centers.

5. The CNI's powers were expanded in 1984 through the Antiterrorist Law, which allowed it to make arrests without a court order.

6. See Comisión Nacional sobre Prisión Política y Tortura (2004). It is likely that this was a result of the fact that the CNI, unlike the DINA, enjoyed closer working relationships with the different branches of the armed forces, especially the army itself.

7. Its best-known bases of operations in Santiago were its headquarters in Avenida República No. 517 and its detention center in Borgoño No. 1470 (Chilean National Commission on Truth and Reconciliation 1993, 640). It also operated out of the DINA's former center in Villa Grimaldi.

8. There is some evidence of informal continuity of some of the networks of cooperation and information sharing established under Cóndor at least until the early-mid 1990s: for example, surrounding the capture and assassination of former DINA agent turned liability Eugenio Berríos. Berríos had escaped to Montevideo to avoid giving testimony against the DINA. His body turned up thirty kilometers from Montevideo on April 13, 1995, and it is likely that his assassination was the work of former DINA and Cóndor operatives (Blixen 1994; Blixen and Bergalli 1998).

9. The Comisión Nacional sobre Prisión Política y Tortura notes that the DINA "sought to systematically eliminate those persons who tried to clandestinely rearticulate those parties or movements that . . . were tainted with the stigma of Marxism" (2004, 195).

10. The timing of this does not completely support Sigmund's claim, insofar as President Carter came into office only in January 1977 and a large number of prisoners had already begun to be released as early as 1975. Nevertheless, the United States did pressure the Chileans on the human rights violations and on the disappearances, with U.S. Ambassador Popper holding high-level meetings with Chilean generals during 1976 and early 1977. See "Additional Documents on Human Rights Prepared by the Vicariate of Solidarity," American Embassy (Popper) to Department of State, August 17, 1976, http://foia.state.gov/documents/pinochet/91ca.PDF; "Chile: Dialogue on Human Rights Matters," American Embassy (Popper), Santiago, to Secretary of State, December 14, 1976, http://foia.state.gov/documents/pinochet/9b96.PDF; and "Chile: A Review of Human Rights," American Embassy (Popper) to Secretary of State, January 18, 1977, http://foia.state.gov/documents/pinochet/9404.PDF.

11. For an analysis of the judiciary's continued support of the regime against international pressures, see Hilbink (1999).

12. For example, in October 1976, U.S. Ambassador Popper cabled Washington to report a dinner meeting with the then–Chilean interior minister (General) Cesar Benavides Escobar and secretary-general of government (Brig. General) Hernán Bejares González, "regarding what might be done by [the government of Chile] to moderate international criticism of Chile on human rights grounds." Popper noted that about three weeks after his meeting the Chilean government "announced release of over 300 political prisoners being held without trial. . . . While we have no basis for connecting the release with the dinner conversation, it was clearly a step designed in

large part to assuage foreign opinion. Subsequently, top GOC [government of Chile] military have continued to express interest in what they might do to improve Chile's position overseas, particularly in the United States." See "Chile: Dialogue on Human Rights Matters," American Embassy (Popper), Santiago, to Secretary of State, December 14, 1976, http://foia.state.gov/documents/pinochet/9b96.PDF. See also "'Interview with Chilean Air Force General Leigh," American Embassy (Popper) to Secretary of State, February 18, 1976, http://foia.state.gov/documents/pinochet/918f.PDF.

13. Reagan at first was far more sympathetic to the Chilean regime than Carter, for whom human rights had been a major policy agenda. Later on, however, the Reagan administration also began to pressure Chile over the human rights problem (Jacoby 1986).

14. Padilla Ballesteros (1995) incorrectly points out that the amnesty benefited *both* the DINA and the CNI. As I discuss later in this book, the CNI benefited from the amnesty only for acts committed during a short period— until 1978. No CNI acts after the promulgation of the amnesty were covered, a lack of legal protection that had profound consequences regarding the application of coercion.

15. Padilla Ballesteros writes that "various reforms were implemented inside the armed forces in order to ensure greater unity and concentration of power in the top command, to permit greater internal cohesion, homogeneity, and a single line of command" (1995, 19).

16. Indeed, the idea that even totalitarian dictatorships are necessarily monolithic was refuted long ago (Moore 1950, 1954; Deutsch 1954; Friedrich and Brzezinski [1956] 1965; Friedrich 1970).

17. See also Cristi (2000) and J. Salazar Salvo (1994).

18. D. L. 2191 was published in *D.O.,* April 19, 1978. Justice Minister Mónica Madariaga, who defended the amnesty on the grounds of bringing national reconciliation and "a new era of peace," drafted the law. Although some political prisoners were released under the law's benefits, the overwhelming majority of those who benefited from the law were state agents. Indeed, until the mid- to late 1990s (when the Supreme Court began to interpret the law in a different way than before), it served as the linchpin to prevent prosecutions into the human rights violations during the 1973–78 period (Mónica Madariaga, interview, January 20, 1997, Santiago, Chile). Also, Miguel Schweitzer, one of Fernandez's top aides at the time (and later Pinochet's counsel in London while he was under arrest there), noted that Pinochet had at first opposed the amnesty (interview, December 17, 1966, Santiago, Chile; also Schweitzer 1998, 205).

19. Also Miguel Schweitzer, interview, December 17, 1996, Santiago, Chile.

20. The extent of Guzmán's criticism of the DINA's human rights violations recently became a subject of some controversy, at the time of the tenth anniversary of his April 1991 assassination. (He was killed by members of the armed wing of the Communist Party, the Frente Patriótico Manuel Rodríguez.) It is true that Guzmán strongly criticized the DINA toward the end of the military regime, in the late 1980s, as the quote above suggests. And his disputes with Contreras on other grounds are well known. Contreras blamed Guzmán for failing to build support for the regime and used the DINA to spy on him and his supporters, a vigilance Guzmán deeply resented. There is also evidence of Guzmán having acted in private on behalf of people he was personally acquainted with and who had been detained by the regime. For example, my review of the archives at the Fundación Jaime Guzmán revealed several letters from public figures in the center and left either requesting aid from Guzmán or thanking him for his intervention on their behalf. But notwithstanding these actions, the evidence does not support his supporters' claim that Guzmán was a strong and principled defender of human rights during the time of the regime. Even though he was deeply religious, Guzmán strongly criticized the church on several occasions for its antiregime stance, and he supported the measures to send several high-profile Christian Democratic critics of the regime into exile. For a thorough discussion of Guzmán's relationship to the regime's coercive policies, see Huneeus (2000a, 342–51).

21. Actas del Consejo del Estado, Santiago, Session 14, March 29, 1977. Debates over human rights violations had taken place within the government from the earliest periods. In the Comisión Constituyente, some members argued for ensuring the protection of citizens' rights (an obvious reference to the then-current situation), while others argued that while defending people's rights was well and good, the "practical exigencies" of rebuilding the country demanded that more pragmatic prescient principles be adopted. República de Chile, Actas Oficiales de la Comisión Constituyente (Santiago: Talleres Gráficos Gendarmería de Chile), esp. Session 9, October 23, 1973.

22. El Mercurio, May 28, 1977, quoted in Quezada (1978, 362).

23. El Mercurio had in fact begun reporting on the human rights–based international critiques as early as 1976, something the U.S. Embassy noted with approval (though noting that El Mercurio made sure to rebut the allegations against the regime); see "El Mercurio and the Chilean Internal Debate on Human Rights," Airgram, American Embassy to Department of State, June 22, 1976: http://foia.state.gov/documents/pinochet/93a6.PDF.

24. Quoted in Quezada (1978, 362).

25. Ercilla, March 28, 1977, quoted in Quezada (1978, 362). As suggested above, government officials abroad also faced embarrassing critiques

over the DINA's human rights record. UN Ambassador Sergio Díez, in a November 1977 speech before the UN Human Rights Commission, admitted, "The most serious situation facing Chile is that of the disappeared." He added, "While the government is certain about the absolute innocence of the Chilean government in any situation having to do with the disappeared . . . we do not want to hide anything, we want to clear everything up, and if the investigations indicate that Chilean government officials are involved, I can assure this commission that, as the president of the republic has affirmed, these people will be severely punished. . . . This problem is of such grave importance and delicacy that I call upon the working group to collaborate with the Chilean government in our investigation on the fate of the disappeared" (Quezada 1978, 362). Quezada added, "One does not make these solemn declarations before such an official without accepting as a premise the existence of serious irregularities" (363). His article was written in the *Vicaría*'s monthly publication, *Mensaje*, and its reflections can be interpreted as a signal that the *Vicaría* itself knew about the growing discontent with the DINA from within government circles.

26. The importance of this cannot be overemphasized. The Chilean military is a rigidly hierarchical institution, and such a disruption of military rank was bound to cause deep resentment (Sohr 1989).

27. General (ret.) Fernando Arancibia stated that "it would have made no sense politically for Chile" to have killed Letelier, that "clearly the CIA was behind it," and that "I would have cut their balls off if I'd found someone here responsible." (interview, October 26, 1995, Santiago, Chile). For the argument that the assassination was a CIA-inspired plot to destabilize the Pinochet government, see Morete Alnar (1987).

28. In the same interview, however, Arancibia also stated that "in order to fight bandits you have to take a tough line. Sometimes you have to hang them up by the balls."

29. The rivalry between the two men went back to the beginning of their military careers, as students in the Military Academy in the 1940s (Frühling 2000).

30. General (ret.) Odlanier Mena, interview, October 7, 1996, Santiago, Chile. Mena was brought out of retirement and out of virtual exile as ambassador to Uruguay in February 1978 to take over the command of the CNI. He had gone to Uruguay in part because of discontent over Contreras's rise (Cavallo Castro, Salazar Salvo, and Sepúlveda Pacheco 1989, 134–36; Comisión Nacional de Verdad y Reconciliación 1991). Jaime Castillo Velasco, a leading opposition figure and a senior member of the Christian Democratic Party, also has come to believe that Contreras "was not a good security chief. He wasn't rigorous. Those people acted with such impunity

that they didn't worry about the details. They improvised. In other words, I actually believe them when they say they have no information on the disappeared" (interview, November 15, 1995, Santiago, Chile).

31. As we saw in chapter 3, at the time of the coup the military lacked a clear vision of what to do with power once it had it. When it took power, the junta announced that it would remain in power for only a short time. Bando No. 5, issued the day of the coup, stated that the purpose of the coup was simply to restore political and economic order and to return power quickly to civilian authorities. General Sergio Arellano's son notes that during this time military officers and civilian allies commented in casual conversation that 1976—the end of Allende's presidential term—would be a likely date to return power to civilians (Arellano Iturriaga 1985; Huneeus 2000a). Nevertheless, a different view soon took hold among the members of the junta. On October 11, 1973, Pinochet delivered a speech in which he noted: "Reconstruction is always slower and harder than destruction. Because of this, we know that our mission will not be as fleeting as we might wish, and as a result we are not stating specific timetables or dates. Only when the country reaches the necessary social peace, to attain the true progress and economic development to which it is entitled, and there are no more hatreds, that is when our mission will have been accomplished" (quoted in Huneeus 2000a).

32. Leigh was more senior than Pinochet, but as head of the air force he commanded fewer resources than Pinochet did as head of the army. Leigh, along with Commander Merino of the navy, had also been one of the original planners of the coup, a plot that Pinochet had joined only at the eleventh hour. Participation in the coup was an important source of legitimacy within the new regime, and this put Pinochet at a distinct disadvantage. Within the army, Pinochet systematically outmaneuvered the entire "coup class," those among his colleagues who had taken part in the coup (Arriagada Herrera 1988; Cavallo Castro, Salazar Salvo, and Sepúlveda Pacheco 1989; Barros 1996; Huneeus 2000a).

33. For a comprehensive analysis of the risks of political involvement for military professionalism, see Stepan (1988).

34. The junta had appointed a commission of constitutional and legal experts to study the possibility of drafting a constitution. The commission was made up mostly of figures closely tied to former right-wing president Jorge Alessandri (1958–64) and to other conservative political sectors. It included Enrique Ortúzar (justice minister under Alessandri, 1958–64), Sergio Diez (National Party senator), and Jaime Guzmán. Jorge Ovalle (former Radical Party member who was a constitutional law expert at the Universidad de Chile) was the sole exception. A few weeks later four more commissioners were added. Of these, two came from the Christian Democratic Party

and one from the Liberal Party. The fourth was a woman who did not belong to any political party but who was an ideological conservative nevertheless (Huneeus 2000a).

35. Moreover, these views are on some level complementary with explanations that focus on international factors. As we saw, the timing of the shifts and some of the particular outcomes can be explained according to international factors.

36. Leigh's departure followed months of increasing tension between the two leaders over the question of how long the regime would last, the division of powers between the executive and the junta, and what Leigh saw as the personalization of power around Pinochet. His fall was triggered by comments Leigh made in an interview with the Italian newspaper *Corriere della Sera*, suggesting that the country could not "keep denying liberty indefinitely" (F. Varas 1979; Cavallo Castro, Salazar Salvo, and Sepúlveda Pacheco 1989, 222–24; Cossio 2005).

37. Critically, throughout the regime the junta retained its unanimity rule, giving veto power to each of its members. Moreover, the commanders in chief of the armed forces retained full control over their respective branches, which Pinochet was unable to override. This meant that as president Pinochet was not given a power that all previous civilian Chilean presidents had enjoyed: the power to appoint the heads of the different armed forces branches (Barros 1996).

SEVEN   Options and Shifts

1. This constraint did not prevent the regime from turning against human rights workers, however. For example, in August 1976 the regime kidnapped and sent into exile two prominent centrist human rights lawyers, Jaime Castillo and Eugenio Velasco.

2. As discussed in the previous chapter, the judiciary received information on human rights violations through the *recursos de amparo* but overwhelmingly failed to use this knowledge to check the executive's use of coercion. A central reason for this was that that the civil courts ruled that cases involving actions of military personnel belonged in the military courts. The cases were closed without further investigation. The military courts, over which the Supreme Court had no jurisdiction, were run by military personnel. Once in the military court system, the cases were simply ignored. In some cases members of the civil courts attempted to carry out their own ad hoc investigations (García Villegas 1990; Hilbink 1999).

3. Mena argued that placing the CNI more clearly under the command of the cabinet established a "guarantee to citizens because one knows for cer-

tain the channels through which information is directed, given the existence of a Ministry accessible to the public" (quoted in United Nations 1978, 32). Mena obviously exaggerates the accessibility of the Ministry of the Interior to the general public at large, but this exaggeration is less than might be imagined. A more precise description would have been "accessible to right-wing civilians." Nevertheless, a civilian-led cabinet was a significant departure for the regime, permitting conservative civilian sectors a great deal of influence and control (Guzmán Errázuriz 1992; Fernández 1994; Huneeus 2000a, 2000b; Barros 2002).

4. The CNI appears to have set up some front organizations (such as Chilean Anti-Communist Action Group, or ACHA, or the September 11 Command). The *Informe Rettig* notes that there are "grounds for presuming that [such] organizations . . . which publicly took credit for some of the killings, were names that the CNI used to conceal its activities or those of people working for it" (Chilean National Commission on Truth and Reconciliation 1993, 639).

5. For example, this included civilian operators such as Michael Townley, Enrique Arancibia Clavel, and Eugenio Berríos (the chemist who led DINA experiments with sarin gas). It also included association with Miami-based anti-Castro Cubans (such as Virgilio Paz and Dionisio Suárez) to carry out the Letelier assassination, and with right-wing paramilitary groups in Italy in the Leighton case. The DINA also built relationships with Argentine paramilitaries such as the Triple A.

6. General Odlanier Mena indicated that one of Contreras's most serious mistakes had been not only to associate with civilians such as Townley but also to allow them to obtain such high-level access within the organization. This turned out to be a grave security risk after Townley turned state's witness in the United States over the Letelier case (General [ret.] Odlanier Mena, interview, October 7, 1996, Santiago, Chile).

7. After the murder, Contreras gave an anonymous interview in the newspaper *La Tercera*, in which he charged Mena with losing the fight against terrorism. Mena retaliated by charging Contreras with corruption (Cavallo Castro, Salazar Salvo, and Sepúlveda Pacheco 1989, 301; Huneeus 2000a, 505, 541 n. 524).

8. For example, a 1981 bank robbery near the Chuquicamata copper mine that was originally attributed to the MIR proved to have been carried out by CNI agents (Huneeus 2000a, 506).

9. In one respect, the full extent of which is hard to gauge at this point without being able to delve inside DINA and CNI archives, it is possible that internal monitoring may have decreased with the CNI. Although the CNI

inherited the bulk of the DINA's personnel and physical infrastructure, it is likely that Contreras took what appears to be a great deal information with him (in the form of archives). How many documents he took, or their relative value, is not clear. Nevertheless, this suggests a reason why, at least with respect to its capacity as information clearinghouse, the CNI might have been less effective than the DINA.

10. General (ret.) Odlanier Mena, interview, October 7, 1996, Santiago, Chile.

11. The nature of the conversation reveals either surprising naïveté or astonishing cynicism on the part of Mena. During the meeting, in response to the bishops' natural inquiries on the matter of the disappeared, Mena told them that "there are people who are not here," but that "there are no political prisoners at this moment." Mena notes that he was disappointed that the bishops did not believe him (General [ret.] Odlanier Mena, interview, October 7, 1996, Santiago, Chile). Given the regime's record, it is not surprising, to put it mildly, that the church authorities did not react kindly to Mena's claim. Still, the fact that such a meeting took place at all signaled an important shift.

12. Jaime Castillo Velasco, interview, November 15, 1995, Santiago, Chile.

13. Ibid; Andrés Domínguez Vial, interview, August 16, 1995, Santiago, Chile.

14. Jaime Castillo Velasco, interview, November 15, 1995, Santiago, Chile.

15. It is unlikely that this contact was established as a way to spy on the CChDH. The CNI did not lack ways to monitor opposition groups. There were far more effective ways to do this (such as the common practice of telephone tapping). The hot line provided the far rarer opportunity for direct communication with the CChDH's leadership.

16. The decree stipulated that because of the "general tranquility, peace, and order" the country now enjoyed, it was necessary to leave "behind hostilities that are now of no importance" (D.L. 2191, April 18, 1978).

17. Indeed, until the mid- to late 1990s (when the Supreme Court began to interpret the law in a different way than before), the decree prevented prosecutions of the human rights violations during the 1973–78 period.

18. However, the case was closed after the court recognized the guilt of the policemen involved.

19. See also García Villegas (1990).

20. For a full account, see García Villegas (1990).

21. For a comprehensive account of the Supreme Court's exercise of its institutional capacities against dissidents, see Hilbink (1999).

22. The circumstances surrounding Leigh's removal suggest such a possibility. He was ousted for publicly criticizing the institutionalization plans, accusing Pinochet of a power grab, and demanding a quick transition to a civilian government (González 2000).

EIGHT   The Politics of Organizing Coercion

1. The Triple A was set up in 1974 by José Lopez Rega, President Isabel Perón's minister of social welfare, often called the "Rasputin of the Pampas" (Andersen 1993, 94–123; Brysk 1994, 30 n. 50–52; CONADEP [1984] 1995, xi–xii). The Triple A was a "loosely organized 'federation' of death squad-style organizations directed or assisted by organs of the state, including SIDE, the state intelligence service, and the Social Welfare Ministry. . . . There were also links to the authoritarian-nationalist current of the army . . . [and] between the Triple A and European fascists and terrorists, including the Franco regime in Spain and the Italian fascist lodge Propaganda-Due (P-2)" (McSherry 1997, 72–73).

2. It is nevertheless telling that the myth of the Dirty War is also perpetuated by sectors within the Peronist Party (Partido Justicialista). The undersecretary for human rights under the (Peronist) Menem government, Dr. Alicia Pierini, argued that the Peronists have a "different view" of human rights than many other sectors in society. "We experienced a civil war," she noted, "where *we* suffered the blunt of the repression." She also argued that the war ended with a "peace treaty" in which each side made compromises. "The military accepted democracy, and we accepted the pardons *(indultos)* [issued by Menem]" (Dr. Alicia Pierini, interview, April 26, 1996, Buenos Aires, Argentina).

3. An official document stated that "the Armed Forces took over the political power *[sic]* of the Argentine Republic, together with the responsibility of curbing the progressive disintegration of the State . . . so as to subsequently redirect the country towards order, productive work, and progress under democracy." República Argentina, Poder Ejecutivo Nacional, *Terrorism in Argentina: Evolution of Terrorist Delinquency in Argentina* (Buenos Aires, 1980), p. 1, quoted in McSherry (1997, 89). The source is an official publication of the Argentine junta published (and translated into English) to counter growing international critiques (McSherry 1997, 325 n. 317).

4. By contrast, the Chilean army is unquestionably the dominant branch within the armed forces. Pinochet, as head of the army and the armed forces at the time of the coup, was also named head of the junta. This appointment was a recognition of his de facto status as primus inter pares

among the junta members, even though, unlike the heads of the navy and air force, he had joined the coup plots only at the last minute.

5. In Chile, only the army and the Carabineros had an organizational reach that extended throughout the country. The navy and air force took and held prisoners in their respective regiments and bases, but their reach was limited by the fact that they had far fewer bases. The navy, however, was essentially given control over the city of Valparaíso, the most important port and the center of naval operations.

6. The quote within this Brysk quotation is from Moncalvillo and Fernández (1985, 29–33).

7. "Despite all the SED's efforts to depict the upheaval as a fascist putsch or the work of West German provocateurs," Maier observes, "the movement revealed how alien and dependent on a continuing Soviet presence the regime remained. Until the disappearance of the GDR, the uprising remained an anxious memory; as their authority evaporated in 1989, Politbüro members repeatedly asked whether unrest had become as serious as it had been in 1953" (1997, 15).

8. On Dzerzhinskii and the Cheka, in English, see Leggett (1981).

9. Which makes him one of the most durable intelligence chiefs in history, perhaps even the most durable.

10. Apartheid law divided the population into four major racial groups: Africans (blacks), whites, coloreds, and Asians. This law was abolished in 1991, but many South Africans still view themselves and each other according to these categories. I use the term *black* instead of *African,* but others whom I cite use the older term.

11. The *Truth and Reconciliation Commission Report* states: "For at least 3.5 million black South Africans [apartheid] meant collective expulsions, forced migration, bulldozing, gutting or seizure of homes, the mandatory carrying of passes, forced removals into rural ghettos and increased poverty and desperation" (Truth and Reconciliation Commission 1999, 34).

12. Nadine Gordimer observed, "We shall not be rid of censorship until we are rid of apartheid. Censorship is the arm of mind control and as necessary to maintain a racist regime as that other arm of internal repression, the secret police" (1980, 27).

13. An official organ of the ANC noted that this coordination network "allows the police, military, National Intelligence Service and Military Intelligence to pool information at a local level. This co-ordinated action of all intelligence systems is new, and gives the racist regime an improved capability in identifying individuals and groups that are opposed to it" (Comrade Ramat 1987, 29, quoted in Herbst 1988, 674).

14. For example, Genghis Khan was extremely effective in wreaking havoc throughout Europe with what amounted to blind coercion over his troops.

15. This is meant strictly in terms of people killed. In terms of number of people affected by coercion, East Germany was undoubtedly the highest, given the Stasi's reach.

16. The exception, of course, is Stepan (1988).

APPENDIX A   Monitoring Indicators, September–December 1973

1. General (ret.) Alejandro Medina Lois, interview, October 26, 1995, Santiago, Chile.

2. Actas de las Sesiones de la Honorable Junta de Gobierno, Santiago, 1973–89, No. 12, April 15, 1974, cited in Barros (1996, 80).

APPENDIX B   Monitoring Indicators, 1974–78

1. A useful contrast may be the archives of Paraguay's Asunción police, uncovered in 1991 and dubbed the "Horror Archives." Coercion in Paraguay during different periods of the Stroessner regime was applied with far less regard for secrecy and in a far less finely targeted fashion than the DINA. The archives contain detailed information regarding who was responsible for a given prisoner, when interrogations took place, and what the results of it were.

2. Besides Contreras, this group included Armando Fernandez Larios, Miguel Krasnoff Marchenko, and others.

3. The question of how much Pinochet knew often tends to get conflated with the question of his legal and ethical responsibility for the DINA's actions. This is an error. Even if Pinochet knew only vague generalities about the DINA's operations, as its titular head, armed forces chief, and president of the country, he undoubtedly bears legal responsibility for it. The point I am making is not an ethical-legal one but an analytical-historical one. To draw a parallel, evidence about the discussions held by the principals at the Wansee Conference indicates that the details of the "final solution" were sketchy at best. Many would be worked out by experiment on the spot and on the ground. But there is no question about the principals' legal and moral responsibility.

4. On the Comando Conjunto, see González (1984), and González and Contreras (1991).

5. As a result of this order, the air force's main detention center, in its Colina Air Base, was dissolved (González and Contreras 1991, 206).

6. The DINA spied on regime supporters, including Jaime Guzmán, because Contreras believed that the civilians had failed to build a solid base of support for the regime and hence could not really be trusted (Guzmán Errázuriz 1992; Huneeus 2000b).

7. This is by contrast to Argentina, for example, where one of the more notorious practices was officers' trade in black-market babies born in captivity to imprisoned pregnant women.

8. General Mena, for example, a prominent critic of the DINA within the army, was made ambassador to Uruguay soon after the DINA gained official status in June 1974. Others met with a worse fate. General Lutz, a prominent coup leader, mysteriously fell ill and died in October 1974. General Bonilla, described by Pinochet aide Federico Willoughby as "the only man who could have stopped Contreras" (Constable and Valenzuela 1991, 101), was a vocal and powerful critic as minister of the interior. He was killed under mysterious circumstances in a helicopter accident in January 1975. The full story of both generals' deaths is still not known, but there is a great deal of speculation about the DINA's and Pinochet's possible role (Constable and Valenzuela 1991).

9. There continues to be some dispute within the human rights community around this issue. Roberto Garretón, one of the leading COPACHI lawyers during this time, defends the individual person–based system on the grounds that it prevents counting victims twice. This may result, for instance, from recording the number of beatings, arrests, and tortures surrounding a given event because one person can suffer more than one kind of human rights violation. On the other hand, he notes that counting only individuals probably results in the total number of human rights violations being undercounted so as not to count individuals twice (R. Garretón Merino 1989, n.d.). The Human Rights Documentation System International (HURIDOCS) in the 1980s developed a method for coding and recording human rights violations across different cases and contexts that include both events and individual-based records (Stormoken 1985); see their Web site at www.huridocs.org. But this has not been universally adopted.

10. Roughly thirty *recursos* were accepted between 1973 and 1978, out of more than eight thousand presented. On why the Chilean courts largely abdicated their responsibility to protect basic human rights and liberties during the dictatorship, see Chilean National Commission on Truth and Reconciliation (1993, 120–26), R. Garretón Merino (1989), and Hilbink (1999).

11. The Chilean regime aimed to have good relations with the church. This was in contrast to places such as El Salvador, where the church was far

more hostile to the regime and thus subject to more severe backlashes. Also, the Chilean Church, in contrast to the church in Argentina, went further in protecting human rights. A great deal of responsibility for the church's position no doubt lies with Cardenal Henríquez, particularly in his ability to have managed to reconcile the deeply conservative (and pro-junta) wing of the clergy with the far more liberal wing that devoted itself fully to the human rights cause (Huneeus 1987, 1988; Constable and Valenzuela 1991; Silva Henríquez and Cavallo 1991).

APPENDIX C   Monitoring Indicators after 1978

1. Jaime Castillo Velasco, interview, November 15, 1995, Santiago, Chile; Andrés Domínguez Vial, interview, August 16, 1995, Santiago, Chile.

2. Jaime Castillo Velasco, interview, November 15, 1995, Santiago, Chile.

3. Indeed, until the mid- to late 1990s (when the Supreme Court began to interpret the law in a different way than before), it served as the linchpin to prevent prosecutions into the human rights violations during the 1973–78 period.

4. The second-best strategy thus far has been far more successful than the first. The principal argument used by human rights lawyers, which the Supreme Court has recently also adopted, is that a disappearance is technically a "kidnapping" until a body turns up. As such, it is a crime that continues *beyond* 1978 and is hence beyond the protection afforded by the amnesty. The Supreme Court's changed interpretation of the Amnesty Decree has thus effected a political sea-change in Chile. It means that now investigations into the particular cases can proceed until a body turns up, whereas previously cases were summarily closed prior to any formal inquiries.

APPENDIX D   Cross-Country Comparisons on Monitoring Indicators

1. An exception was the English-language paper the *Buenos Aires Herald*.

2. Al Capone hired a variety of out-of-town assassins to ensure that the hired gun would feel he was killing one of "them" rather than one of "us" (Diamond 1992, 298).

3. See also Rosenberg (1991).

4. The most notorious difference between Chile and Argentina in this regard was the Argentine practice of keeping the babies of detained expectant

mothers. The search for these children, many of whom were brought up by military officers' families, has been championed by the Grandmothers of Plaza de Mayo (Las Abuelas). The well-known movie *La historia oficial* centers on the crisis of one military officer's wife who realizes that their adopted daughter was illegally taken from a woman in detention.

5. In 1968 the MfS changed the classification of its informers. Previously referred to as *Geheime Informatoren* (secret informants), the new title became *Inoffizielle Mitarbeiter* unofficial colleagues, or collaborators). Mielke intended this shift as a way to ease the psychological burden of informing and to allow the number of informants to increase (Childs and Popplewell 1996, 83).

6. Garton Ash adds: "Allow just one dependent per person, and you're up to one in twenty-five" (1997, 84).

7. Koehler points out that in the Soviet system in general the secret police are a powerful kingmaker and that "no Soviet leader had ever been removed from office without the active support of the secret police" (1999, 71). But in East Germany the fragility of the state contributed to an especially strong leverage by Moscow, through the secret police, over the SED leadership. Mielke was crucial to this. Koehler argues that Mielke was a master at switching personal allegiances and that he was loyal not to a particular person per se but rather to the joint KGB/Stasi goal of building and cementing communist power (72).

8. The relationship with the main black opposition shifted in the mid-late 1980s; that was when the NP began to hold secret talks with the ANC leadership, including Mandela.

Bibliography

Abbott, Andrew, 1992. "What Do Cases Do?" In *What Is a Case? Exploring the Foundations of Social Science*, edited by C. Ragin and H. Becker. New York: Cambridge University Press.

Agüero, Felipe. 1991. "The Assertion of Civilian Supremacy in Post-authoritarian Contexts: Spain in Comparative Perspective." PhD diss., Duke University.

Ahumada, Eugenio, Rodrigo Atria, Javier Luis Egaña, Augusto Góngora, Carmen Quesney, Gustavo Saball, and Gustavo Villalobos. 1989. *Chile: La memoria prohibida*. 3 vols. Santiago, Chile: Pehuén Editores.

Alchian, Armen A., and Harold Demsetz. 1973. "Production, Information Costs, and Economic Organization." *American Economic Review* 62:777-95.

Allison, Graham T., and Philip Zelikow. 1999. *Essence of Decision: Explaining the Cuban Missile Crisis*. 2nd ed. New York: Longman.

Ambier, John Stewart. 1966. *The French Army in Politics, 1945-1962*. Columbus: Ohio University Press.

Ancelovici, Gastón, dir. 1990. *Chile en transición*. Montreal: Imaginavision Films.

Andersen, Martin Edwin. 1993. *Dossier Secreto: Argentina's Desaparecidos and the Myth of the "Dirty War."* Boulder, CO: Westview Press.

Aoki, Masahiko. 1984. *The Co-operative Game Theory of the Firm*. New York: Oxford University Press.

Archivo Chile. n.d. "Chile: Organismos de represión durante la dictadura militar (1973-1990)." www.archivochile.com/Dictadura_militar/org_repre/DMorgrepre0003.pdf.

Arellano Iturriaga, Sergio. 1985. *Más allá del abismo: Un testimonio y una perspectiva*. Santiago, Chile: Editorial Proyección.

Arriagada Herrera, Genaro. 1985. *La política militar de Pinochet*. Santiago, Chile: Editorial Aconcagua.

———. 1986. *El pensamiento político de los militares: Estudios sobre Chile, Argentina, Brasil y Uruguay*. Santiago, Chile: Editorial Aconcagua.

———. 1988. *Pinochet: The Politics of Power*. Translated by Nancy Morris. Boston: Unwin Hyman.

Associated Press. 2004. "Former Chilean Agent Gets 12-Year Sentence for Pair of 1977 Kidnappings Dating to Military Era." September 30.

Bailey, John, and Lucía Dammert. 2006. *Public Security and Police Reform in the Americas*. Pittsburgh: University of Pittsburgh Press.

Barnard, Chester. 1938. *The Functions of the Executive*. Cambridge, MA: Harvard University Press.

Barros, Robert J. 1996. "By Reason and Force: Military Constitutionalism in Chile, 1973–1989." PhD diss., University of Chicago.

———. 2001. "Personalization and Institutional Constraints: Pinochet, the Military Junta, and the 1980 Constitution." *Latin American Politics and Society* 43 (Spring): 5–28.

———. 2002. *Constitutionalism and Dictatorship: Pinochet, the Junta, and the 1980 Constitution*. Cambridge: Cambridge University Press.

Bayley, David H. 1975. "The Police and Political Development in Europe." In *The Formation of National States in Europe*, edited by Charles Tilly. Princeton: Princeton University Press.

———. 1985. *Patterns of Policing: A Comparative International Analysis*. New Brunswick: Rutgers University Press.

Bennett, Andrew. 1997. "Lost in the Translation: Big (N) Misinterpretations of Case Study Research." Paper presented at the annual meeting of the International Studies Association, Toronto, March 18–22.

———. 1999. "Causal Inference in Case Studies: From Mill's Methods to Causal Mechanisms." Paper presented at the annual meeting of the American Political Science Association, Atlanta, September 2–5.

Bethell, Leslie, ed. 1993. *Chile since Independence*. New York: Cambridge University Press.

Blau, Peter M. 1955. *The Dynamics of Bureaucracy: A Study of Interpersonal Relations in Two Government Agencies*. Chicago: University of Chicago Press.

Blixen, Samuel. 1994. *El vientre del Cóndor: Del archivo del terror al Caso Berríos*. Montevideo, Uruguay: Ediciones de Brecha.

———. 1996. "El avestruz levanta cabeza." *Brecha*, January 20.

———. 1997a. "El poder bajo el Quepis." *Brecha*, May 30.

———. 1997b. "La sombra del General Timmerman." *Brecha*, June 1.

———. 1998. "A la sombra del Cóndor." *Noticias Aliadas*, November 12.

Blixen, Samuel, and Roberto Bergalli. 1998. *Operación Cóndor: Del Archivo del Terror y el asesinato de Letelier al Caso Berríos*. Montevideo, Uruguay: Ediciones de Brecha.

Bob, Clifford. 2005. *The Marketing of Rebellion: Insurgents, Media and International Activism*. Cambridge: Cambridge University Press.

Branch, Taylor, and Eugene M. Propper. 1983. *Labyrinth*. New York: Penguin Books.

Brysk, Alison. 1994. *The Politics of Human Rights in Argentina: Protest, Change, and Democratization*. Stanford: Stanford University Press.

Calloni, Stella. 1994. "The Horror Archives of Operation Condor." *Covert Action*, no. 50 (Fall).

Calvert, Randall, Matthew D. McCubbins, and Barry R. Weingast. 1989. "A Theory of Political Control and Agency Discretion." *American Journal of Political Science* 33 (3): 588–611.

Carvajal, Patricio. 1993. *Téngase presente*. Valparaíso, Chile: Arquén.

Caucoto Pereira, Nelson, and Héctor Salazar Ardiles. 1994. *Un verde manto de impunidad*. Santiago, Chile: FASIC and Ediciones Academia de Humanismo Cristiano.

Cavallo Castro, Ascanio, Manuel Salazar Salvo, and Oscar Sepúlveda Pacheco. 1989. *Chile, 1973–1988: La historia oculta del régimen militar*. Santiago, Chile: Editorial Antártica.

Centeno, Miguel Angel. 2002. *Blood and Debt: War and the Nation-State in Latin America*. University Park: Pennsylvania State University Press.

Central Intelligence Agency. 1974. "Treatment of Prisoners by Intelligence Services." Intelligence Report, April 13. http://foia.state.gov/documents/pcia/9d6e.PDF.

———. 1975. "Efforts to Rein in DINA." Intelligence Report, January 31. http://foia.state.gov/documents/pcia/9cf2.PDF.

Chevigny, Paul. 1995. *Edge of the Knife: Police Violence in the Americas*. New York: New Press.

———. 1999. "Defining the Role of the Police in Latin America." In *The (Un) Rule of Law and the Underprivileged in Latin America*, edited by J. E. Méndez, G. O'Donnell, and P. S. Pinheiro. Notre Dame: Notre Dame University Press.

Childs, David. 1966. *From Schumacher to Brandt: The Story of German Socialism, 1945–1965*. New York: Pergamon Press.

———. 1983. *The GDR: Moscow's German Ally*. Boston: Allen and Unwin.

———. 1985. *Honecker's Germany*. Boston: Allen and Unwin.

Childs, David, and Richard J. Popplewell. 1996. *The Stasi: The East German Intelligence and Security Service*. New York: New York University Press.

Chilean National Commission on Truth and Reconciliation. 1993. *Report of the Chilean National Commission on Truth and Reconciliation*. Notre Dame: University of Notre Dame Press.

Coase, R. H. 1937. "The Nature of the Firm." *Economica* 4 (16): 386–405.

CODEPU-DIT. 1994. *La gran mentira: El caso de las "Listas de los 119."* Santiago, Chile: CODEPU.

Collier, David, ed. 1979. *The New Authoritarianism in Latin America*. Princeton: Princeton University Press.

Collier, Simon, and William F. Sater. 1996. *A History of Chile, 1808–1994*. New York: Cambridge University Press.

Comisión Nacional de Verdad y Reconciliación. 1991. *Informe Rettig: Informe de la Comisión Nacional de Verdad y Reconciliación*. 2 vols. Santiago, Chile: La Nación and Ediciones Ornitorrinco.

Comisión Nacional sobre Prisión Política y Tortura. 2004. *Informe de la Comisión Nacional sobre Prisión Política y Tortura*. Santiago, Chile.

Comrade Ramat. 1987. "Pretoria's Security System: The Network That Spreads across the Country." *Sechaba*, January.

CONADEP. [1984] 1995. *Nunca más: Informe de la Comisión Nacional sobre la Desaparición de Personas*. Buenos Aires: Editorial Universitaria de Buenos Aires.

Constable, Pamela, and Arturo Valenzuela. 1991. *A Nation of Enemies: Chile under Pinochet*. New York: W. W. Norton.

Corder, Hugh. 1987. "The Supreme Court: Arena of Struggle." In *The State of Apartheid*, edited by W. G. James. Boulder, CO: Lynne Rienner.

Corporación Nacional de Reparación y Reconciliación. 1996. *Informe sobre calificación de víctimas de derechos humanos y de la violencia política*. Santiago, Chile: Corporación Nacional de Reparación y Reconciliación.

Cossio, Hector. 2005. "Pinochet: "Dios me perdonará si me excedí alguna vez, que no creo." *La Tercera*, November 17.

Crawford, Vincent P., and Joel Sobel. 1982. "Strategic Information Transmission." *Econometrica* 50 (6): 1431–51.

Cristi, Renato. 2000. *El pensamiento político de Jaime Guzmán: Autoridad y libertad*. Santiago: LOM.

Cross, Robert, and Sam B. Israelit. 2000. *Strategic Learning in a Knowledge Economy: Individual, Collective, and Organizational Learning Process*. Boston: Butterworth-Heinemann.

Crozier, Michel. 1964. *The Bureaucratic Phenomenon*. Chicago: University of Chicago Press.

———. 1973. *The World of the Office Worker*. New York: Schocken Books.

Cuya, Esteban. 1993. "La Operación Cóndor: El terrorismo de estado de alcance transnacional." *Ko'aga Roñe'eta*, ser. 7. www.derechos.org/koaga/vii/2/cuya.html.

Davis, Diane E. 1994. *Urban Leviathan: Mexico City in the Twentieth Century*. Philadelphia: Temple University Press.

Davis, Diane E., and Anthony W. Pereira. 2003. *Irregular Armed Forces and Their Role in Politics and State Formation*. New York: Cambridge University Press.

de Luigi, María Angélica. 1989. "La CNI hace sus maletas." *El Mercurio*, October 8, D1–D2.

de Vylder, Stefan. 1976. *Allende's Chile: The Political Economy of the Rise and Fall of the Unidad Popular*. New York: Cambridge University Press.

Délano, Manuel. 2007. "Un general chileno se declara en rebeldía contra un fallo que le condena a 5 años." *El País*, June 14.

Derechos Chile. 2002. "The Judiciary under the Dictatorship." www.chipsites.com/derechos/dictadura_poder_eng.html.

Deutsch, Karl W. 1954. "Cracks in the Monolith: Possibilities and Patterns of Disintegration in Totalitarian Systems." In *Totalitarianism: Proceedings of a Conference Held at the American Academy of Arts and Sciences, March 1953*, edited by Carl J. Friedrich. Cambridge, MA: Harvard University Press.

Diamond, Jared M. 1992. *The Third Chimpanzee: The Evolution and Future of the Human Animal*. New York: HarperCollins.

Dinges, John. 2004. *The Condor Years*. New York: New Press.

Dinges, John, and Saul Landau. 1980. *Assassination on Embassy Row*. New York: Pantheon Books.

Eckstein, Harry. 1975. "Case Study and Theory in Political Science." In *Handbook of Political Science*, edited by Fred I. Greenstein and Nelson W. Polsby, vol. 7, pp. 79–138. Reading, MA: Addison-Wesley.

Economist. 2004. "Pinochet's Tarnished Coin." August 7.

———. 2006. "Augusto Pinochet: The Passing of a Tyrant." December 13.

Elster, Jon. 1989. *Nuts and Bolts for the Social Sciences*. New York: Cambridge University Press.

Ensalaco, Mark. 1999. *Chile under Pinochet: Recovering the Truth*. Philadelphia: University of Pennsylvania Press.

Fernández, Sergio. 1994. *Mi lucha por la democracia*. Santiago, Chile: Editorial Los Andes.

———. 1998. "Génesis de la Constitución de 1980." In *Análisis crítico del régimen militar*, edited by Gonzalo Vial. Santiago, Chile: Universidad Finis Terrae.

Freedom House. 2008. "Freedom in the World 2008: Global Freedom in Retreat." Press release, January 16. www.freedomhouse.org/template.cfm?page=70&release=612.

Friedrich, Carl J. 1970. "The Failure of a One-Party System: Hitler Germany." In *Authoritarian Politics in Modern Society: The Dynamics of*

Established One-Party Systems, edited by Samuel P. Huntington and C. H. Moore. New York: Basic Books.

Friedrich, Carl J., and Zbigniew K. Brzezinski. [1956] 1965. *Totalitarian Dictatorship and Autocracy*. 2nd ed. Cambridge, MA: Harvard University Press.

Frontalini, Daniel, and Maria Cristina Caiati. 1984. *El mito de la Guerra Sucia*. Buenos Aires: Centro de Estudios Legales y Sociales.

Frühling, Hugo. 1983. "Stages of Repression and Legal Strategy for the Defense of Human Rights in Chile." *Human Rights Quarterly* 5:510–33.

———. 1984. "Repressive Policies and Legal Dissent in Authoritarian Regimes: Chile 1973–1981." *International Journal of Sociology of Law* 12:351–74.

———. 1986. *Represión política y defensa de los derechos humanos*. Santiago, Chile: Programa de Derechos Humanos Academia de Humanismo Cristiano Centros de Estudios Sociales Ediciones Chile y América.

———. 2000. "Determinants of Gross Human Rights Violations by State and State-Sponsored Actors in Chile, 1960–1990." In *Determinants of Gross Human Rights Violations by State and State-Sponsored Actors in Brazil, Uruguay, Chile, and Argentina, 1960–1990*, edited by W. S. Heinz and H. Frühling. The Hague: Martinus Nijhoff.

Frühling, Hugo, Carlos Portales, and Augusto Varas. 1982. *Estado y fuerzas armadas*. Santiago, Chile: Facultad Latinoamericana de Ciencias Sociales.

Fulbrook, Mary. 1995. *Anatomy of a Dictatorship: Inside the GDR, 1949–1989*. New York: Oxford University Press.

García Villegas, René. 1990. *Soy testigo: Dictadura, tortura, injusticia*. Santiago, Chile: Amerinda.

Garretón Merino, Manuel Antonio. 1989. *The Chilean Political Process*. Boston: Unwin Hyman.

Garretón Merino, Manuel A., Roberto Garretón Merino, and Carmen Garretón Merino. 1998. *Por la fuerza sin la razón: Análisis y textos de los bandos de la dictadura militar*. Santiago, Chile: LOM.

Garretón Merino, Roberto. 1989. *El poder judicial chileno y la violación de los derechos humanos*. Santiago, Chile: Corporación de Promoción Universitaria.

———. n.d. "Informe Global sobre las Más Graves Violaciones a los Derechos Humanos, 1973–1990." Mimeo, Santiago, Chile.

Garton Ash, Timothy. 1997. *The File: A Personal History*. New York: Random House.

George, Alexander, and Andrew Bennett. 2005. *Case Studies and Theory Development in the Social Sciences*. Cambridge, MA: MIT Press.

Gill, Lesley. 2004. *The School of the Americas: Military Training and Political Violence in the Americas*. Durham: Duke University Press.

González, Mónica. 1984. "Confesiones de un agente de seguridad." *El Diario de Caracas*, December 7–10.

———. 2000. *La conjura: Los mil y un días del golpe*. Santiago, Chile: Ediciones B, Grupo Z.

———. 2001a. "'Caravana de la Muerte': Documentos inéditos acusan a Pinochet." *El Mostrador*, February 7.

———. 2001b. "Un militar reveló atrocidades de la dictadura chilena." *Clarín*, January 27.

González, Mónica, and Héctor Contreras. 1991. *Los secretos del Comando Conjunto*. Santiago, Chile: Las Ediciones del Ornitorrinco.

Gordimer, Nadine. 1980. "New Forms of Strategy—No Change of Heart." *Critical Arts*, June.

Guzmán Errázuriz, Jaime. 1992. *Escritos personales*. Santiago, Chile: Zig-Zag.

Hachten, William A., C. Anthony Giffard, and Harva Hachten. 1984. *The Press and Apartheid: Repression and Propaganda in South Africa*. Madison: University of Wisconsin Press.

Harrington, Edwin, and Mónica González. 1987. *Bomba en una calle de Palermo*. Santiago, Chile: Emisión.

Hawkins, Darren. 1994. "International Influence and Human Rights in Chile: Explaining the Disappearance of the DINA in 1977." Paper presented at the annual meeting of the American Political Science Association, New York, September 1–4.

———. 1996. "The International and Domestic Struggle for Legitimacy in Authoritarian Chile." PhD diss., University of Wisconsin–Madison.

Hedström, Peter, and Richard Swedberg, eds. 1998. *Social Mechanisms: An Analytical Approach to Social Theory*. New York: Cambridge University Press.

Herbst, Jeffrey. 1988. "Prospects for Revolution in South Africa." *Political Science Quarterly* 103 (4): 665–85.

———. 2000. *States and Power in Africa: Comparative Lessons in Authority and Control*. Princeton: Princeton University Press.

Hersh, Seymour. 1982. "The Price of Power: Kissinger, Nixon, and Chile." *Atlantic Monthly*, December, 21–58.

Hilbink, Elisabeth C. 1999. "Legalism against Democracy: The Political Role of the Judiciary in Chile, 1964–94." PhD diss., University of California, San Diego.

Hitchens, Cristopher. 2001a. "The Case against Henry Kissinger, Part I: The Making of a War Criminal." *Harper's Magazine*, February, 33–58.

———. 2001b. "The Case against Henry Kissinger, Part II: Crimes against Humanity." *Harper's Magazine*, March, 49–74.

Hudson, James R. 1972. "Organizational Aspects of Internal and External Review of the Police." *Journal of Criminal Law, Criminology, and Police Science* 63 (3): 427–33.

Huidobro, Sergio. 1989. *Decisión naval*. Valparaíso: Editorial Impresa de la Armada.

Human Rights Watch. 2000. *Under Orders: War Crimes in Kosovo*. New York: Human Rights Watch.

Huneeus, Carlos. 1985. *La Unión de Centro Democrático y la transición a la democracia en España*. Madrid: Centro de Investigaciones Sociológicas, Siglo Veintiuno de España Editores.

———. 1987. *Los Chilenos y la política: Cambio y continuidad bajo el autoritarismo*. Santiago, Chile: Centro de Estudios de la Realidad Contemporánea Academia de Humanismo Cristiano, Instituto Chileno de Estudios Humanísticos.

———. 1988. "El ejército y la política en el Chile de Pinochet: Su magnitud y alcances." *Opciones* 14:89–136.

———. 2000a. *El régimen de Pinochet*. Santiago, Chile: Sudamericana.

———. 2000b. "Technocrats and Politicians in an Authoritarian Regime: The 'Odeplan Boys' and the 'Gremialistas' in Pinochet's Chile." *Journal of Latin American Studies* 32 (2): 461–501.

Jacoby, Tamar. 1986. "The Reagan Turnaround on Human Rights." *Foreign Affairs* 64 (5): 1066–86.

Jervis, Robert. 1976. *Perception and Misperception in International Politics*. Princeton: Princeton University Press.

Johnson, Ronald N., and Gary D. Libecap. 1994. *The Federal Civil Service System and the Problem of Bureaucracy: The Economics and Politics of Institutional Change*. Chicago: University of Chicago Press.

Keck, Margaret E., and Kathryn Sikkink. 1998. *Activists beyond Borders: Advocacy Networks in International Politics*. Ithaca: Cornell University Press.

Kiewiet, R. D., and M. D. McCubbins. 1991. *The Logic of Delegation*. Chicago: Chicago University Press.

King, Gary, Robert Keohane, and Sidney Verba. 1994. *Designing Social Inquiry: Scientific Inference in Qualitative Research*. Princeton: Princeton University Press.

Kirk, Jerome, and Marc L. Miller. 1986. *Reliability and Validity in Qualitative Research*. Vol. 1. Beverly Hills, CA: Sage Publications.

Koehler, John O. 1999. *Stasi: The Untold Story of the East German Secret Police*. Boulder, CO: Westview Press.

Kornbluh, Peter. 2003. *The Pinochet File: A Declassified Dossier on Atrocity and Accountability*. New York: New Press.

Krehbiel, Keith. 1991. *Information and Legislative Organization*. Ann Arbor: University of Michigan Press.

Kritzer, Herbert M. 1996. "Interpretation and Validity Assessment in Qualitative Research: The Case of H. W. Perry's *Deciding to Decide.*" *Law and Social Inquiry* 19 (Summer): 687–724.

La Nación. 2007. "Parlamentarios repudian rebeldía de General Iturriaga Neumann." June 13.

Lebow, Richard Ned. 2001. "Social Science and History: Ranchers versus Farmers." In *Bridges and Boundaries: Historians, Political Scientists, and the Study of International Relations*, edited by Colin Elman and Miriam Fendius Elman. Cambridge, MA: MIT Press.

Leggett, George. 1981. *The Cheka: Lenin's Political Police: The All-Russian Extraordinary Commission for Combating Counter-revolution and Sabotage, December 1917 to February 1922*. New York: Clarendon Press.

Lieberson, Stanley. 1992. "Small N's and Big Conclusions: An Examination of the Reasoning in Comparative Studies Based on a Small Number of Cases." In *What Is a Case? Exploring the Foundations of Social Inquiry*, edited by Charles C. Ragin and Howard S. Becker. New York: Cambridge University Press.

Linz, Juan. 1975. "Totalitarian and Authoritarian Regimes." In *Handbook of Political Science*, edited by Fred I. Greenstein and Nelson W. Polsby, vol. 3, 175–357. Reading, MA: Addison-Wesley.

Linz, Juan J., Alfred Stepan, and Richard Gunther. 1994. "Democratic Transitions and Consolidation in Southern Europe (with Reflections on Latin America and Eastern Europe)." In *The Politics of Democratic Consolidation: Southern Europe in Comparative Perspective*, edited by Richard Gunther, P. Nikiforos Diamandouros and Hans-Jurgen Puhle. Baltimore: Johns Hopkins University Press.

Loveman, Brian. 1993. *The Constitution of Tyranny: Regimes of Exception in Spanish America*. Pittsburgh: University of Pittsburgh Press.

———. 1999. *For La Patria: Politics and the Armed Forces in Latin America*. Wilmington, DE: SR Books.

Lowenthal, Abraham F., and J. Samuel Fitch, eds. 1986. *Armies and Politics in Latin America*. New York: Holmes and Meier.

Macey, Jonathan R. 1992. "Organizational Design and the Political Control of Administrative Agencies." *Journal of Law, Economics and Organization* 8 (1): 93–110.

Machiavelli, Niccolo. 1950. *The Prince and the Discourses*. New York: Modern Library.

Mahoney, James. 1999a. "Nominal, Ordinal, and Narrative Appraisal in Macrocausal Analysis." *American Journal of Sociology* 104 (January): 1154–96.

———. 1999b. "Uses of Path Dependence in Historical Sociology." Paper presented at the annual meeting of the American Political Science Association, Atlanta, September 2–5.

Maier, Charles S. 1997. *Dissolution: The Crisis of Communism and the End of East Germany*. Princeton: Princeton University Press.

Mainwaring, Scott. 1994. *Democracy in Brazil and the Southern Cone: Achievements and Problems*. Notre Dame: University of Notre Dame, Helen Kellogg Institute for International Studies.

Mainwaring, Scott, J. Samuel Valenzuela, and Guillermo A. O'Donnell. 1992. *Issues in Democratic Consolidation: The New South American Democracies in Comparative Perspective*. Notre Dame: University of Notre Dame Press.

Maldonado, Carlos. 1990. "Los Carabineros de Chile: Historia de una policía militarizada." *Ibero-Americana, Nordic Journal of Latin American Studies* 20 (3): 3–31.

Mannix, Daniel P. 1986. *The History of Torture*. New York: Dorset Press.

Maravall, José María. 1978. *Dictatorship and Political Dissent*. London: Tavistock.

Maravall, José María, and Julián Santamaría. 1986. "Political Change in Spain and the Prospects for Democracy." In *Transitions from Authoritarian Rule: Southern Europe*, edited by Guillermo O'Donnell, Philippe C. Schmitter, and Laurence Whitehead. Baltimore: Johns Hopkins University Press.

Marchak, Patricia. 1999. *God's Assassins: State Terrorism in Argentina in the 1970s*. Montreal: McGill-Queen's University Press.

Marenin, Otwin. 1990. "The Police and the Coercive Nature of the State." In *Changes in the State: Causes and Consequences*, edited by Edward S. Greenberg and Thomas F. Mayer. Newbury Park, CA: Sage Publications.

Marquis, Christopher, and Diana Jean Schemo. 2000. "Documents Shed Light on Assassination of Chilean in U.S." *New York Times*, November 14.

Martorell, Francisco. 1999. *Operación Cóndor*. Santiago, Chile: LOM.

Matus, Alejandra. 1999. *El libro negro de la justicia chilena*. Santiago: Planeta.

McCubbins, Matthew D., and Barry R. Weingast. 1984. "Congressional Oversight Overlooked: Police Patrols versus Fire Alarms." *American Journal of Political Science* 28 (1):165–79.

McSherry, J. Patrice. 1997. *Incomplete Transition: Military Power and Democracy in Argentina*. New York: St. Martin's Press.

———. 2000. "Analyzing Operation Condor: A Covert Interamerican Structure." Paper presented at the 22nd International Congress of the Latin American Studies Association, Miami, March 16–19.

———. 2005. *Predatory States: Operation Condor and Covert War in Latin America* Boulder, CO: Rowman and Littlefield.

Meilinger de Sannemann, Gladys. 1993. *Paraguay en el Operativo Condor: Represión e intercambio clandestino de prisioneros políticos en el Cono Sur*. Asunción, Paraguay: RP Ediciones.

Memoria y Justicia. 2001. "Letter from Dr. Luis Fornazzari." April 9. www. memoriayjusticia.cl/english/en_docs-fornazzari.html.

———. 2002. "Caravan of Death," February. www.memoriayjusticia.cl/english/en_focus-caravan.html.

Mery Figueroa, Nelson. 1996. *Policía de investigaciones de Chile: Discurso del Director General de la Policía de Investigaciones de Chile, Don Nelson Mery Figueroa, en el 63˚ aniversario de la institución*. Santiago, Chile: n.p.

Mignone, Emilio F. 1991. *Derechos humanos y sociedad: El caso argentino*. Buenos Aires: CELS.

Mill, John Stuart. [1859] 1955. *On Liberty*. Gateway ed. Chicago: Henry Regnery.

Moncalvillo, Mona, and Alberto Fernández. 1985. *La renovación fundacional*. Buenos Aires: El Cid Editor.

Moore, Barrington. 1950. *Soviet Politics: The Dilemma of Power. The Role of Ideas in Social Change*. Cambridge, MA: Harvard University Press.

———. 1954. *Terror and Progress USSR: Some Sources of Change and Stability in the Soviet Dictatorship*. Cambridge, MA: Harvard University Press.

Morete Alnar, Alfonso. 1987. *CIA: ¿Mito O Realidad?* Madrid: Ediciones Piedra Buena.

North, Liisa. 1986. "The Military in Chilean Politics." In *Armies and Politics in Latin America*, edited by Abraham F. Lowenthal and J. Samuel Fitch. New York: Holmes and Meier.

Nunn, Frederick M. 1994. "The South American Military Tradition: Preprofessional Armies in Argentina, Chile, Peru, and Brazil." In *Rank and Privilege: The Military and Society in Latin America*, edited by L. Alexander Rodríguez. Wilmington, DE: Scholarly Resources.

———. 1997. "The Military in Chilean Politics, 1924–32." In *The Politics of Antipolitics: The Military in Latin America*, edited by Brian Loveman and Thomas M. Davies Jr. Wilmington, DE: Scholarly Resources.

O'Donnell, Guillermo. 1973. *Modernization and Bureaucratic-Authoritarianism: Studies in South American Politics.* Berkeley: Institute of International Studies, University of California.

———. 1993. "On the State, Democratization and Some Conceptual Problems: A Latin American View with Glances at Some Postcommunist Countries." *World Development* 21 (8): 1355–70.

O'Rourke, Dara. 2000. "Monitoring the Monitors: A Critique of PricewaterhouseCoopers (PwC) Labor Monitoring." Report for the Independent University Initiative, September 28, Massachusetts Institute of Technology, Cambridge, MA.

O'Shaughnessy, Hugh. 2000. *Pinochet: The Politics of Torture.* New York: New York University Press.

Olmeda, José Antonio. 1988. *Las fuerzas armadas en el estado franquista.* Madrid: Ediciones el Arquero.

Orellana, Patricio, and Elizabeth Quay Hutchison. 1991. *El movimiento de derechos humanos en Chile, 1973–1990.* Santiago, Chile: Centro de Estudios Políticos Latinoamericanos Simón Bolívar.

Pacheco, Máximo. 1979. *Lonquén.* Santiago, Chile: Editorial Aconcagua.

Padilla Ballesteros, Elías. 1995. *La memoria y el olvido: Detenidos desaparecidos en Chile.* Santiago, Chile: Ediciones Orígenes.

Phelan, John M. 1987. *Apartheid Media: Disinformation and Dissent in South Africa.* Westport, CT: L. Hill.

Pinheiro, Paulo Sérgio. 1999. "Introduction: The Rule of Law and the Underprivileged in Latin America." In *The (Un)Rule of Law and the Underprivileged in Latin America,* edited by Juan E. Méndez, Guillermo O'Donnell, and Paulo S. Pinheiro. Notre Dame: University of Notre Dame Press.

Pinochet Ugarte, Augusto. 1974. "Interview." *Veja,* February.

———. 1979. *El día decisivo, 11 de septiembre de 1973.* Santiago, Chile: Editorial Andrés Bello.

Pion-Berlin, David. 1989. *The Ideology of State Terror: Economic Doctrine and Political Repression in Argentina and Peru.* Boulder, CO: Lyne Rienner.

Policzer, Pablo. 2003. "The Charter vs. Constitutional Military Involvement in Politics." *Canadian Foreign Policy* 10 (3): 75–86.

———. 2006. "Human Rights Violations beyond the State." *Journal of Human Rights* 5 (2): 215–33.

———. 2007a. "Chile: The Price of Democracy." *New English Review,* January.

———. 2007b. "La dictadura que casi tuvimos." *El Mostrador*, January 3.

Prats González, Carlos. 1974. *Memorias: Testimonio de un soldado.* Santiago, Chile: Pehuén.

Proyecto Internacional de Derechos Humanos. 2008. "Raúl Iturriaga Neumman." Memoria Viva. Updated June 3. http://memoriaviva.com/culpables/criminales%20i/Raul_Iturriaga.htm.

Quezada, Alejandro. 1978. "La lección de la DINA." *Mensaje*, July.

Ragin, Charles. 1997. "Turning the Tables: How Case-Oriented Research Challenges Variable-Oriented Research." *Comparative Social Research* 16:27–42.

Remmer, Karen. 1991. *Military Rule in Latin America.* Boulder, CO: Westview Press.

Reno, William. 1995. *Corruption and State Politics in Sierra Leone.* New York: Cambridge University Press.

———. 1998. *Warlord Politics and African States.* Boulder, CO: Lynne Rienner.

Rojas, María Eugenia. 1988. *La represión política en Chile: Los hechos.* Madrid: IEPALA.

Roniger, Luis, and Mario Sznajder. 1999. *The Legacy of Human-Rights Violations in the Southern Cone: Argentina, Chile, and Uruguay.* New York: Oxford University Press.

Rosberg, James H. 1995. "The Rise of an Independent Judiciary in Egypt." PhD diss., Massachusetts Institute of Technology, Cambridge, MA.

Rosenberg, Tina. 1991. *Children of Cain: Violence and the Violent in Latin America.* New York: William Morrow.

———. 1995. *The Haunted Land: Facing Europe's Ghosts after Communism.* New York: Random House.

Rosenzweig, Luc, and Yacine Le Forestier. 1992. *L'empire des mouchards: Les dossiers de la Stasi.* Paris: J. Bertoin.

Ross, Stephen A. 1973. "The Economic Theory of Agency: The Principal's Problem." *American Economic Review* 63:134–39.

Rudgers, David F. 2000. *Creating the Secret State.* Lawrence: University of Kansas Press.

Russett, Bruce. 1974. "International Behavior Research: Case Studies and Cumulation." In *Power and Community in World Politics*, edited by Bruce M. Russett. San Francisco: W. H. Freeman.

Sabel, Charles F. 1993. "Learning by Monitoring: The Institutions of Economic Development." In *The Handbook of Economic Sociology*, edited by Neil J. Smelser and Richard Swedberg. Princeton: Princeton University Press.

Salazar Salvo, Jaime. 1994. *Guzmán: Quien, cómo, por qué.* Santiago, Chile: Ediciones BAT.

Salazar Salvo, Manuel. 1995. *Contreras: Historia de un intocable.* Santiago, Chile: Grijalbo.

Schemo, Diana Jean. 2001. "New Files Tie U.S. to Deaths of Latin Leftists in 1970's." *New York Times*, March 6.

Schweitzer, Miguel. 1998. "El gobierno militar ante el problema de los derechos humanos." In *Análisis crítico del régimen militar*, edited by Gonzalo Vial. Santiago: Universidad Finis Terrae.

Seegers, Annette. 1996. *The Military in the Making of Modern South Africa.* New York: Tauris Academic Studies.

Sigmund, Paul. 1977. *The Overthrow of Allende and the Politics of Chile.* Pittsburgh: University of Pittsburgh Press.

———. 1993. *The United States and Democracy in Chile.* Baltimore: Johns Hopkins University Press.

Sikkink, Kathryn. 1993. "Human Rights, Principled Issue-Networks, and Sovereignty in Latin America." *International Organization* 47 (3): 411–41.

Silva Henríquez, Raúl, and Ascanio Cavallo. 1991. *Memorias.* Santiago, Chile: Copygraph.

Simon, José Luis. 1992. *La dictadura de Stroessner y los derechos humanos.* Vol. 1. Asunción, Paraguay: Comité de Iglesias.

Slack, Keith M. 1996. "Operation Condor and Human Rights: A Report from Paraguay's Archive of Terror." *Human Rights Quarterly* 18:492–506.

Smith, Bradley F. 1983. *The Shadow Warriors: OSS and the Origins of the CIA.* New York: Basic Books.

Sohr, Raúl. 1989. *Para entender a los militares.* Santiago, Chile: Ediciones Melquíades, Comisión Sudamericana de Paz.

Stalnaker, Robert. 1996. "Knowledge, Belief and Counterfactual Reasoning in Games." *Economics and Philosophy* 12:133–62.

Stanbridge, Roland. 1980. "Contemporary African Political Organizations and Movements." In *The Apartheid Regime*, edited by Robert M. Price and Carl G. Rosberg. Berkeley: University of California Press.

Stepan, Alfred. 1971. *The Military in Politics: Changing Patterns in Brazil.* Princeton: Princeton University Press.

———. 1986. "The New Professionalism of Internal Warfare and Military Role Expansion." In *Armies and Politics in Latin America*, edited by Abraham F. Lowenthal and J. Samuel Fitch. New York: Holmes and Meier.

———. 1988. *Rethinking Military Politics: Brazil and the Southern Cone.* Princeton: Princeton University Press.

Stinchcombe, Arthur L. 1990. *Information and Organizations*. Berkeley: University of California Press.

Stormoken, Bjørn. 1985. *HURIDOCS Standard Formats for the Recording and Exchange of Information on Human Rights*. Boston: Martinus Nijhoff.

Tanner, Murray Scott. 2000. "Will the State Bring *You* Back In?" *Comparative Politics* 33 (1): 101–25.

Téllez, General Indalecio. 1949. *Recuerdos militares*. Santiago, Chile: Instituto Geográfico Militar.

Tetlock, Philip E., and Aaron Belkin, eds. 1996. *Counterfactual Thought Experiments in World Politics: Logical, Methodological, and Psychological Perspectives*. Princeton: Princeton University Press.

Tilly, Charles. 1986. "State Making and War Making as Organized Crime." In *Bringing the State Back In*, edited by Peter B. Evans, Dietrich Rueschmeyer and Theda Skocpol. New York: Cambridge University Press.

———. 1992. *Coercion, Capital, and European States, AD 990–1992*. Cambridge, MA: Blackwell.

———. 2000a. "Historical Analysis of Political Process." In *Handbook of Sociological Theory*, edited by Jonathan H. Turner. New York: Plenum.

———. 2000b. "Mechanisms in Political Processes." Consortium on Qualitative Research Methods (CQRM), Arizona State University. www.asu.edu/clas/polisci/cqrm/papers/Tilly/TillyMechs.pdf.

———. 2000c. "Violent and Nonviolent Trajectories in Contentious Politics." Paper presented at the Symposium on States in Transition and the Challenge of Ethnic Conflict, Moscow, December 29.

Tilly, Charles, and Gabriel Ardant. 1975. *The Formation of National States in Western Europe*. Princeton: Princeton University Press.

Trinquier, Roger. 1980. *La Guerre*. Paris: A. Michel.

———. n.d. *La guerra moderna*. Buenos Aires: Editorial Rioplatense.

Truth and Reconciliation Commission. 1999. *Truth and Reconciliation Commission of South Africa Report*. Vol. 2. New York: Macmillan.

United Nations. 1978. *Informe del Consejo Económico y Social: Protección de los derechos humanos en Chile*. New York: United Nations.

U.S. Senate. Church Committee. 1975. "Interim Report: Alleged Assassination Plots Involving Foreign Leaders." http://history-matters.com/archive/church/reports/ir/contents.htm.

U.S. Senate. Committee on Homeland Security and Governmental Affairs. 2005. "Money Laundering and Foreign Corruption: Enforcement and Effectiveness of the Patriot Act. Supplemental Staff Report on U.S. Accounts Used by Augusto Pinochet." http://levin.senate.gov/newsroom/supporting/2005/pinochetreport.pdf.

U.S. Senate. Select Committee to Study Governmental Operations with Respect to Intelligence Activities. 1975. "Covert Action in Chile, 1963–73: Staff Report." www.fas.org/irp/ops/policy/church-chile.htm.

Valenzuela, Arturo. 1978. *Chile*. Baltimore: Johns Hopkins University Press.

Varas, Augusto. 1987. *Los militares en el poder: Régimen y gobierno militar en Chile, 1973–1986*. Santiago, Chile: Pehuén and FLACSO.

Varas, Florencia. 1979. *Gustavo Leigh: El general disidente*. Santiago: Editorial Aconcagua.

Vega, Luis. n.d. *Anatomía de un golpe de estado*. Jerusalém: La Semana.

Verbitsky, Horacio. 1995. *El vuelo*. Buenos Aires: Planeta.

Verdugo, Patricia. 1989. *Caso Arellano: Los zarpazos del puma*. Santiago: Ediciones ChileAmérica CESOC.

Vicaría de la Solidaridad. 1975. *Los servicios de inteligencia del gobierno militar y los derechos humanos fundamentales*. Santiago, Chile: Vicaría de la Solidaridad.

Weber, Max. 1946. "Bureaucracy." In *From Max Weber: Essays in Sociology*, edited by H. H. Gerth and C. Wright Mills. New York: Oxford University Press.

Weiss Fagen, Patricia. 1992. "Repression and State Security." In *Fear at the Edge: State Terror and Resistance in Latin America*, edited by Juan E. Corradi, Patricia Weiss Fagen, and Manuel Antonio Garretón. Berkeley: University of California Press.

Whelan, James R. 1993. *Desde las cenizas: Vida, muerte y transfiguración de la democracia en Chile, 1833–1988*. Santiago, Chile: Zig-Zag.

Williamson, Oliver E. 1975. *Markets and Hierarchies*. New York: Free Press.

———. 1990. *Industrial Organization*. Aldershot: E. Elgar.

Wilson, James Q. 1989. *Bureaucracy: What Government Agencies Do and Why They Do It*. New York: Basic Books.

Woods, Donald. 1991. *Biko*. New York: Henry Holt.

Zegart, Amy B. 1999. *Flawed by Design: The Evolution of the CIA, JCS, and NSC*. Stanford: Stanford University Press.

Index

PABLO POLICZER

is assistant professor in political science and Canada Research Chair in Latin American Politics at the University of Calgary.